Presence of Mind

Education and the Politics of Deception

Pepi Leistyna

University of Massachusetts, Boston

Westview Press
A Member of the Perseus Books Group

The Edge: Critical Studies in Educational Theory

Copyright © 1999 by Westview Press, A Member of the Perseus Books Group

Published in 1999 in the United States of America by Westview Press, 5500 Central Avenue, Boulder, Colorado 80301-2877, and in the United Kingdom by Westview Press, 12 Hid's Copse Road, Cumnor Hill, Oxford OX2 9JJ

Library of Congress Cataloging-in-Publication Data
Leistyna, Pepi.
  Presence of mind : education and the politics of deception / by
Pepi Leistyna.
    p.   cm. — (The edge, critical studies in educational theory)
  Includes bibliographical references and index.
  ISBN 0-8133-3475-6 (hardcover). — ISBN 0-8133-3476-4 (pbk.)
  1. Critical pedagogy.   2. Politics and education.   I. Title.
II. Series.
LC196.L45   1999
370.11'5—dc21   98-34588
                                                                               CIP

The paper used in this publication meets the requirements of the American National Standard for Permanence of Paper for Printed Library Materials Z39.48-1984.

PERSEUS
POD
ON DEMAND   10   9   8   7   6   5   4   3   2

Contents

Foreword
Critical Pedagogy and the
Project of Exemplary Prophecy

Henry A. Giroux
Penn State University

These are hard times for educators and advocates of democratic school-ing. Besieged by the growing forces of vocationalism and the culture wars, prospective and existing classroom teachers are caught in an ideo-logical crossfire regarding the civic and political responsibilities they as-sume through their roles as engaged critics and cultural theorists. Asked to define themselves either through the language of the marketplace or through a discourse that abstracts the political from the realm of the cul-tural or the sphere of the social, educators are increasingly being pres-sured to become either servants of corporate power or disengaged spe-cialists wedded to the imperatives of a resurgent and debasing academic professionalism. These two positions demand further elaboration.

According to right-wing advocates of school–business partnerships, schools should be viewed as a private rather than a public good, tied to the dictates of the marketplace and run just like any other business. For many who support this position, schools should either be turned over to for-profit corporations—exercising complete control over their organi-zation, curricula, and classroom practices—or organized through strate-gies that favor educational choice, vouchers, and private charter schools. Within the language of privatization and market reforms, there is a strong emphasis on standards, measurements of outcomes, and holding teachers and students more accountable. Privatization is an ap-pealing prospect for legislators who do not want to spend money on schools and for those Americans who do not want to support public ed-ucation through increased taxes. Such appeals are reductive in nature and hollow in substance. Not only do they abstract questions of equity and equality from the discourse of standards, they appropriate the democratic rhetoric of choice and freedom without addressing issues of power and inequality. There is little concern in these discourses with who has access to the resources, wealth, and power that make the available range of choices more viable for some groups and not others. The ideas and images that permeate this corporate model of schooling reek with the rhetoric of insincerity and the politics of social indifference.

Stripped of a language of social responsibility, the advocates of privatization reject the assumption that school failure might be better understood within the political, economic, and social dynamics of poverty, joblessness, sexism, race and class discrimination, unequal funding, or a diminished tax base. Rather, student failure, especially the failure of poor minority group students, is often attributed to a genetically encoded lack of intelligence, a culture of deprivation, or simply pathology.

The second threat to democratic schooling and the role that educators might play as critically engaged intellectuals can be seen in the recent interventions by a growing number of progressives and conservatives who attempt to either reduce pedagogy to the technical formalism and hermetic task of simply teaching the text (test, method, etc.), or have narrowly defined politics and pedagogy within a dichotomy that pits the alleged "real" material issues of class and labor against a fragmenting and marginalizing identity politics, on the one hand, and a range of diverse, ineffective side-show battles over culture on the other. The latter politicized model is characteristic of a resurgent economism rooted in a totalizing concept of class in which it is argued that "we can do class or culture, but not both."[1] Unfortunately, this model not only fails to recognize how issues of race, gender, age, sexual orientation, and class are intertwined, it also refuses to acknowledge the pedagogical function of culture as the site where identities are constructed, desires are mobilized, and moral values are shaped.

Ellen Willis rightly argues in opposition to this position that if people "are not ready to defend their right to freedom and equality in their personal relations, they will not fight consistently for their economic interests, either."[2] In short, this totalizing model of class functions largely to cancel out how culture as a terrain of struggle shapes our sense of political agency and mediates the relations between materially based protests and structures of power and the contexts of daily struggles. This position is evident in the works of Jim Sleeper, Todd Gitlin, Michael Lind, and others who argue that cultural struggles, especially those dealing with recent social movements organized around sexuality, gender, race, the politics of representation, and multiculturalism, are nothing more than a weak substitute for "real" politics, notably those that focus on class, labor, and inequality. According to this position, movements that fail to organize around economic issues have given politics a bad name. The notion that struggles over culture are at the heart of struggles over meaning, agency, and resistance and represent a different but no less important site where political struggles take place is completely lost here. Moreover, if identity politics poses a threat to the endearing transcendent, universal category that class appears to represent to some critics, as the historian Robin Kelley argues, it may be because such critics either fail to understand how class is lived through race, sexual orientation, and gender or it may be that the return to a form of class warfare against the corporations represents simply another form of identity politics, that is, a form of white male angst that cannot imagine movements led by African-Americans, women, Latinos, or gays and lesbians speaking for the whole or even embracing radical humanism.[3]

Culture matters because it is the site where desire is mobilized, knowledge is formed, and identities are made and unmade. Culture matters because it also represents the terrain where alliances can be constructed among diverse cultural workers who can unite in a movement for democracy, freedom, and the pursuit of happiness, a movement that would transcend the untenable distinction between economics and culture, and regard movements organized around distinct oppressions as potential allies rather than as competitors and antagonists.

Another version of the attack on culture as a site of pedagogical and political struggle and resistance is evident in the work of traditionalists such as Harold Bloom and progressives such as Richard Rorty, both of whom bemoan the death of romance, inspiration, and hope as casualties of the discourse of power, politics, and multiculturalism. For Bloom, literary criticism has been replaced by cultural criticism in the academy and the result is nothing less than the death of criticism. Bloom cannot bear the politics of what he calls "identity clubs" and argues that "multiculturalism is a lie, a mask for mediocrity for the thought-control academic police, the Gestapo of our campuses."[4] Bloom wants to remove culture to the sphere of aesthetic transcendence, unhampered and uncorrupted by the politics of representation, the struggle over public memory, or the democratic imperative for constant self- and social criticism.

Although Richard Rorty does not evacuate the political as a meaningful category of public life, he does abstract it from culture and in doing so legitimates a conservative reading of pedagogy and the aesthetic. According to Rorty, you cannot "find inspirational value in a text at the same time as you are viewing it as a . . . mechanism of cultural production."[5] Of course, this view has not gone unchallenged. Critical educators such as Paulo Freire, bell hooks, Donaldo Macedo, Peter McLaren, Roger Simon, and others have steadfastly rejected so rigid a division between understanding and hope, mind and heart, thought and action. For these critical educators hope was a practice of witnessing, an act of moral imagination that enabled educators and other cultural workers to think otherwise in order to act otherwise. Hope demanded an anchoring in transformative practices, and one of the tasks of the progressive educator was to unveil opportunities for hope as part of a broader pedagogical and political project.

Underlying this form of cultural politics of hope was a view of radical pedagogy that located itself on the dividing lines where the relations between domination and oppression, power and powerlessness continued to be produced and reproduced. As a defining element of politics and pedagogy, hope for many cultural workers always meant listening to and working with the poor and other subordinate groups so that they might speak and act in order to alter oppressive relations of power. But professionalist relegitimation in a troubled time seems to be the order of the day as an increasing number of academics both refuse to recognize the university or public schools as critical public spheres and offer little or no resistance to the ongoing vocationalization of schooling, the continuing evisceration of the intellectual labor force, and the current assaults on the poor, the elderly, children, people of color, and working people in this country.[6]

It is against the current onslaught on public schooling, democratic culture, multiculturalism, and the role that teachers might play as public intellectuals that Pepi Leistyna's important book must be read. At the risk of repeating some of the crucial insights that Leistyna provides in this book, I want to highlight some of the more insightful interventions and comment on their importance for those of us concerned about the fate of democracy, teachers, students, and public education.

Central to Leistyna's notion of critical pedagogy is the assumption that pedagogy is the outcome of diverse struggles and not simply an a priori discourse that has to be discovered, unveiled, and then simply mastered as a set of prescriptions to be implemented. Viewed as a set of theoretical assumptions, practices, and body of knowledge that is inventive, contextual, and ongoing, Leistyna offers his readers a notion of critical pedagogy that locates itself in the interplay among symbolic representations, everyday life, and material relations of power. As a form of cultural politics, critical pedagogy for Leistyna engages culture not as a transcendent category or as a depoliticized social sphere but as a crucial site for "the production and struggle over power."[7] Within this discourse, pedagogy becomes a form of social practice that arises out of particular historical conditions, social contexts, and cultural relations.

Rooted in an ethical and political vision that attempts to take students beyond the world they already know, critical pedagogy for Leistyna is concerned with producing knowledge, values, and social relations that enable students to take up the tasks of becoming critical citizens able to negotiate and participate in the broader structures of power that shape public life. But Leistyna does more than simply present a compelling argument for viewing critical pedagogy as a form of cultural politics tied to the project of active and democratic citizenship; he also demonstrates how this pedagogical project is mediated, given legitimacy, and challenged in the work of a range of educators, including Paulo Freire, Noam Chomsky, and E. D. Hirsch Jr. Ever attentive to the concept of pedagogy as a social discourse grounded in broader public struggles, Leistyna fashions his own language of critique and possibility to demystify the common-sense assumptions and social practices underlying dominant models of schooling and teacher education. But he also takes great pains to provide through the work of Freire and others what Max Weber once called models of "exemplary prophecy."[8]

Hope looms large in this text but not through the simple call for clear prose, easy technological fixes, or objectivity. Free of the jargon of undigested concepts, Leistyna embraces critical theory as an indispensable tool for allowing teachers, students, and others to intervene and act strategically to change the contexts that enable or restrict their capacities to be critical agents, to keep alive the hope of pedagogy as an act of critical citizenship and social justice. For Leistyna, theory is tantamount to a form of critical literacy that must remain open, partial, and deconstructive so as to question authority, dismantle relations of domination, and provide options for people to understand and intervene in the conditions that shape their lives. But literacy and language in this context must also be self-critical, open to speculation, and never prone to shutting down discussion.

Leistyna provides an important theoretical service for those interested in education by stressing the importance of dialogue as a pedagogical practice and a performative act designed to confront history, politics, and society while reclaiming education as a project inextricably related to the expansion of democratic values, identities, and social relations. But dialogue in this context is not simply a pretext for a discussion or conversation. On the contrary, dialogue presupposes an object of analysis, the use of theory to bridge the gap between intellectual rigor and social relevance, and it makes problematic the beliefs and practices through which teachers and students engage particular issues without reducing what we believe to belief itself. That is, dialogue is in part motivated by the assumption that there are reasons for engaging in a dialogue, being educated, and being able to discriminate between what is right or wrong, valuable or useless.

For Leistyna, dialogue and the pedagogical practices it suggests, in part, must be grounded in what Robert Scholes calls a notion of truthfulness that "begins in a rigorous attention to the grounds of our own beliefs and a willingness to be corrected."[9] This is not an argument for absolute truth but for the need to maintain intellectual rigorousness and authority in the face of relativism. For Leistyna, dialogue only becomes meaningful through a disciplined authority that draws upon diverse and rigorous strategies of historical understanding, empirical and qualitative work, theoretical engagement, and comparative analysis in order to provide better understandings of the conditions through which people participate in the making of their own lives and a democratic and just society.

Pedagogy for Leistyna represents a moral and political practice rather than merely a technical procedure. Hence, it always has to be understood within the project that informs it along with the historical and social formations that give rise to such a project. At stake here is not only the call to link critical pedagogy to practices that are interdisciplinary, transgressive, and oppositional, but also to connect such practices to broader projects designed to further racial, economic, and political democracy.[10] The project that informs Leistyna's *Presence of Mind* is grounded in strategies of understanding, engagement, and transformation that address the most pressing social problems of our time, particularly issues of economic inequality and racial injustice. Central to such a project is the need to begin at those intersections where people actually live their lives. Critical literacy in this context becomes part of a public pedagogy designed to understand the social context of everyday life as lived relations of power. But literacy also represents a pedagogy of disruption fashioned to persuade teachers and students to address and bear witness to the ethical and political dilemmas that animate the particularities of their lives and their connection to the larger social landscape. Implicit in this notion of the project is an affirmation of the public nature of education as a form of cultural politics and the importance of culture as a struggle over meaning and identity—a struggle that is essential to the formation of public memory, oppositional ideologies, and a multicultural democracy. Within the parameters of such a project, Leistyna argues persuasively that if educators are to define public education as essential to the creation of a vibrant democracy, they will have to make racial justice central to any discourse on education.

Critical pedagogy for Leistyna opens a space for disputing conventional academic borders and raising questions "beyond the institutional boundaries of the disciplinary organization of questions and answers."[11] Such a pedagogy does not separate issues of culture from systematic relations of power, nor does it overlook the risk involved when teachers and students challenge existing beliefs, ideas, and values, particularly as they often frame relatively conservative schools of education. In fact, Leistyna provides a firsthand account of the type of pedagogical terrorism at work in his own graduate program in education at Harvard University. But Leistyna is far too smart to treat his experience as simply a historical memoir. On the contrary, he recognizes that the meaning of schooling, including his own, is not inscribed inside its own context but is made meaningful through its connection and state of play with wider social and pedagogical relations. Hence, Leistyna critically engages his own experiences at Harvard as part of a broader public discourse about the conservative ideologies and teaching practices that characterize schools of education throughout this country.

Refusing to stay within the safe confines of his Harvard Graduate School training, Leistyna's intellectual restlessness and daring lead him to explore a generation of critical theorists and radical educators whose work has always been marginal to established educational discourses. Rather than reward him for such work, many of his professors deride and criticize it by dismissing it as either political or unscientific. Fortunately, Leistyna is unwilling to look upon his own punishing graduate experiences through the lens of despair or cynicism and draws upon them to provide his readers with a moving example of the power of oppositional discourse in challenging such practices and the possibilities at work within such theories for students to develop enclaves of resistance under the most reactionary institutional pressures.

Leistyna's own graduate experience represents part of a larger challenge to American education—to get educators to make explicit the moral and political aims at work in their practice and to develop pedagogies that critically address how knowledge is related to the power of self-definition and social transformation. Leistyna's graduate experience also reinforces his argument for educating teachers and students to move within and across disciplinary, political, and cultural borders in order to raise new questions, to produce diverse contexts in which to organize the energies of a moral vision, and to draw upon the intellectual resources needed to understand and transform those institutions and forces that keep "making the lives we live, and the societies we live in, profoundly and deeply antihumane."[12] Public and higher education need to foster enclaves of deliberation and resistance so that democracy is not viewed as a surplus but as essential to the process of learning itself.

Underlying this important book is the recognition that the crisis of democracy is more than an educational problem, but it is a crisis that cannot be understood and challenged unless teachers and students learn how to be critically attentive to the connection between pedagogy and historical processes, knowledge and the production of competing identities, and the relationship between "academic traditions" and the process of myth making. Pedagogy in this context is neither neutral nor apolitical, but a form of cultural production and cultural politics that is interdisciplinary and continually involved in border crossings, transgressive in its challenge to authority and power, and intertextual in its attempt to link the specific with the national and transnational. The project underlying such a pedagogy may take many forms, but its deepest impulse is rooted in issues of compassion and social responsibility aimed at deepening and expanding the possibilities for human happiness, critical agency, racial justice, and economic and political democracy.

Presence of Mind is a challenging and instructive book. It is refreshingly interdisciplinary, theoretical, contextual, biographical, and rigorous—it is accessible but refuses easy answers. But most importantly, it is courageous because it makes hope the foundation of pedagogy and freedom and social justice the mechanisms that frame its project. This is a book that instructs and disrupts, opening a dialogue but refusing to stick so close to a position that it closes down deliberation and reflection. Given the current assault on public education, Leistyna offers both those who are unfamiliar with critical pedagogy as well as those who are well versed in its diverse traditions a welcomed opportunity to rethink what it means for educators to take up the challenge, as the philosopher and Czech president Vaclav Havel puts it, to create "a society that makes room for the richest possible self-restructuring and the richest possible participation in public life."[13]

Notes

1. Ellen Willis, "We Need a Radical Left," *The Nation* (June 29, 1998), p. 19.

2. Ellen Willis, op. cit., p. 19.

3. Robin D.G. Kelley, *Yo' Mama's Disfunktional! Fighting the Culture Wars in America*. Boston: Beacon Press, 1998.

4. Harold Bloom, "They Have the Numbers; We Have the Heights," *Boston Review* (April/May 1998), p. 27.

5. Richard Rorty, "The Inspirational Value of Great Works of Literature," *Raritan* 16:1 (1996), p. 13 (8–17).

6. The term *professionalist legitimation* comes from a personal correspondence with Professor Jeff Williams of East Carolina University.

7. Lawrence Grossberg, "Bringing It All Back Home—Pedagogy and Cultural Studies." In: *Between Borders: Pedagogy and the Politics of Cultural Studies*, Henry A. Giroux and Peter McLaren (eds.). New York: Routledge, 1994.

8. Max Weber cited in Pierre Bourdieu and Hans Haacke, *Free Exchange*. Stanford, CA: Stanford University Press, 1995, p. 83.

9. Robert Scholes, *The Rise and Fall of English*. New Haven, CT: Yale University Press, 1998, p. 57.

10. My notion of transdisciplinary comes from Mas'ud Zavarzadeh and Donald Morton, "Theory, Pedagogy, Politics: The Crisis of the 'Subject' in the Humanities." In: *Theory/Pedagogy/Politics: Texts for Change*, Mas'ud Zavarzadeh and Donald Morton (eds.). Urbana: University of Illinois Press, 1992, p. 10. At issue here is neither ignoring the boundaries of discipline-based knowledge nor simply fusing different disciplines, but creating theoretical paradigms, questions, and knowledge that cannot be taken up within the policed boundaries of the existing disciplines.

11. Lawrence Grossberg, "Toward a Genealogy of the State of Cultural Studies." In: *Disciplinarity and Dissent in Cultural Studies*, Cary Nelson and Dilip Parameshwar Gaonkar (eds.). New York: Routledge, 1996, p. 145.

12. Stuart Hall, "Race, Culture, and Communications: Looking Backward and Forward at Cultural Studies," *Rethinking Marxism*, Vol. 5, No. 1, Spring 1992, p. 18.

13. Vaclav Havel, "The State of the Republic." *The New York Review of Books* (June 22, 1998), p. 45.

Preface

I wrote these essays when I was a graduate student at Harvard, not that the school of education initiated or promoted these ideas; rather it inspired them by trying to dull my senses. The title of this book, *Presence of Mind*, refers to people's developing awareness of the social, historical, and political realities that shape our lives. It is my conviction that only through critical consciousness can citizens of a democratic society resist falling prey to the deceptive lip service that has been paid to official efforts to inform the public, create civic responsibility, encourage political participation, and achieve social justice.

The central goal of this book is to point out some of the different and multiple ways in which power has been wielded in insidious and destructive fashions. All of the chapters address, through a language of critique and possibility, the need for critical pedagogy to contribute to the expansion of democratic relations, identities, and values. The book is an urgent call for us to engage and transform the nature of what we as educators bring to teaching, that is, for developing what C. Wright Mills referred to as the "sociological imagination"—to be able to read and act upon the world around us by connecting the microcontext of the classroom with the larger macropolitical structures and struggles that shape the everyday realities of cultural politics.

Chapter 1 introduces the reader to the basic ideas of critical education. I set the stage by covering what critical pedagogy embraces and what it rejects from mainstream models of multicultural education. The intention is to scaffold the unfamiliar into the debates over diversity and schooling, and to present a clear idea of what critical pedagogy, in general, sets out to accomplish. In this way, educators are better able to understand how any kind of education that limits the dynamics of culture to the apolitical exotics of food, dance, and cut-and-paste add-ons to existing curricula can never lead to more democratic and transformative structures.

Any discussion of critical pedagogy and multiculturalism is greatly lacking without covering, to some degree, the work of Paulo Freire, perhaps the best-known critical educator of this century—it would be like discussing physics without recognizing the contributions of Albert Einstein. While Freire's name is synonymous with critical pedagogy, far too often his important work is misunderstood and distorted. Chapter 2 sets out to explore some of the basic tenets of his philosophy, and to rupture the myths and uncritical appropriations of his ideas. We explore the concept of dialogue, unity in diversity, democracy and leadership, love, and the need for critical consciousness in the process of learning and knowing. We also rebut the critique that Freire fails to name the oppressive nature of racism.

Mainstream models of education, including liberal multicultural efforts, do fail to adequately recognize and challenge the realities of racism and racialization in the United States, especially within the socializing institutions of schools, government, and the media. When public education, in its many forms, does deal with racism, it is treated as if it were a result of individual acts of mean spiritedness or ignorance, rather than the product of socially sanctioned and institutionalized practices of a historically racist society.

Chapter 3 interrogates the results of the antagonistic social relations caused by the unequal distribution of power throughout society along racial lines. "Racenicity," I argue, is the product and driving force of an ideology in which "whiteness"—which I show has been a sociopolitically and institutionally sanctioned marker of status in the United States—in part shapes ethnic identities, that is, the values, beliefs, languages, and so on, through which we come to see and experience the world around us. I contend that any form of education abstracted from critical engagement with the ideology of white supremacy, with all forms of oppression across a politics of identity and difference (e.g., class, gender, sexuality, ability, and so forth), is nothing more than a distracter from the real possibilities of democratizing society.

Chapter 4 echoes this book's emphasis on the importance of forging a larger conception of pedagogy and politics. The dialogue with Chomsky frames the lives of youth in the United States, and the culture of violence that permeates much of U.S. society, within an interdisciplinary perspective that explores the historical, sociopolitical, economic, and cultural conditions of this country, laying bare the ideologies that drive such conditions. It is the first time that Chomsky's work has been brought into the field of education.

After being exposed to readings by such critical social theorists as Chomsky, hooks, and Freire, graduate students (future and practicing teachers) often ask me what I think schools of education can do to mitigate the complex problems that this society has been facing. I always emphasize the importance of nurturing presence of mind. However, I explain to them that schools of education in this country usually do exactly the opposite, working to deskill teachers from understanding the complexities, and inherently political realities, that they face.

Chapter 5 explores my experiences (seven years) at the Harvard Graduate School of Education. I use theoretical portions of the dialogue with Chomsky (in the previous chapter) as a cornerstone of analysis for explaining how positivism is used to maintain the status quo by manipulating developing minds into believing that science and objectivity are the keys to social justice and equality. I link critical social theory to practice by sharing with the reader not only my trials and tribulations at Harvard, but also how I was able to make sense of them—thus moving beyond mere description and into praxis.

As I argue throughout this book, critical literacy—that is, the ability to recognize and engage the values, beliefs, and interests embedded in the information that we are exposed to—is crucial to meaningful and transformative education. However, often educators are confused as to what this kind of analysis entails. Chapter 6 provides not only a juxtpositioning of dominant and critical educational traditions (the reader having already been exposed to Freire and Chomsky), but also an illustrative example of/exercise in critical pedagogy. In this chapter I deconstruct the work of E. D. Hirsch Jr. in order to show how critical analysis and theorizing function in action. I investigate and challenge, through a literature review, Hirsch's perspectives on democracy in public education in the United States, and consequently provide a clear picture of what his approach is attempting to accomplish and why. I describe his position on *culture, multicultural education,* and *language.* Each of these discussions is accompanied by an analysis of the central points raised, as well as a critique of the limitations and contradictions. In essence, I reveal the deceptive and fundamentally antidemocratic nature of Hirsch's work by looking at what is there, what is not there, and what could and should be there.

At the close of this book I provide the reader with a glossary. All the complex terms throughout the text are boldface to indicate they are defined in the glossary. The glossary is not meant to offer fixed definitions, but rather, it is intended to illuminate semantic signposts that can help scaffold the reader into existing debates and discussions.

A critical reading of these six chapters should create an experience in which theory, that is, how we make sense of the world around us—the why of what we do—can work through critical educators in interdisciplinary ways. The book should suggest what teachers can do to link commitment to theoretical rigor, reflection to practice, and context with pedagogy. A cover-to-cover read should help all of us interested in reviving the democratic process—beyond the deceptive politics of domestication, anti-intellectualism, and passivity—bring the light of awareness and possibility, that is, the presence of mind necessary for achieving a more just world.

Pepi Leistyna

Acknowledgments

I would like to dedicate this book to my mother, Rita, whose life, though cut short at the age of fifty-one, was lived with great generosity, love, and unselfishness—qualities so lacking in this world.

I would like to express a special thanks to the entire Kubik family, especially Ritzy and Brushie, whose warmth and openness have given me the heart—to say nothing of the delicious meals—to take on such a task. I also want to show my undying gratitude to Lilia Bartolomé and Donaldo Macedo. It has been their exemplary mentoring and endless encouragement that got me through to the end of this book while writing my doctoral thesis and teaching three graduate courses. Many thanks also go to the folks at Westview Press, Lisa Wigutoff, Sarah Warner, Cathy Murphy, Todd Tobias, and Mary Dorian, for having such faith in my first solo flight.

From the bottom of my heart, I want to thank Susan Kubik. It has been her love, patience, and humor in my everyday life that have made all of this possible.

P. L.

What's Past, What's Present, a Look into the Future: Remembering Paulo 1921–1997

I like to live, to live my life intensely. I am the type of person who loves his life passionately. Of course, someday, I will die, but I have the impression that when I die, I will die intensely as well. I will die experimenting with myself intensely. For this reason I am going to die with an immense longing for life, since this is the way I have been living.

—Paulo Freire

It is May 31, 1997, my birthday. Birthday mornings have a tendency to bring intense and vivid reflections. At thirty-four, I find myself digging through my past, excavating buried memories. For a brief moment, I wonder if *remembering*—exposing my scars and the pains that I have caused—will only bring me to my knees. Then Paulo reminds me that without trying to trace and make sense of the outside world within me, I become a mere spectator of my own existence—passive, easily diverted and toyed with, unable to engage my life and others around me. As such, I can no longer care and have compassion, be concerned with social justice, take a stance, or love. . . . I can no longer be truly alive. With Paulo's words, I remember that remembering—to be conscious, reflective, ever hopeful, and willing to change—is the only way to truly live. In this way, I can "live my life intensely." This is what Paulo has taught me, and I will forever remember him and reinvent his wisdom and love for life.

Pepi Leistyna

Pepi Leistyna and Paulo Freire. (Photo by Susan Kubik)

1 Back to the Basics: An Introduction to the Fundamental Tenets of Critical Pedagogy

During the Civil Rights movement of the 1960s, various groups, motivated by the contention that educational institutions were systematically denying certain people fair and equal treatment, demanded the revision of curricula and pedagogy in primary and secondary schools.[1] Ostensibly, the goal was to provide all students, regardless of their background, with an equal opportunity to learn. Although a majority of educators across the **ideological** spectrum have subscribed to the idea of equality for all students, they by no means have agreed on the content or purposes of public education, that is, on whose terms equality will exist. Often referred to as culture wars (Buchanan, 1992; Gates, 1992; Giroux, 1994c), the struggle over which bodies of knowledge, values, and interests are to be legitimized through the educational process has represented a terrain of fierce debate in the United States.

Caught in the middle of these culture wars, and ill-prepared to accommodate the demographics and mitigate the antagonistic social relations in their communities, educators and school systems are increasingly turning to the evolving literature in multiculturalism to help ensure cross-cultural understanding, academic success, and overall school/public harmony.[2] Those involved with such efforts immediately confront the confusing reality that, over the years, multicultural education has come to mean many different things.

Using a typology generated by Christine Sleeter and Carl Grant (1988), I discuss in this chapter the myriad of **theoretical** and practical approaches for addressing diversity within schools. The basic components of the different camps are interpreted as presented by Sleeter and Grant, and the individual strengths and weaknesses of each of these models are revealed via a critical pedagogical lens. This process results in a clear elaboration of the basic theoretical tenets of critical pedagogy, which inform the analysis and vision of this entire book.

Examining the Underlying Conceptual Framework of Various Models of Multicultural Education

Multicultural education: Schooling that helps students understand and relate to cultural, ethnic, and other diversity. . . . Multicultural education should be a process to work together and to celebrate differences, not to be separated by them.

—*The Language of Learning: A Guide to Education Terms*
(**McBrien & Brandt, 1997, p. 66**)

Although multicultural education is often talked about as if it were a monolithic entity, as illustrated in the above definition, in fact, the rubric contains a multiplicity of theoretical and practical insights that may even be contradictory. Over the years, educators have developed a plethora of approaches for categorizing cultural diversity (Gibson, 1976; McCarthy, 1993; McLaren, 1994; Pratte, 1983; Sleeter & Grant, 1988). After an extensive review of the literature, Sleeter and Grant (1988) divided the available insights into five groups:

1. Teaching the exceptional and the culturally different
2. Human relations
3. Single-group studies
4. Multicultural education
5. Education that is multicultural and social reconstructionist

This chapter presents a brief overview of the first four of these existing models in a way that allows me to juxtapose them to what I refer to as (borrowing Paulo Freire's term) *critical pedagogy,* or *critical multiculturalism.*[3] Although I make use of the above typology, I am not implying that it takes into account the details of every possible attempt at multicultural education. As Peter McLaren (1995) argues:

These are, to be sure, ideal-typical labels meant to serve only as a "heuristic" device. In reality the characteristics of each position tend to blend into each other within the general horizon of our social lifeworld. As with all typologies and criteriologies, one must risk monolithically projecting them onto all spheres of cultural production and instantiating an overly abstract totality that dangerously reduces the complexity of the issues at stake. My effort should be understood only as an initial attempt at transcoding and mapping . . . so as to formulate a tentative theoretical grid that can help discern the multiple ways in which difference is both constructed and engaged. (p. 120)

Once I have interpreted Sleeter and Grant's (1988) first four models, I show which tenets critical pedagogy appropriates and which it rejects, as well as articulate some additional concerns.

Teaching the Exceptional and the Culturally Different

Proponents of teaching the exceptional and the culturally different are concerned with helping students from diverse cultural backgrounds, including those with "disabilities," adapt to the mainstream demands of public schooling and society. The ultimate goal of this approach is to "remediate deficiencies or build bridges between the student and the school" (Sleeter & Grant, 1988, p. 35).

Viewing public education as systemically sound, just, and democratic, teachers who embrace this multicultural model believe in **meritocracy**—where the so-called talented are advanced by virtue of their achievements. They feel that the only reason culturally different people are not succeeding academically, and consequently in the workforce, is that they do not possess the necessary, standard human capital to navigate the everyday demands of society, for example, language and bodies of knowledge.[4] Consequently, advocates of this type of education attempt to prepare "in-need" students with the necessary skills, values, and knowledge to compete in the classroom, and eventually in the job market, arguing that their success will eradicate the larger national problems of poverty and discrimination.

The initial stress of teaching the exceptional and the culturally different by using educational approaches that are culturally compatible with learners' backgrounds is intended to "teach traditional school knowledge more effectively by building on knowledge and skills students bring with them" (Sleeter & Grant, 1988, p. 43). Therefore, as a process of remediation, educators who work within this paradigm use what information, skills, learning styles, and languages (which may include the implementation of transitional bilingual education) students possess only to the extent that they act as vehicles for more efficiently transferring the learner into the "regular" classroom. Such background information is not intended to displace or transform more conventional school content. Although this multicultural philosophy does not overtly discourage people from maintaining their native cultures and languages outside of public institutions, parents/caregivers are encouraged to show support for the school's agenda.

Human Relations

The main goal of the intergroup education approach to multiculturalism is to promote positive relations among groups in schools by eradicating stereotypes and encouraging tolerance and unity. The basic idea is to bring about the realization that, as human beings, we all have something in common. It is this universal connection, combined with a newly acquired appreciation for difference, that is thought to lead to social harmony within existing societal structures. Intended to be implemented schoolwide, according to Sleeter and Grant (1988),

> the *Human Relations* approach is directed toward helping students communicate with, accept, and get along with people who are different from themselves; reducing or eliminating stereotypes that students have about people; and helping students feel good about themselves and about groups of which they are members without putting others down in the process. This approach is aimed mainly at the affective level: at attitudes and feelings people have about self and others. (p. 77)

Heterogeneous grouping, cooperative learning, and role-playing are considered important elements of this philosophy of education, as is the open invitation to community members to come into the schools and share information about their cultural backgrounds.

Single-Group Studies

Single-group studies are based on **identity politics,** that is, they promote an in-depth exploration of the lived experiences of an individual group, for example, women, gays, blacks, or the working class. Unlike the two previous models, advocates of single-group studies argue that schools are socializing institutions, and thus, inherently political sites. To engage the ideological nature of public education—that is, the basic values, beliefs, and interests that inform the learning process—this kind of multiculturalism embraces **critical thinking,** cultural analysis, and social action and transformation.

"Essentially, the *Single-Group Studies* approach attempts to change attitudes and provide a basis for social action by providing information (in this case through schooling) about the group and about the effects of discrimination on the group" (Sleeter & Grant, 1988, p. 105). As such, students and teachers are encouraged to question bodies of knowledge in a way that links power, ideology, legitimization, and **marginalization,** offering an alternative view of the **dominant culture** and history of the country from the perspective of the group under study.

Differing from the model of teaching the exceptional and the culturally different, single-group studies is not solely intended for marginalized students. However, unlike human relations, which is also meant for all students, this more critical model serves the purpose of "empowering group members, developing in them a sense of pride and group consciousness, and helping members of the dominant groups appreciate the experiences of others and recognize how their groups have oppressed others" (Sleeter & Grant, 1988, p. 116). This approach also demands that teachers develop a more profound understanding of students' existential realities and needs, helping them to actualize a better sense of their own histories and the sociopolitical influences that shape their lives in the United States—the logic being that when people possess a deeper understanding of themselves and their communities, they are more adequately equipped to bring about positive social change.

Multicultural Education

Multicultural education encompasses educational policies and practices that attempt to affirm cultural pluralism across differences in gender, ability, class, race, sexuality, and so forth. Educators who embrace such an approach stress the importance of cultural diversity, alternative lifestyles, native cultures, universal human rights, social justice, equal opportunity (in terms of actual outcomes from social institutions), and equal distribution of power among groups. Teaching diverse traditions and perspectives, questioning stereotypes, learning the appropriate cultural codes in order to function within a variety of settings, recognizing the contributions of all groups to society (especially those that have been traditionally excluded), encouraging teachers to learn more about their students' experiences and realities, and eliminating negative biases from materials are all deemed important everyday practices. This model also embraces cooperative learning, having high expectations for all participants involved in the learning process, nurturing a positive self-concept among students, and developing forms of evaluation that are free of stereotypical language and that reflect a multicultural curriculum.

Proponents of multicultural education recognize the sociocultural nature of behavioral patterns, literacy practices, bodies of knowledge, language use, and cognitive skills. They demand culturally compatible forms of teaching that build on students' learning styles, needs, and realities. In order to accomplish this goal, there is a call to diversify the faculty and staff so that they better reflect the students and their communities.

Similar to human relations, though far more involved, multicultural education also aspires to bring the community into the schools, and vice versa. Unlike teaching the exceptional and the culturally different, which simply solicits the passive acquiescence of parents, proponents of this model

> believe that when it comes to the education of their children, parents and community members must be more than mere spectators, simply attending graduation ceremonies, open house, or sporting events. They argue that just as citizen participation is fundamental to American democracy, so is it fundamental to school success. . . . Advocates of the *Multicultural Education* approach want to see the community involved in budgetary procedures, the selection of school personnel, and curriculum development. (Sleeter & Grant, 1988, p. 160)

The ultimate task of multicultural education is to transform the entire academic environment, and not just the curriculum or the attitudes of individuals.

Critical Pedagogy

Contrary to common misperceptions of critical pedagogy as a monolithic discourse—that is, one particular way of seeing and engaging the world—the vast literature and positions that generally fall under this category not only demonstrate that there are multiple theoretical camps and differences but also that there is no generic definition that can be applied to the term. Even the conceptual descriptors used to name such educational endeavors vary a great deal. While most critical educators make reference to critical pedagogy in their work, they also use a multiplicity of other related terms to describe their efforts: McLaren (1994) sometimes prefers to use "critical and resistance multiculturalism"; Henry Giroux (1994a) often uses the title "insurgent multiculturalism"; Donaldo Macedo (1994) speaks of "liberatory pedagogy"; bell hooks

(1994) embraces the idea of "engaged pedagogy"; and Lilia Bartolomé (1994) calls for "a humanizing pedagogy."[5]

Regardless of the abundance of names that are summoned to describe critical pedagogy (or critical multiculturalism), there are important theoretical insights and practices that are woven throughout these various concepts, which often grow out of a common set of issues and conditions that provide the focus for critical education within shifting spheres of political conflict. It is with these basic tenets, and through the voices of a number of critical social theorists, that I analyze the first four models in Sleeter and Grant's (1988) typology. However, first it is important to present critical pedagogy's rejection of conventional schooling.

A Critique of the Traditional Classroom

Critical educators (Apple, 1996; Aronowitz, 1992; Bartolomé, 1994; Darder, 1991; Freire, 1985; Giroux, 1993; Goldberg, 1994; hooks, 1989; Leistyna, Woodrum, & Sherblom, 1996; Macedo, 1994; Marable, 1992; McCarthy & Crinchlow, 1993; McLaren, 1995; Mohanty, 1990; Simon, 1992; Sleeter & McLaren, 1995)[6] have argued that traditional, conservative, **technocratic** models that dominate mainstream educational programs, which narrowly conceptualize teaching and learning as a discrete and scientific undertaking, embrace depersonalized methods for educating students that often translate into the regulation and standardization of teacher practices and curricula. As such, the role of the teacher, who is "trained" instead of actively educated, is reduced to that of a passive, "objective," and efficient distributor of information.

Endorsing a mechanical approach to reading, writing, and math, critical pedagogues have argued that this movement, referred to as "back to basics," has focused primarily on the transfer of basic skills from the instructor to the student, through mindless drills and rote memorization of selected "facts" that can easily be measured by standardized testing.[7] Such educators often depict how this pedagogical model, which focuses exclusively on preparing students for the workforce, abstracts education from the challenges of developing a critically conscious, socially responsible, and politically active student body and citizenry. Embodying this tone, Giroux (1994c) asserts,

> Anyone who has been following the culture wars of the past eight years is well aware of the conservative agenda for reordering public and higher education around the commercial goal of promoting economic growth for the

nation while simultaneously supporting the values of Western civilization as a common culture designed to undermine the ravages of calls for equity and multiculturalism. (p. 308)

Many conservatives, who wholeheartedly support traditional pedagogy and curricula (Bennett, 1992, 1996; Bloom, 1987; Cheney, 1988; D'Souza, 1992, 1995; Hirsch, 1996; Kimbal, 1990; Lefkowitz, 1996; Lipman, 1994; Molnar, 1995; Ravitch, 1983, 1995a, 1995b; Rodriguez, 1982; Schlesinger, 1991,1992),[8] have argued that attempts to reveal the underlying values, interests, and power relationships that structure educational policies and practices have corrupted the academic environment.[9] As a rebuttal, critical educators assert that such efforts to "depoliticize" the public's understanding of social institutions, especially schools, in the name of neutrality and democracy, is merely a reactionary ploy to maintain the status quo.

It is important to note that conservatives are not the only ones guilty of this unwillingness, or failure, to name the inherently political nature of formal education. Take, for example, President Bill Clinton's two separate and contradicting statements:

Politics must stop at the schoolhouse door!
I support efforts to empower local school districts to experiment with chartering their schools . . . or having more public school choice, or to do whatever they wish to do as long as we measure every school by one high standard: Are our children learning what they need to know to compete and win in the global economy?[10]

Clinton is complicit in perpetuating the idea that politics can be left at the schoolhouse door, though he is placing the central value of public education on careerism and global capitalism: "Are our children learning what they need to know to compete and win in the global economy?" Even if he chooses the language of democracy and civic responsibility, when speaking openly about educating the public, Clinton would nonetheless be taking a political stance. As Sleeter and Grant (1988) point out, "Schooling that teaches about democracy is not neutral, but offers a particular point of view. Although this view may be related to freedom, justice, and equality, it is nevertheless a point of view" (p. 110).

Critical pedagogues insist that, as a consequence of mainstream technocratic models of public education, the larger historical, ideological, economic, and cultural conditions out of which today's social and institutional crises have grown generally go unquestioned. It is precisely this lack of inquiry, analysis, and agency that a critical philosophy of learning and teaching hopes to reverse.

Critiquing and Appropriating from Four Mainstream Models of Multicultural Education

Critiquing Teaching the Exceptional and the Culturally Different

Teaching the exceptional and the culturally different, like traditional pedagogy and curriculum in the United States, is based on an assimilationist agenda. This is clearly the case when any and all materials that are relevant to learners from "different" backgrounds are used only temporarily and are ultimately discarded. From a critical point of view, this culturally homogenizing process, which implies that students completely wipe out who they are in order to become "Americans," is fundamentally antimulticultural and antidemocratic.[11]

Similar in many ways to conventional schooling, this depoliticized model of multicultural education also embraces the existence of an objective/neutral and universal body of knowledge, which is referred to as *human capital.* Rejecting the idea of a universal **foundation** for truth and culture, as well as any claim to objectivity, critical pedagogy reveals that educational practices and knowledge are always produced within particular social and historical conditions, and therefore any understanding of their production and dissemination must be accompanied by an investigation of their relation to ideology and power (Foucault, 1972). Education, for example, as an integral part of the socialization process, is directed by particular beliefs, values, and interests. Knowledge, which in broad terms is understood as the way a person explains or interprets reality, is similarly constructed. The following questions are posed by critical educators:

Whose values, interpretations, and goals constitute the foundation of formal education—the "official" core curriculum?
How is this body of knowledge, which is often falsely represented as being objective and universal, imposed on the public?

Examining schooling, not as a neutral process but rather as a form of **cultural politics,** critical pedagogues argue that, as microcosms of the larger society, educational institutions reflect and produce social turmoil by maintaining dominant beliefs, values, and interests—cultural identities—through particular teaching practices and bodies of knowledge that are legitimized in classroom content. This surreptitious mirroring of dominant values, at the exclusion of others, is often referred to in the literature as the **hidden curriculum** (Anyon, 1988; Apple, 1990;

Giroux, 1983; Giroux & Penna, 1979; Giroux & Purple, 1982; Simon & Willensky, 1980; Vallance, 1973).[12] Giroux (1983) broadly defines the hidden curriculum as

> those unstated norms, values, and beliefs embedded in and transmitted to students through the underlying rules that structure the routines and social relationships in school and classroom life. The hidden curriculum functions not simply as a vehicle of socialization but also as an agency of social control, one that functions to provide differential forms of schooling to different classes of students. (p. 47)[13]

This covert agenda also works to erase or distort the experiences and perceptions of individuals and groups from other social realities that are shaped by the ideologically constructed categories of race, gender, and sexual orientation.[14]

Critical pedagogy reveals how only those characteristics and practices reflecting that dominant ideology will potentially facilitate academic achievement in mainstream schools (Anyon, 1988; Apple, 1990; Au & Jordan, 1981; Bourdieu & Passeron, 1977; Bowles & Gintis, 1976; Gee, 1996; Villegas, 1988). With this in mind, the idea of universal human capital that is enthusiastically embraced by proponents of teaching the exceptional and the culturally different needs to be **problematized** and replaced. The more appropriate use of the term **cultural capital** is extremely helpful in openly naming how different practices, behaviors, forms of language, and meaning are ideologically produced and hierarchically valued in society (Bourdieu & Passeron, 1977). From this perspective, knowledge is accurately portrayed as being generated within historical relations of power and not as some form of universal human understanding.

Contesting **modernist** traditions based on the notion that emancipation is only realizable through objective inquiry, universal reason, and absolute truth, students and teachers involved in critical multicultural learning and teaching are encouraged to examine the values, assumptions, and interests reflected in bodies of knowledge and **representations;** link such information to their own experiences if possible; and subsequently pose questions about the construction of knowledge concerning whose interests are served and whose voices and narratives have been systematically excluded.[15] For example, educators should immediately question descriptors such as "normal" or "regular," which are often used to compare the bilingual and special education programs to the so-called mainstream—terms that **dialectically** imply that everyone outside of this dominant category is "abnormal" or "irregular." In their efforts to understand the sociopolitical, economic, and historical realities that shape their lives and the lives of others, students and teachers need to struggle to make new meaning and develop cultural practices that are engaging, transformative, and liberatory.

Proponents of critical multicultural education would agree with the idea embraced by teaching the exceptional and the culturally different that all students should possess the tools necessary for navigating the current social order. However, unlike the conservative model that never questions the status quo, there is a call within critical pedagogy for the selective appropriation of dominant **discourses**—language and interaction styles—so that people of all backgrounds are not only able to survive within the mainstream, but more importantly, they are armed to transform it. In this way, teachers and students do not fall into what Paulo Freire (1970) refers to as the **banking model** of education, which occurs when educators perceive students as empty containers that need to be filled with preestablished bodies of knowledge. Within the confines of a pedagogy of transmission, learners are treated as **objects** that are acted upon, rather than as knowledgeable participants in the construction of deep, meaningful, and transformative learning experiences.

By accepting the status quo, teaching the exceptional and the culturally different neglects, or simply ignores, the institutional and socially sanctioned practices of discrimination and oppression. Instead, this model perpetuates the myths of meritocracy and life in a melting pot where the patterns of a so-called common culture miraculously emerge. Through a critical lens, any conservative effort to enforce a common culture (Bennett, 1992, 1996; Hirsch, 1996; Massachusetts Department of Education, 1997; Ravitch, 1995a, 1995b),[16] which is understood as an unnegotiated foundation of values, ethics, meaning, histories, and representations, is viewed as the imposition of a homogenizing social paradigm that severely limits the possibility for a participatory democracy within a pluralistic society.[17] In fact, as Macedo (1994) points out throughout his work, *common* and *democracy* are a contradiction in terms.

The reactionary idea of commonality disregards the real inter- and intragroup cultural differences and histories that exist in the United States. For example, as race and culture, class and culture, and gender and culture are inextricably related via discrimination, it should come as no surprise that racially subordinated realities are substantially different from those of whites, as well as different between the ruling class and the working class, and between men and women. The key question is: Whose perspectives and interests are defining societal norms—common culture—as well as what it means to be an American?

Focusing on the imposition of particular values in society, as well as on the antagonistic relations and the **resistance** (opposition) that surfaces as a response to such domination, critical multicultural educators view the contemporary cultural landscape not as a vista of common traditions and memories but as a terrain of conflict. Democracy is the common element intended to unite the nation and eradicate the inequities that create social antagonisms. However, it is crucial to acknowledge that a participatory democracy thrives on diversity and dissent, and not on coercive acts that rely on symbolic and physical violence to enforce conformity.

Ignoring the fact that U.S. society is not built on a level playing field for all groups, and that the elements of race, gender, class, ability, and sexuality have been used systematically to marginalize or exclude many people, conservative approaches to multicultural education never engage the **politics of difference.** Although "teaching the exceptional and the culturally different" uses the word *different,* the model disallows any exploration of how difference is constructed within unequal relations of power. Working from such a limited and limiting framework, one that focuses exclusively on the so-called other, the concept of difference is often not taken up in terms of recognizing and critically engaging the dominant referent group—the invisible norm of the white, affluent, heterosexual male by which all others are measured. Without ever questioning the inhibiting aspects of this dominant referent, teaching the exceptional and the culturally different implicitly works from a **deficit model** orientation that equates different cognitive and learning styles, literacies, language use, and low academic achievement of students from certain groups with individual or group pathology, cultural deprivation, or genetic limitations. As Bartolomé (1994) describes, students perceived in this fashion are "in need of fixing (if we could only find the right recipe!), or, at worst, culturally and genetically deficient and beyond fixing" (p. 180).

Instead of recognizing schools as a product of the larger society of inequities and struggles, they are viewed within this reactionary multicultural model as the great equalizers, the all-encompassing panaceas to "cultural and physical deficiencies," as well as to societal problems. Educational institutions are thus understood as the solution to, rather than the perpetuators of, social injustice and demise.

Critiquing Human Relations

There are a number of qualities that critical pedagogy appropriates from the human relations approach to diversity: the idea that education of this kind is for all students and not just those on the margins, the stress on infusing such principles systemwide, and the use of heterogeneous grouping, cooperative learning, and role-playing in the classroom. The two models also mutually embrace teaching social skills and providing an open invitation to community members to come into the schools and share information about their cultural backgrounds. However, human relations, like teaching the exceptional and the culturally different, neglects to analyze the larger social and institutional structures that create intergroup tensions, poverty, disenfranchisement, and oppression. Instead, this multicultural model is built around the idea of **cultural relativism,** a philosophy in which all cultures are valued equally.

By not addressing structural inequalities, and the reality that all groups and experiences are not treated with the same respect in society, human relations implicitly accepts the present social order.[18] In fact, by using the word *human* in place of the term *cultural,* this educational model avoids any kind of engagement with antagonistic intergroup relations, collapsing into a kind of benign universal humanism (McCarthy, 1993). As a result, proponents openly reject talking about oppressive practices, claiming that exploration of this sort will exacerbate differences, tensions, and hostility among groups. In reference to such approaches, Paul Gilroy (1987) argues, "They have been concerned not directly with the enhancement of the power of the oppressed or disadvantaged groups but with the development of racially harmonious social and political relations" (p. 117).

In actual practice, human relations rarely moves beyond the surface features of traditional foods, clothing, and music. Schooling is consequently, and naively, dealt with as a public ground where people, given the opportunity, can remove themselves from the turmoil of the rest of the world. Sleeter and Grant (1988) contend that within multicultural practices of this type

> students may learn to interact pleasantly with Victor and to enjoy Chinese food, but this is no guarantee that they will learn about issues such as the poverty of Chinatown or the psychological devastation many Asian immigrants face when they realize they must surrender much of their identity to assimilate into American society. (p. 98)

Grounded in a relativistic stance on culture and identity, a major problem with human relations in the classroom is that the attitudes and beliefs of educators are often taken for granted. When advocates of this approach identify the need to question the affective domain of teachers, this often translates into an innocuous call for individuals to be more sensitive to differences and more inclusive. In fact, many well-intentioned educators, working from within this conceptual framework, naively believe that they can be more welcoming and just by miraculously leaving their own cultural baggage and biases at the schoolhouse door.[19] Rather than confronting any potentially negative, inhibiting, and exclusionary ideologies that inevitably enter the classroom, they are, in many cases, rendered invisible.

From a more critical perspective, teachers are viewed as working and speaking from within historically and socially determined relations of power and privilege that are based on such markers as their race, class, ability, sexuality, and gender. Diametrically opposed to ignoring educators' attitudes and beliefs, critical pedagogues call for the ongoing process of self-reflection and self-actualization. This evolving awareness, which I refer to as *presence of mind,* is intended to help us not only understand the social nature of our own cultural assumptions, and how they may affect the educational process, our students, and the school's overall social relations, but also the asymmetries of power that exist within the institutions where we work and live. Reinventing Freire's insights around the idea of "conscientization," or teacher awareness and political clarity, Bartolomé (1994) elaborates:

> *Political clarity* refers to the process by which individuals achieve a deepening awareness of the sociopolitical and economic realities that shape their lives and their capacity to recreate them. In addition, it refers to the process by which individuals come to better understand possible linkages between macro-level political, economic, and social variables and subordinated groups' academic performance at the micro-level classroom. Thus, it invariably requires linkages between sociocultural structures and schooling. (p. 235)[20]

Such presence of mind also allows us to recognize the ideology of groups, such as teachers' unions and school committees, that control school life, as well as "the hierarchical and often authoritarian relationships of school management, the conservative nature of school ideology, the material conditions of the classroom, the structural isolation teachers often face, and the fiscal and ideological constraints imposed by school boards on faculty" (Giroux, 1983, p. 56).

As educators, we need to reflect deeply on the assumptions that we carry about learning, evaluation, and different cultural identities. Self-actualization and prejudice reduction are essential to social transformation. However, self-actualization and prejudice reduction do not in and of themselves address where the self or the prejudice came from: By solely looking within oneself, an individual is unable to make the links to the larger sociopolitical reality that shapes the psychological so as to be able to change it.

It is also crucial to recognize that consciousness raising is not simply about the process of unlearning. Of equal importance is developing an understanding of where and how such values and beliefs were produced so that any such sources can be confronted and eradicated if need be. For example, when it comes to actual classroom practices, Antonia Darder (1991) argues, "Another significant factor in the production of self-awareness in teachers is the ability to decode and critique the ideologies inscribed in the forms of structuring principles behind the presentation of images in curriculum materials" (p. 87).

When human relations manages to move beyond the mere sensitizing of teachers and students, and focuses on changing their attitudes, such a philosophy in action often implicitly individualizes and psychologizes oppression, abstracting one's personality from the **sociohistorical** factors that in fact shape human **subjectivities.** Instead of examining the inherently ideological and thus political nature of identities and educational practices, and the systemic nature of multicultural tensions, this approach abstracts the historical from the present, the institutional from the personal, and thus, the social from the psychological. It deals with discrimination as if it were the product of ignorance or personal acts of mean-spiritedness, rather than the result of socially sanctioned practices and institutions. Cameron McCarthy (1993) observes:

> Within these frameworks, school reform and reform in race relations depend almost exclusively on the reversal of values, attitudes, and the human nature of social actors understood as "individuals." Schools for example are not conceptualized as sites of power or contestation in which differential resources and capacities determine the maneuverability of competing racial groups and the possibility and pace of change. (p. 293)

Trapped by the inherent myopia of this paradigm, it is no wonder that there is little to no call for a radical transformation of the ways in which society and public education have been organized. If discrimination can be reduced to the level of personal attitudes, abstracted from the cultural institutions and everyday practices that have in fact shaped those personality traits (what I refer to as the outside within), then there is no need to question reality beyond an individual's consciousness and actions. Reducing any real opportunity for social agency to psychological reconstruction, as if the two exist apart from each other, is a major flaw in any project of change.

The use of the term *ignorance*, by apologists who are looking for excuses for particular forms of individual behavior, actually conjures up images of a lack of experience, as if a person simply does not know any better. However, the experience of ignorance is not empty of content. On the contrary, it is full of information that is worked deeply into the fabric and texture of identity. Such experience not only distorts social reality but also deskills people from understanding what guides their thoughts and feelings.[21]

Psychologizing the world also manages to create an individualized and relativistic understanding of difference, which has the tendency to lead to a "color-blindness" mentality that disarticulates students' identities in the classroom from the diverse social realities of every day. When educators argue, "I value all of my students in the same way!" as well intentioned as this may be, the lack of acknowledging and engaging the ideological markers of difference, especially within a project of social change, has negative consequences (Nieto, 1992). That is, teachers cannot value all students if they deny any engagement with their different life experiences, especially those related to and shaped by homophobia, ableism, sexism, classism, and racism. Unfortunately, the human relations philosophy of empty humanism and benign pluralism obfuscates the reality that difference exists within historically determined asymmetries of power in which some identities are valued and encouraged, while others are disparaged and discouraged (McCarthy, 1993; Villegas, 1988). In working toward more democratic structures and social justice, as responsible educators we cannot simply hide behind what appears to be an objective and just way of interacting with all students—the idea that "I value all people as human beings."

The process of individualization also creates a distorted understanding of the concept of self-esteem. As argued, the self does not exist in a cognitive and affective vacuum, but rather, it is produced in relation to sociohistorical forces. As such, achieving the goal of raising students' self-esteem, which is often a priority of most mainstream multicultural models, is not simply realized through exposure to a feel-good pedagogy in which we create some superficial context where the learner suddenly finds internal satisfaction. Teachers need to use multicultural education as a way to equip people with the necessary tools to reappropriate their history/cultural past, so as to be able to understand the sociopolitical nature of the self and engage and transform the present realities that they face. However, accomplishing such a critical task presupposes the ability to theorize—that is, to make sense of the world around and within us in a way that we are able to explain the *why* of *what* happens in our lives.

One of the major obstacles of critical transformative education in the United States is that theory of any kind is often devalued among educators. Such ambivalence is not surprising when it comes to schooling, considering the fact that most educational theory has been removed from everyday practice and left in the hands of academic "experts" who have little contact with the actual classroom dynamic. Further, theories of learning and teaching are often uncritically passed down to future teachers to inform more "efficient" ways that students can assimilate basic skills. When asked about education in the United States, Freire responded, "There are always the mechanistic questions, how tos, how tos with no theory behind them. They want to know the facts. I like facts too, but I like to know where they came from" (personal communication, 1994, as cited in Leistyna, Woodrum, & Sherblom, 1996, p. 6).

This divorce of theory and practice is reflected in a system of public primary and secondary schooling that continues to be inundated with the practical: prepackaged methods, teacher-proof materials, and standardized evaluation. Within these rigid and disempowering pedagogical conditions, educators generally have no opportunity, nor are we encouraged, to develop an understanding of the historical specificities and presuppositions that inform such practices (Bartolomé, 1994), let alone those that inform the larger social order.

Advocates of the human relations approach to multicultural education actually work against the possibility of understanding and creating social theory. Psychologizing people's behavior—collapsing the world into the realm of the individual, at the expense of recognizing the sociohistorical construction of the psyche—makes it virtually impossible to interpret, critique, and draw generalizations about what socially takes place around and within us. Educators who exclusively embrace the individualization of life thus run the risk of crippling the possibilities for theorizing what it means to be associated with a particular group or shared experience. Consequently, cultural politics are often undertheorized in ways that lead to a premature search for practical solutions. For example, the basic theoretical underpinning of human relations is that educators need to be more sensitive. The inherent problem with this conceptual approach, in practice, is that striving solely for sensitivity and a safe environment creates a paradigm of interaction that is based on the idea of good relations, and not necessarily on consciousness, social critique, and action. In most cases, the formation of a comfort zone—an inevitable outcome of a sensitivity model—does not allow for critical interrogation of ideas and assumptions. This not only limits the possibilities for critical **dialogue** but also allows discriminatory values, beliefs, and actions to go uncontested. Multicultural education is thus reduced to what I refer to as "the nice and neat." As Ana Maria Villegas (1988) states, "Culturally sensitive remedies to the educational problems of oppressed minority students that ignore the political aspect of schooling are doomed to failure. Worse still, they give the illusion of progress while perpetuating the academic problem, and by extension, the social inequalities they mask" (p. 263).

Perhaps creating comfort zones is a strategy to keep ears open to the issues being discussed; however, if education never moves into the unknown and the uncomfortable, and silenced voices are never heard from, then oppressive institutions and identities remain virtually unchallenged. It is crucial that multiculturalism gets beyond the politeness muzzle of solely affirming diversity, which discourages individuals from intellectually rigorous discussions. This is not intended to be an argument against acknowledging where people come from, being sensitive to the plight of others, or creating a safe environment to dialogue. Rather, it is simply a contention that without critical engagement, sensitivity alone cannot adequately address what needs to be changed in schools and society.

Educators need to create a space that allows for a more critical and democratic exchange of ideas in which everyone's location, experiences, and perceptions in their private and public lives become the point of departure for dialogue and a **text** for debate. In examining the social construction of knowledge, values, and interaction across difference, the idea is not for the process to be abusive by silencing participants or placing their identities on trial. Rather, the process is to be unsettling only to the degree that it forces all of those involved to recognize and challenge their role in accepting and perpetuating oppression of any kind. By not confronting the sources of stereotypes, and by hiding behind superficial, positive portrayals of all groups, human relations works to create and perpetuate what Macedo (1994) refers to as "the social construction of not seeing" and "complicity through denial"—both of which contribute to **cultural reproduction** of the status quo.

Critiquing Single-Group Studies

Single-group studies, in theory, have a good deal in common with critical pedagogy. These two approaches embrace a schoolwide discussion of a group's contributions and struggles in society. Perhaps the strongest connection between the two camps is the mutual recognition of, and engagement with, the ideological and thus inherently political nature of schooling. This entails questioning bodies of knowledge and providing alternative perspectives and **counterdiscourses** (languages of critique, demystification, and agency capable of contesting oppressive beliefs and practices). Such interaction is intended to rupture stereotypes, myths, and cultural and institutional biases.

Single-group studies and critical pedagogy also call for the development of political awareness (presence of mind) among classroom participants, which necessitates constant engagement with history, as well as with teachers' and students' existential realities, in ways that develop the kinds of cultural analyses and personal connections that are fundamental to critical education. Unfortunately, instead of having students explicitly link their actual lives to the legacy of discrimination being explored in the classroom, single-group studies, in practice, has a tendency to deal with oppression in an abstract way—disarticulated from the here and now. Even worse, as noted by Sleeter and Grant (1988), a softer form of this model often turns into "the four Fs: fairs, festivals, food, and folk tales" (p. 121). Generally collapsed into one course, such an approach to diversity and discrimination frequently consists of simply adding on to the existing curriculum, instead of achieving the ostensible goal of challenging and changing the entire educational process.

One of the major flaws of single-group studies—a common problem among all mainstream models of multicultural education—is that it has a tendency to **essentialize** and thus objectify and stereotype identities. Essentialism ascribes a fundamental nature, or a biological determinism, to humans (e.g., men are naturally aggressive, women are naturally nurturing) through attitudes about experience, knowledge, and cognitive development. From a monolithic and homogenizing point of view, the category of gender, for example, appears as a gross generalization and single-cause explanation for individual character and behavior. As such, this model is inclined to ignore intragroup differences across class, ability, race, sexuality, and so forth. Pointing out the limitations of such a **reductionistic** propensity, Sleeter and Grant (1988) observe, "Specifically, ethnic studies often focus on the males of a given ethnic group; labor studies often focus on the working-class males; and women's studies often focus on White, middle-class women" (p. 129). It is as if the multiple forms of diversity—the complex and interconnecting relationships that speak to a more dialectical understanding of the politics of difference—exist in isolation from each other.[22]

An additional, recurring problem with a pedagogy based on identity politics is that experience is often left at the level of description, that is, storytelling is welcomed at the expense of theoretical analysis. Such an atheoretical posture gives the erroneous perception that **subject position** (the place that a person occupies within a set of social relationships, often determined by gender, class, race, language, sexual orientation, age, and ability) leads to presence of mind. In other words, when a **subordinated** person shares experiences of discrimination, this narration, in and of itself, would necessarily bring about the intra- and interpersonal political awareness to understand such oppressive acts. McLaren (1995) articulates this very pitfall:

> Either a person's physical proximity to the oppressed or their own location as an oppressed person is supposed to offer a special authority from which to speak. . . . Here the political is often reduced only to the personal where theory is dismissed in favor of one's own personal and cultural identity— abstracted from the ideological and discursive complexity of their formation. (p. 125)

The pretense that location predisposes presence of mind is like saying that a patient who is sick, who feels the pain, necessarily understands why the disease exists, how it works, and how to combat it. If subject position ensured consciousness, then the white working class and white women would not be so easily diverted, as they historically have been, by issues of race and sexuality, and would rise up in solidarity with others against their own oppression (Allen, 1994; Anzaldúa,1990; Du Bois, 1935; Feagin & Vera, 1995; Fine, Weis, Powell, & Wong, 1997; Frankenburg, 1993, 1994, 1997; Goldfield, 1992; Hill, 1997; hooks, 1981; McIntyre, 1997; Minh-ha, 1989; Mohanty, Russo, & Torres, 1991; Roediger, 1991, 1994; Wallace, 1990).[23] It is only with exposure to a multitude of competing information, and in dialogue with the powerless, that all of those opposed to the present social order can work from a position of awareness to one of informed solidarity.[24]

Countering the reductionistic tendency to conflate location and consciousness, critical pedagogy requires the kinds of theoretical analyses and dialogue necessary for explaining why something (a particular experience) occurred in the first place. As we will see in Chapter 2, for educators influenced by Freire's wisdom, it is important to keep in mind that the concept of dialogue is not simply about having a conversation with students and their respective communities. Rather, this type of discursive relationship is meant to facilitate critical interaction that focuses on the kinds of ideological analyses of knowledge and experience that lead to political awareness and action capable of eradicating oppressive practices, institutions, and identities both in schools and society.

Critiquing Multicultural Education

Critical pedagogy, like multicultural education, recognizes the importance of cultural diversity, alternative lifestyles, maintaining native cultures, universal human rights, social justice, equal opportunity (in terms of actual outcomes from social institutions), and equal distribution of power among groups. Both models call for teaching diverse traditions and perspectives, questioning stereotypes, learning the cultural codes to function within a variety of settings, recognizing the contributions that all groups have made to society (especially those that have been traditionally excluded), and encouraging teachers to learn more about their students' experiences and realities. They also embrace learning cooperatively, having high expectations for all classroom participants, nurturing a positive self-concept among students, and developing forms of evaluation that are free of stereotypical language and reflect a diverse curriculum.[25]

Although multicultural education and critical pedagogy, in theory, have a great deal in common, critical educators argue that in practice this is not the case. Similar to human relations, multicultural education often endeavors to simply affirm diversity and identities through positive images of subordinated groups, and does so in a limited fashion, focusing on color coordination (abstracted from issues of ideological differences among people from the same racial/ethnic group), food festivals (in which multicultural education is reduced to having fun), cut-and-paste add-ons to the existing canon, and group-based methodologies (which often essentialize and objectify students by making them fit to the method, rather than the other way around).

Not paying enough attention to structural inequalities and student agency, multicultural education, through a superficial pedagogy of inclusion, often becomes a romanticization and celebration of differences without any interrogation of the power differentials that give rise to exclusive practices, distorted representations of otherness, and social strife. As previously discussed in the critique of human relations, the insistence on solely affirming diversity creates a pedagogical process that is reduced to an empty form of pluralism that largely ignores the workings of power and privilege. Consequently, diversity is not experienced as a politic of cultural criticism and change—a process of engaging all lived experiences for their strengths and weaknesses—nor is it embraced as an ongoing democratic struggle to achieve social justice. When activities in schools are solely based on games, role-plays, and cultural fairs that are sanitized of any engagement with institutional structures, social practices, and identities, there can never be the kinds of edifying conditions that generate presence of mind and social activism among educators and students. Giroux (1994a) warns of this radical omission:

> In opposition to quaint liberalism, a critical multiculturalism means more than simply acknowledging differences and analyzing stereotypes; more fundamentally, it means understanding, engaging, and transforming the diverse histories, cultural narratives, representations, and institutions that produce racism and other forms of discrimination. (p. 328)

As argued earlier, curricula and pedagogy can either affirm or exclude certain voices and lifestyles. What is worse, in the hands of unreflective teachers, they can demean, deny, or disfigure the lived experience of many people who are not part of dominant groups. Instead of simply adding elements of diversity to existing classroom content, educators need to recognize that the ways in which conventional subject matter often blatantly ignore or distort the realities of the oppressed are not matters of circumstance or oversight, but rather, they are systematic ideological impositions intended to shape public memory along the lines of race, gender, class, sexual orientation, and disability. Otherwise, we risk embracing a pedagogy of content addition that does not question the basic structures of public schooling, nor does it contest the ways in which such institutions are implicated in the politics of difference and domination.

Multicultural educators often mention the importance of not treating lightly such events as Black History Month—that is, any philosophy of diversity should be interdisciplinary and ever-present throughout the curriculum. However, far too often, there is little effort to point out and insist upon utilizing the very political nature of these historical markers to generate year-round discussions in schools about oppression in society. As Darder (1991) states,

> Often the dominant culture is able to manipulate alternative and oppositional ideologies in a manner that more readily secures its hegemony. The celebrations of Cinco de Mayo and Martin Luther King's birthday are prime examples of how these initially radical concepts—intended to resist cultural invasion—have been appropriated in such a fashion that they now do little to challenge the real basis of power of the dominant culture. (p. 43)

It is extremely important that teachers and students develop a more critical sense of knowledge and its inextricable link to ideology and power. It is only then that we will be able to avoid the pitfalls of liberal multiculturalism that Darder warns against, and move into a more liberatory process of learning and knowing.

When mainstream models of multicultural education address the politics of the curriculum, it is usually in a limited fashion, superficially pointing out the problems with Eurocentrism. However, instead of using *Eurocentrism* to name white supremacy, the term functions in a relativistic manner to simply quantify and balance out classroom content by focusing on how often a certain worldview is or is not mentioned. This level of critique does not confront and challenge knowledge bases and the construction of identities, but rather, it collapses into the benign idea that we need to teach all cultures. One seriously debilitating result of this relativistic approach to difference is that white students are not encouraged to recognize the fact that they are also racialized, gendered, sexualized, historically, and thus ideologically driven. Louis Castenell and William Pinar (1993) maintain that, "The 'Eurocentric' character of the school curriculum functions not only to deny 'role models' to non-European American students, but to deny self-understanding to 'white' students as well" (p. 5). With this in mind, any model of multicultural education based on a pedagogy of inclusion that simply functions to raise self-esteem is not only working to raise the confidence of stigmatized students but also to celebrate the development of oppressive identities.

Rather than merely filling in the blanks of the existing Eurocentric curriculum with superficial elements of diversity, educators need to encourage a great deal of self-reflection and self-actualization among all students. This, in part, entails a discussion about content omissions and structured silences, as well as why history has been written in certain ways. It is important to recognize that the call to critically examine existing curricula is not a demand to throw the baby out with the bath water, so to speak. That is, "We need not necessarily indiscriminately abandon the traditions of Western civilization; instead, we need to engage the strengths and weaknesses of such a complex and contradictory tradition as part of a wider effort to deepen the discourse of critical democracy and responsible citizenship" (Giroux, 1992, p. 105).[26]

It is not only what we teach that is important but how we teach. Educators can have very progressive content but an authoritarian style of interaction that excludes the perspectives of students. Regardless of intention, this style represents a pedagogy of imposition rather than exposition. By including all voices in the classroom and having theory work through students rather than on them, teachers can move away from the traditional relational restraints. Real dialogue, which demands critical reflection, debate, and negotiation, affords the necessary conditions for everyone, especially students, to act as knowers, learners, and teachers, and to reach beyond our own cultural boundaries. It is extremely important for teachers to participate as learners if we hope to truly discover who our students are, what they need, and how best to accommodate those needs.

Unfortunately, instead of tapping learners as rich sources of information and guidance, the majority of curricula activities within uncritical approaches to multicultural education attempt to affirm diversity by randomly providing such superficial aspects as Japanese Doll Day, flag displays, and units on particular countries.[27] Educators seem to prefer to use abstract objects and practices from the outside world, rather than the living, breathing, cultural entities—the students themselves—as text for exploration and debate. Although affirming aspects of distant cultures is a step in the right direction (as long as they are not stripped of their actual meaning), without serious consideration of the existential realities of people in the United States, multicultural education can accomplish very little, if anything. For example, how can the study of Cape Verde (especially abstracted from the history of colonization) be expected to reveal the discourse styles, literacies, knowledge bases, and cultural experiences (Gee, 1996; Heath, 1983; Michaels, 1981), which, to a large extent, develop within the antagonistic social relations that create the ghettos where many of these students actually live and grow up in this country? A great majority of the people who are perceived as culturally different in schools in the United States have roots elsewhere, but the reality is that many of their cultural characteristics are more the result of local developments than we care to recognize or believe. Thus, a central problem with multicultural education—and with all mainstream approaches for that matter—is its proponents usually work from an atheoretical, ahistorical, and apolitical understanding of culture.

While the first four models in Sleeter and Grant's (1988) typology readily make use of the word *culture,* none of them, even the more progressive approach of single-group studies, offers a comprehensive explanation of the term.[28] One certainly cannot rely on a dictionary for a definition, regardless of erroneous claims that it is a universal, neutral, and fixed source of meaning:

Culture: (1) A particular form of civilization, esp. the beliefs, customs, arts, and institutions of a society at a given time. (2) Refinement in intellectual and artistic taste. (3) The act of developing the intellectual faculties through education. (*Webster's II New Riverside Dictionary*, 1984, p. 171)

Beyond this vacuous conception of artifacts, social practices, and traditions, culture in the critical sense also embodies the lived experiences and behaviors that are the result of the unequal distribution of power along such lines as race, class, gender, sexuality, and ability (Freire, 1970; Giroux, 1983). Therefore, culture is perceived as being shaped by the lived experiences and institutional forms organized around diverse elements of struggle and domination. Critical pedagogues argue that as people interact with existing institutions and social practices in which the values, beliefs, bodies of knowledge, styles of communication, and biases of the dominant culture are imposed, they are often stripped of their power to articulate and realize, or are forced to rearticulate, their own goals. From this perspective, cultures in the United States develop in relation to (whether it is actual human contact, or via institutionalized norms), and not in abstraction from, each other.[29]

It seems that many of those who participate in current multicultural practices reduce the idea of culture to national origin—as witnessed by the celebration of Japanese Doll Day, flag displays, and units on particular countries. This assumption not only boils down the multiplicity of identities within a nation to one homogenized portrait but also fragments groups of people via real borders, pulling culture out of its antagonistic intergroup relations and institutional formations. For example, talking about Nigeria to a young black man, born and raised in the Bronx, often removes the classroom from the immediacy of the lived experiences of the learner. Even worse, such an exercise risks implying that there is some genetic link between the student and a faraway land—a deterministic connection that is fundamentally racist.[30]

If well-intentioned teachers want to create a culturally compatible/responsive model of education that links history and home life to school life, they are compelled to engage in the actual conditions within which people live, and not solely in the abstract and romanticized version of culture elsewhere. Hopefully, critical multicultural education will lead to a recognition of the real living community learning patterns and worldviews: the different discourses, bodies of knowledge, cognitive styles, and literacies that kids bring to school with them (Au & Jordan, 1981;

Heath, 1983; Moll, Diaz, Estrada, & Lopes, 1991; Gee, 1996). As Joyce King (1994) states, "Teachers need sufficient in-depth understanding of their students' background to select and incorporate into the education process those forms of cultural knowledge and competence that facilitate meaningful, transformative learning" (p. 42).

The reduction of culture to the idea of nation has also led to a trend in mainstream discussions of multiculturalism regarding immigrant experiences. Although an understanding needs to develop about students who have recently endured cultural and geographical transitions, such an effort should not obfuscate the reality that many of the people who are not academically succeeding in public schools have been in the United States for generations—blacks, Native Americans, Native Hawaiians, Chicano/as, Puerto Ricans, Filipinos, and so on. These are not histories of immigration, but rather, they are the products of enslavement, genocide, colonization, and conquest. They should stand as testimonies and challenges to simplistic notions of pluralism, as well as to the liberal call to satisfy the needs of so-called newcomers.

If we are to address immigration, and we should, I think that it is crucial that educators problematize their understanding of this phenomenon. Contrary to researcher John Ogbu's (1987) idea of "voluntary immigrants," most groups do not come to the United States by choice. In fact, U.S. foreign policy, in places such as Latin America, Southeast Asia, Africa, and the Caribbean, has led to mass destruction and chaos, forcing people away from their homes (Chomsky, 1992, 1993). Teachers need to develop a more profound awareness as to why people come to this country. Then we can better understand the relative insignificance of "nice things" such as food and dance that define mainstream definitions of culture and delve into the realities of what many of our students have experienced—war, starvation, displacement, and so forth. We need to move beyond the antimulticultural, conservative ideology that claims, "You [immigrants] came to our house for dinner and now you want to decide what's on the menu." The reality for many is that we went into their homes and took more than we can ever give back.

Although multicultural education, in theory, is intended to encompass issues of race, gender, class, ability, and sexuality, often this approach reduces culture to unelaborated inclusions of race and ethnicity, at the exclusion of all other markers of identity.[31] As such, it neglects to engage how these multiple and interconnecting relationships that define a politics of identity and difference shape the cultural realities of everyday life. For example, frequently the relationship between gender and culture—

that is, how sex-role socialization situates men and women in particular ways of speaking and acting—is neglected. Some advocates of mainstream models actually choose not to see the category as cultural at all.[32]

Along these same lines, capitalism and social class are often not considered significant issues when dealing with raising consciousness about multiculturalism. In fact, like gender, they are generally not understood as culturally formative entities. Consequently, economic exploitation and the concomitant social antagonisms and cultural values, beliefs, languages, and worldviews that are shaped by class relations (hooks, 1994) are rendered invisible, as are the ways in which schools act as socializing agencies for capitalist logic and as sorting machines for a hierarchically divided labor force (Anyon, 1988; Spener, 1996).[33] For that matter, the same is true of the ways in which the working classes have historically been diverted away, via scapegoating, from the real sources of power that affect their lives, and are consequently used to incite ethnocentrism, racism, sexism, and other forms of oppression (Allen, 1994; Du Bois, 1935; Feagin & Vera, 1995; Goldfield, 1992; Roediger, 1991, 1994). In fact, uncritical approaches to multicultural education neglect to understand how social strife and injustice often generate new cultural patterns and oppositional/resistant identities (Darder, 1991; Everhart, 1983; Fine, 1991; Fordham, 1988; Giroux, 1988; MacLeod, 1987; McLaren, 1986; Ogbu, 1987; Solomon, 1992; Willis, 1977).

The ways in which culture is produced via the media are also overlooked by most models of multicultural education. From a critical perspective, pedagogy—that is, how, and in what context, we learn what we learn—does not simply take place in schools. The electronic media—for example, television news, movies, and music—not only serve up information but also shape our perceptions. These media are not simply expressive or reflective but are also formative, in that they can influence how we see ourselves and others. What inevitably becomes a struggle over identity and representation (that is, over who has the power to articulate experience, fashion identities, define the nature of problems, and legitimate solutions) contributes to shaping the sociocultural relations of everyday life—how we look at, feel about, fear, and interact with each other, and how we perceive ourselves. Educators must keep in mind that identity and culture are not simply the products of self-perception but also how we are perceived. Such social, rather than self-, representations lead to all kinds of patterns of behavior.

As popular culture has a tendency to produce and maintain stereotypes and destructive identities, critical pedagogues argue that there is a serious need in public education to have students develop critical media skills (critical literacy) so as to be able to **deconstruct** the ideologies embedded in the images to which they are constantly subjected, and protect themselves against, and rewrite, any harmful messages (Davies, 1996; Dines & Humez, 1995; Freire & Macedo, 1987; Giroux, 1994b; Herman & Chomsky, 1988; Lankshear & McLaren, 1993; Mitchell & Weiler, 1991; Sholle & Denski, 1994). Citing a number of ways in which the media works to distort cultural realities, shape public memory, and situate debates over multiculturalism, McCarthy (1993) states that,

> All of these are examples of a larger system of representation and production of images in the media and popular culture and school texts that position minorities, women, and the third world people in relation to dominant whites. In many cases our students depend on the media, more so than on textbooks or the classroom, for their understanding of existing relations of dominance and subordination in the world. We must therefore find some way to interrogate the current production of images in the popular culture; we must find some way critically to examine film, TV, the newspaper, and popular music in the classroom. (p. 297)

As promoted by a number of critical educators and social theorists, the ideal pedagogical format for developing critical literacies would be to have a stronger cultural studies approach to education that invites students to critically engage the politics of representation in popular culture—in all cultural artifacts for that matter (Aronowitz, 1993; Dent, 1992; Dines & Humez, 1995; During, 1993; Dyer, 1993; Giroux, 1994b, 1996, 1997; Giroux, Simon, & Contributors, 1989; Gray & McGuigan, 1993; Grossberg, Nelson, & Treichler, 1992; Said, 1993; Strinati, 1995). By investigating the historical situatedness of particular forms of representation, and how such images are constructed and for whom, the class can examine and extend their understanding of the ways in which multimedia can work toward both a liberatory self and collective definition, and toward distorting perceptions of social reality that can act maliciously as agents of containment and cultural reproduction. Thus, students develop the ability to recognize and confront their own cultural assumptions, especially those that are the result of the vicarious teachings of popular culture.

Embracing a critical pedagogy of the media, David Sholle and Stan Denski (1994) argue that, as active participants, we should be posing such questions in the classroom as:

What names do the media give as they define the world? What language do they speak as they shape the central concepts of our culture? How does the symbolic system work? And who does it work for? What are the institutional determinants of media messages? Under what constraints do media producers work? How do the prevalent symbolic and institutional systems mesh with other systems? How do they mesh with other such social values as democracy, freedom, equality, culture, progress? (p. 141)

These are the kinds of inquiry that lead to a deeper understanding of the sociopolitical realities that shape our lives. They demand a great deal of self-reflection about the ways in which our subjectivities, desires, and actions are mobilized via social interaction and discursive bodies.

As previously mentioned, proponents of multicultural education and critical pedagogy recognize the social construction of behavioral patterns, literacy practices, bodies of knowledge, language use, and cognitive skills. Advocates of such models demand culturally compatible forms of teaching that build on students' learning styles, and that adjust to their needs and cultural realities. In order to accomplish such goals, there is a concerted effort to diversify the faculty and staff of schools so that they reflect the student body and the public at large. The basic idea is that teachers from marginalized groups could potentially bring a great deal to the school community in terms of providing role models, alternative worldviews, critiques of oppressive practices, and ideas and energy for reworking the system in order to meet the needs and interests of all students (Ladson-Billings & Henry, 1990; Sleeter, 1993).

While the struggle to gain representation of different groups on school faculties and staff is crucial, educators should be weary of the misconception that the mere presence of "different" people implies presence of mind, or that color coordination ensures ideological diversity. In other words, having Colin Powell, Linda Chavez, and Richard Rodriguez at the table—three extremely conservative public figures from racially subordinated populations—would not represent the interests of many racially subordinated people, women, the poor, or gays and lesbians. Rebutting the assumption that skin color somehow implies multicultural education, Sleeter (1993) states that,

> Some teachers of color who have successfully entered the middle class accept much about the social class structure that ought to be questioned. Further, there are bodies of content knowledge and pedagogical practice that teachers of color often find very useful but do not simply know without being taught. (p. 169)

Along these same lines, when it comes to socioeconomic status, one cannot guarantee that having working-class representation will ensure the affirmation and engagement of diverse human experience.[34] As Stanley Aronowitz (1992) observes,

> With the increasing identification of class fate with subculture, working-class life appears increasingly distinct, but "class consciousness," encased in largely segregated and culturally homogeneous neighborhoods, tends to become ideologically conservative and politically authoritarian. This is not the result of "inherent" tendencies in the constitution of the working-class, but may be considered as part of a specific conjuncture of the strengthening of corporate capitalist hegemony and the profound weakness of the labor movement. (p. 68)

The malicious strategy of color coordination, at the expense of ideological diversity, is frequently employed in the national debates over education. For example, E. D. Hirsch Jr., in his successful call for a "Core Knowledge Sequence" in education, has argued that his curriculum was democratically conceived by virtue of the fact that he invited voices from a number of backgrounds to contribute to his lists of "What Every American Needs to Know." However, when looking more deeply at the character of the people who actually participated in this project, the political tendencies, for the most part, are one and the same. On the contrary, multicultural education of any kind should not be only interdisciplinary in content but should also draw upon the lived experience of people from a variety of backgrounds and ideologies who cross and engage the multiple and shifting interconnecting relationships that constitute a pedagogy and politics of identity and difference. Multicultural education needs to develop from, and thus reflect, the plethora of communities that inhabit this country.

Beyond simply expanding the faculty and staff, critical forms of education also call for bringing the public into the schools. Like human relations and multicultural education, critical pedagogy embraces the active participation of parents/caregivers and the communities at large in the process of schooling. As Sonia Nieto (1992) states,

> The research is quite clear on the effectiveness of parent and community involvement: In programs with a strong component of parent involvement, students are consistently better achievers than in otherwise identical programs with less parent involvement. In addition, students in schools that maintain frequent contact with their communities outperform those in other schools. (p. 81)

The problem is that most mainstream multicultural research and literature fails to define what exactly "involvement" and "community" mean.

There are multiple, even contradicting, definitions of *parent involvement* in public education. As Marianne Bloch and Robert Tabachnick (1994) observe, "Some (e.g., the Hmong families with whom we worked) perceive the roles of parents and teachers as distinct, with little overlap, while other parents believe there should be more shared visions, communication, or collaboration between teachers and parents over the education of their children" (p. 285). While both multicultural education and critical pedagogy support the idea of being sensitive to diverse needs and perceptions of parents and caregivers, they also call for a more profound relationship between families and schools—one that moves beyond parent/teacher conferences, bake sales, and extracurricular activities such as sports (Bloch & Tabachnick, 1994; Delgado-Gaitan, 1990; Pink & Borman, 1994).[35] They mutually call for shared responsibility and decision-making power in the conceptualization, implementation, and evaluation of school change. This collaboration (not competition) is intended to be based on respect for parents'/caregivers' insights about their children and the educational process. Both models want to move away from the reality that parent involvement policies and opportunities are usually controlled by very particular contingencies in the schools that neglect to solicit decision-making input from the individuals and groups that they claim to serve (Miramontes, Nadeau, & Commins, 1997).

Unfortunately, far too often, in practice, the rhetoric of parent/community involvement in mainstream practices of power sharing reduces concrete engagements of deliberation and action to mere lip service. Consequently, many efforts to democratize schools do not go beyond the inclusion of a few token parents (Borman & Greenman, 1994). Dale Snauwaert (1993) warns "that the so-called community empowerment approaches to school restructuring and school-based management are also designed primarily to increase efficiency rather than to empower the community" (p. 95).

The critical problem is that parental involvement is often not recognized as being determined within specific and unequal relations of power (Bloch & Tabachnick, 1994), when, in fact, attempts at school/ community partnerships are "often based on a mainstream, middle-class model that assumes that parents have particular outlooks, resources, and time frames available for schoolwork" (Miramontes, Nadeau, & Commins, 1997, p. 202). In their research, Bloch & Tabachnick (1994) argue that,

> The rhetoric and the reality of parent involvement, despite the good intentions of actors and participants in such programs, appear to us to be symbolic reform. The concept of parent involvement, as currently used in the schools we've examined, is an "educational quick fix" that is constrained by economic, ideological, and social relationships of power as well as perceptions of unequal expertise. (Bloch & Tabachnick, 1994, p. 289)

These constraints of social class, language, gender, race, and so forth, which act as boundaries between school personnel and parents, dramatically affect the ways in which people are actually able to participate in the educational process. As Thomas Popkewitz (1992) argues, "The rituals of participation are bound to the discourse contained in institutional relations" (p. 140). He explains, "While the purpose of the project was to give community people representation in school policy-making, the discourse about change legitimated the status, privileges, and initiative of those who could authoritatively define the content of schooling" (p. 141).

In relation to larger political struggles in society, Nancy Fraser (1994) adds, "Discursive interaction within the bourgeois public sphere was governed by protocols of style and decorum that were themselves correlates and markers of status inequality. These functioned informally to marginalize women and members of the plebeian classes and to prevent them from participating as peers" (p. 81). Taking into consideration these subtle and not so subtle forms of exclusion, let alone more overt forms of cultural devaluation, indigence, and disrespect, it should come as no surprise that low-income and "minority" families are rarely found on school boards or at PTA/PTO meetings (Bloch & Tabachnick, 1994). As Malcolm Levin (1987) states, "Parents also know that they are helpless in the face of the schools' power to evaluate them, their children, and their culture" (p. 273).

Refusing to acknowledge that society unjustly values certain cultures over others only serves to reproduce the very same hierarchy of power and exclusion in the guise of participation. In the best interest of democratic deliberations, Fraser (1994) argues that we cannot simply set aside inequalities of status, as if we are all on the same playing field—what she refers to as "a space of zero-degree culture" (p. 82). Such discrepancies should be acknowledged and dismantled.[36]

As with the lack of definition of *parental involvement,* many mainstream multicultural efforts to create a partnership with communities rarely supply an adequate definition of *community.* Are they referring to particular racial/ethnic groups, neighborhoods, socioeconomically equivalent groups, women, gay and lesbian populations (with all of their diversity), local businesses, and so forth? Is there support for reciprocity among these multifaceted communities (different voices and conceptions of the world) that in fact inhabit the area?[37]

Arguing in favor of the term *public* in place of *community* (using Jurgen Habermas's [1962] concept of a **public sphere**), Fraser (1994) states,

> The concept of a public differs from that of community. "Community" suggests a bounded and fairly homogenous group, and it often connotes consensus. "Public," in contrast, emphasizes discursive interaction that is in principle unbounded and open-ended, and this in turn implies a plurality of perspectives. Thus the idea of a public, better than that of a community, can accommodate internal differences, antagonisms, and debates. (p. 97)

It is crucial to recognize the multiplicity of groups and issues that are present in every town and city. Without being open to all differences of opinion and perspective, the idea of community involvement and public deliberation collapses into a paradigm of containment. Elizabeth Kelly (1995) insists that political life should be interpreted "not as a process that could be preordained, but rather as necessarily resulting from the constant interaction of human beings with each other in day-to-day life" (p. 49).

If democracy is to thrive, then there should be no set boundaries as to who can and cannot participate in public deliberations, and as to which issues and interests are appropriate for discussion. As witnessed in the not-so-distant past, the concerns of women regarding the oppressive nature of patriarchy (and more recently of gays and lesbians facing heterosexism, and the "don't ask, don't tell" mentality of the federal government) have been considered private and not public matters by the powers that be. This type of preclusion and the disdain for "difference" fall into what Dennis Carlson (1997) calls a "normalizing community":

> Throughout much of this century, the dominant idea of community in America was represented by what I will call the *normalizing community.* Within normalizing communities, some individuals and subject positions (i.e., white, middle class, male, heterosexual, etc.) are privileged and represented as "normal," while other individuals and subject positions (i.e., Black, working class, female, homosexual, etc.) are disempowered and represented as deviant, sick, neurotic, criminal, lazy, lacking in intelligence, and in other ways "abnormal." (p. 99)

Public institutions of education have historically promulgated "normalizing" conceptualizations of community, and in doing so, they have reproduced an exclusionary model of participation in the name of public good and cultural commonality. Instead, educators need to understand the concept of community/public as a space of difference and diversity. The idea of inclusion should ensure that all groups, especially those that have historically been left out of so-called public debates, can participate. As a positive sign, research shows that when outreach is organized specifically to engage parents from low-income and traditionally marginalized groups, their levels of involvement and participation in school affairs increase (Brandt, 1989; McCaleb, 1994).

One important multidimensional constituency that is readily disenfranchised in public/school decision-making processes is the student body. From a critical pedagogical perspective, mobilizing students is especially important because they are extremely diverse in backgrounds, cultures, and experiences—unlike the overall makeup of most faculty and staff. Thus, if the majority of educators in schools that are overwhelmingly white and middle class choose not to push the teachers' union or school committee to make democratic changes, then the students can.

Another important critical insight around creating public spheres that are inclusive of all voices is not to essentialize the idea of community (Greene, 1996; Pink & Borman, 1994). As Maxine Greene (1996) argues,

> Wherever we are trying to build a democratic community, we cannot settle for conditioning or merely imposing uniform behaviors from without. Nor can we ascribe fixed essences to people or treat them as "representative" of given groups, cultures, or even genders. Treating them as various and situated, we have to take into account a diversity of perspectives and realities. (p. 28)

Essentializing communities risks creating the false binarism of "us" (the public) against "them" (the schools). Thus, it can produce the misconception that there are only two competing interest groups and agendas (Szkudlarek, 1993).

In critical pedagogical theories of schooling and society, multiple publics are preferable to the idea of a comprehensive community. Fraser (1994) argues that we must "eradicate the underlying assumption that the institutional confinement of public life to a single, overarching public sphere is a positive and desirable state of affairs, whereas the proliferation of a multiplicity of publics represents a departure from, rather than an advance toward, democracy" (p. 83). From this perspective, diverse communities of struggle should not be accused of separatism and disuniting the nation as they readily are by reactionaries and jingoists who wish to maintain the status quo.[38] For example, Arthur Schlesinger (1991) wrongly asserts, "The cult of ethnicity exaggerates differences, intensifies resentments and antagonisms, drives ever deeper the awful wedges between races and nationalities. The end game is self-pity and self-ghettoization" (p. 29).

In fact, according to their own logic, Western legionaries—the E. D. Hirsch Jr.'s, Lynn Cheneys, William Bennetts, Chester Finns, and Diane Ravitches, among others, who support standardization and canonization of knowledge—are advocating a form of separatism (which they readily accuse multiculturalists of doing). In other words, categories such as Western and canon by their very nature are exclusive.

Instead of blaming the victim by viewing segregation and ghetto life as a choice, multiple communities of resistance and struggle need to be understood as oppositional groups working from historically marginalized positions of power in the United States. They are bodies of people struggling in solidarity to resist the dominant center so as to be able to democratize and transform it. Strongly in favor of using the imposed margins as sites of possibility, withdrawal, and recruitment, bell hooks (1990) insists that such a space "offers to one the possibility of radical perspective from which to see and create, to imagine alternatives, new worlds" (p. 150).[39] There is a serious need to get schools involved with such potentially democratizing spaces.[40]

A fundamental tenet of multicultural education and critical pedagogy is having students and teachers actively involved in community service. Both models mutually support the idea of a two-way street in which parents/caregivers (communities at large) do not solely hold the responsibility of coming into the schools if they hope to effect change (Hollins, King, & Hayman, 1994). Schools are also compelled to move the classrooms into the communities in the form of parent professional development and student/teacher community service.

There are a number of examples in the educational research and literature of schools involving themselves in community service and transforming the society at large.[41] Jay MacLeod (1991) provides educators, interested in extending the walls of schools, with pedagogical insight for bridging the classroom with the street. He has come up with strategies for high school students to study the local cultures and histories of their towns and cities, and in doing so, they develop the necessary presence of mind to understand the sociopolitical realities around and within them. It is this kind of awareness that can successfully guide new forms of social agency and transformation.

Maria Torres-Guzman, Carmen Mercado, Ana Helvia Quintero, and Diana Rivera Viera (1994) also talk about the importance of linking classroom learning with community action. They describe a typical class:

> The learner had to apply what was learned in the classroom to what happened in the community, and their community action informed and gave meaning to the classroom learning. The students' actions were embedded in the passion, morality, and caring they felt for what happened to their family and friends in the community. Reflecting on the significance of what occurred permitted the students to distance themselves sufficiently so as to gain understanding of the political, social, and scientific complexity of their work . . . students themselves were creating change within the school and in the community. (p. 114)[42]

While I wholeheartedly support these kinds of critical pedagogical considerations and activism, I do not want to give the impression that I believe that urban/suburban renewal should occur only with the sweat and blood of those who are already disempowered in society. That would be like saying that African-Americans should clean up the mess that whites created with the institution of slavery and segregation. Poverty and discrimination are not the products of subordinated groups; they are the results, and thus problems, of dominant cultures' oppressive practices.

If including the public (multiple communities) in the educational process, and vice versa, is to be realized, critical dialogue needs to be at the center of political participation and deliberation. In order to achieve such dialogue, people need to be literate in multiple ways of perceiving and speaking about reality. Engaging a full range of perspectives is not an argument for a particular position or ideology, but, rather, it leads us to recognize that there are multiple audiences, and demands a willingness to strive to understand and make ourselves understood in speaking and acting across our differences. As argued earlier in this chapter, those educators who hope to engage in critical dialogue (so as to reclaim the past and create opportunities for communities to participate in the transformation of present realities) need to include the multiple languages that express diverse worldviews as part of the process of bringing the so-called community into the schools and the schools into the community.

Unfortunately, as Sleeter and Grant (1988) point out, language is only dealt with peripherally in multicultural education. This mainstream approach tends to generalize the complexities of multiple discourses (Gee, 1996) through which people operate in their everyday lives to grand categories, such as English, Spanish, and German, assuming that there are some universal and objective standards by which all languages exist.[43] From a more critical perspective, Jim Gee (1996) argues,

> At the outset, however, we need to be clear that any language—English, for example—is not one monolithic thing. Rather, each and every language is composed of many sub-languages, which I will call social languages. . . . This sounds simple, but it is not. First, we are all, despite our common illusions about the matter, not a single *who*, but a great many, different *whos* in different contexts. . . . We accomplish different whos and whats through using different social languages. (p. 66)[44]

Homogenizing definitions of language abstract systems of communication from issues of gender, class, race, and so forth, which in part shape the discourse styles that are used by all humans.[45] Most proponents of mainstream multicultural education do not even recognize the reality that they do not speak a standard—each person has his or her own accent and a particular take on language that surely represents the communities in which he or she has been apprenticed (Gee, 1996).

Multicultural education's uncritical approach to language neglects to engage the inherent relationship among ideology, power, language, and experience. Such a perspective fails to recognize the fact that language is inextricably related to culture and identity (Anzaldúa, 1990; Bakhtin, 1981; Gee, 1996; Halliday, 1976; Heath, 1983; Macedo, 1994; Voloshinov, 1986; Vygotsky, 1978). That is, it ignores the way that systems of communication, which are all social and historical constructions informed by particular ideologies, play a significant role in shaping (rather than simply reflecting) human perceptions and worldviews, and can work either to confirm or deny the life histories and experiences of the people who use them.[46]

Rather than emphasizing the need to interact with a diversity of perspectives and modes of expression, many progressive educators in the United States assume that multicultural education can take place solely in English. As such, they discount the insights, contributions, and legitimacy of experience of all those who do not speak or write in a particular fashion. This has potentially devastating consequences. As Gloria Anzaldúa (1990) attests:

> If you really want to hurt me, talk badly about my language. Ethnic identity is twin skin to linguistic identity—I am my language. Until I can take pride in my language, I cannot take pride in myself . . . as long as I have to accommodate the English speakers rather than having them accommodate me, my tongue will be illegitimate. (p. 207)

If collective deliberation is to become a reality, then critical educators and other public intellectuals need to work toward recognizing disparate discourses, bringing them together, "creating bridge discourses and in opening new hybrid publics and arenas of struggle" (Fraser, 1989, p. 11). We need to acknowledge and challenge the ways in which social status and asymmetrical relations of power, if uncontested, inevitably and detrimentally shape school/public relations.[47]

Concluding Comments

It would be impossible to capture the diversity of perspectives and issues that are part and parcel of a critical philosophy of education, especially since there is no universal theory of critical pedagogy. However, it is my hope that this introductory chapter has helped people to jump on board the debates over diversity and democracy, that we realize that any uncritical approaches to multicultural education can invite surface reforms, but merely recognizing our differences and ignoring such related problems as racism, social justice, and power as a broader set of political and pedagogical concerns will not lead to a transformation of the exclusionary structural and ideological patterns of our unequal society.

Critical pedagogy is enormously important for developing theoretical frameworks that historically and socially situate the deeply embedded roots of racism, discrimination, violence, and disempowerment in the United States. Rather than perpetuating the assumption that such realities are inevitable, avoidable, or easily dissolvable, this philosophy of education invites all of us, especially teachers and students, across all disciplines and spaces, to further explore and act upon the relationship between these larger historic, economic, and social constructs and their inextricable connection to ideology, power, and identity. In this way, we can engage in real praxis and develop, as we interact with each other, our own possibilities for the future.

Notes

In writing this chapter, I am deeply indebted to Christine Sleeter and Carl Grant for their painstaking research and insight. As all interpretations of their models are mine, I hold myself accountable for any potential variation that may occur in the initial descriptions. This is not an attempt to take credit for their work—it is simply to hold myself responsible for any interpretations that they may not have intended.

1. By no means am I arguing that multicultural education evolved out of the 1960s. There have been significant efforts to democratize schooling throughout U.S. colonial history, especially during the Reconstruction Era. It was during the 1960s that many of the issues dealt with in multiculturalism came to center stage.

2. I do not want to imply that there is a cause-and-effect relationship between demographics and social deterioration. This is a common ahistorical, atheoretical, and fundamentally racist assumption. As we will see throughout this book, cultural politics and oppressive social practices have been at the heart of this country since its inception as a colony.

3. It is important to note that I am only using four of Sleeter and Grant's (1988) models. The fifth approach, *Education That is Multicultural and Social Reconstructionist*, has been incorporated and expanded in my discussion of critical pedagogy. The four that are explicitly deconstructed here were chosen because they represent what I refer to as more mainstream (i.e., more widely accepted) multicultural practices.

4. "Culture" in this sense appears to imply ethnic differences.

5. Many of these theorists actually use a combination of these terms in their work.

6. The number of influential critical pedagogues is far too vast to list here. See the annotated bibliography of *Breaking Free: The Transformative Power of Critical Pedagogy* for a more extensive and interdisciplinary collection of work.

7. The use of "back to the basics" in the title of this chapter is a sarcastic rebuttal to this conservative agenda. My point is that functional literacy and ciphering should never be disarticulated from reading the world and human agency. As such, the real basics of education should be to raise critical consciousness. How else can one make informed decisions so as to effectively participate in a democracy?

8. I recognize the fact that there is a great deal of diversity within this analytic distinction "conservative." However, because of the limits of language, and for the sake of drawing generalizations along ideological lines, I have chosen to use this term. The same logic goes for my use of "liberal," as well as to the ambiguities now present in the words political "left" and "right."

9. For an interesting discussion, see Gless & Smith (1992); Newfield & Strickland (1995); Wilson (1995); Berube & Nelson (1995).

10. As the ideological spectrum in national politics is so small, Republicans and Democrats basically belong to the same party—the business party. As such, they have the same class interest. This point is emphasized in Chapter 4.

11. I believe that assimilation is not the real long-term goal of reactionary models of education. Assimilation is merely used as a mechanism to get people to lose the only tools of resistance to domination that they possess—culture and language. Groups that are marked by race, class, gender, and so forth, are meant to be segregated and exploited. In rhetoric, advocates of this model claim that people can do whatever they want in their homes, but that in public they must abide by certain codes. However, it is naive at best, and malicious at worst, to assume that the two spheres can exist in isolation from each other.

12. The idea of cultural reproduction is used to specify this very process. The list of theorists, researchers, and educators who refer to this concept in their work is far too extensive to mention here. I have chosen to use the term *hidden curriculum* in this particular discussion because it directly implicates schooling in the process of social control and oppression.

13. Whereas many of the early theories of cultural reproduction were based solely on social class analysis, the way that I am using the idea of hidden curriculum here is also meant to include the specific social practices, discourse styles, and representations that maintain discrimination along the lines of race, sexual orientation, gender, health, and so forth. I am by no means arguing that social class does not cut across these other categories—categories that are multiple and interconnecting.

14. The idea of ideological construction is not meant to dismiss the biological aspects of these categories, especially sexual orientation. My point is that dominant perceptions of these social markers (as opposed to genetic makeup) lead to oppressive practices. It is also important to point out that the words *gender* and *sexual orientation* are problematic. To my ears, *gender* only implies biology and is often used in reference to women, as if men are not gendered. The reason I prefer *gendered* is that it assumes an agent—that is, someone is ascribing the characteristics onto others. *Sexual orientation,* on the other hand, gives the immediate impression that the complex cultural identities of gay, lesbian, bisexual, and transgendered people can be reduced to acts of sex. I have similar problems with the connotations in the word *disabled.* It falls within a deficit model that I try not to support. Because of the current limitations of language and the lack of alternatives, I apologize for any future use of these terms.

15. The idea that any and all experience or knowledge can necessarily be linked to one's own life inhibits the need for learners to cross into the unknown. Grounding theory in experience is important; however, by no means should it be the end-all to critical analysis.

16. The number of conservative educators who support this notion of common cultural heritage is far too extensive to list here.

17. To illustrate the power and influence of these individuals, a brief biography is needed. E. D. Hirsch Jr. is author of *Cultural Literacy: What Every American Needs to Know* (a national bestseller), *The Dictionary of Cultural Literacy,* and *The Schools We Need and Why We Don't Have Them.* He has been a senior fellow of the National Endowment for the Humanities and is a member of the federally sponsored Foundations of Literacy Project. His conceptual and curricular framework has already been implemented in dozens of school districts nationwide. Dr. William Bennett, the former chairman of the National Endowment for the Humanities, and secretary of education in President Ronald Reagan's second administration, has championed Hirsch's ideas on cultural literacy. Diane Ravitch, who is presently a visiting fellow at the Brookings Institution in Washington, D.C., served from 1991 to 1993 as the assistant secretary for educational research and improvement and counselor to the secretary at the U.S. Department of Education. An educational historian and professor at Teachers College, Columbia University, she worked as codirector of the Educational Excellence Network and co-authored *What Do Our 17-Year-Olds Know?* with Chester Finn Jr.—

the assistant secretary and counselor to the secretary of the U.S. Department of Education from 1985 to 1988. Ravitch was principal writer of the California K–12 history–social science curriculum.

18. Advocates of a human relations approach to multicultural education embrace the idea of tolerance. But they do not recognize that tolerance also exists within relations of power—who is in the position of privilege to decide who will be "put up with" and who won't.

19. The idea that subjectivities can be left at the door gives the erroneous impression that teachers can in fact be neutral distributors of information, that objective truth is attainable.

20. One of the problems that I have with the descriptor *political clarity* is that it is too closely related in sound to *political correctness.* It also gives the impression that there is only one kind of clarity. Although I am certain that these are not Bartolomé's intentions, language is easily manipulated so as to distort the ways in which we had ostensibly hoped to describe the world around us.

21. It is interesting to note that the word *ignorance* contains the word *ignore.* Only people in positions of privilege have the option of turning their backs on oppression.

22. For the sake of theory and developing analytic distinctions, we are compelled to abstract individual categories from the rest of the phenomenon under study. However, as theorists, we must be vigilantly weary of the fine line between a generalization and a stereotype. We must also be honest about the limits of an isolated analytic distinction in relation to, and the actual complexities of what constitutes, the overall object under analysis.

23. By arguing that subject position does not predispose one to presence of mind, I am not implying that there is *a* critical group that should lead the misled, or that there is only one form of, and road to, political awareness. Karl Marx's notion of "false consciousness"—the point at which members of society buy into their own exploitation and subordination, and become uncritical tools of production and consumption—falls into this trap. This modernist concept is no longer readily used because the dialectic of *false* implies that there is a *true* consciousness. In that emancipation is always uncertain, contextual, and incomplete, this idea of universal truth is rejected by many critical pedagogues. More contemporary concepts referring to the phenomenon of ideological manipulation are *domesticated, mystification of social reality, dysconsciousness, anesthetized, the social construction of not seeing, manufactured consent,* and *colonization of the mind.*

24. I strongly believe that people of any background can speak *in solidarity* with others, and *to* or *about* issues, but they should never speak *for* people whose experiences are not their own. I also don't want the reader to assume that the medical metaphor implies that the oppressed are sick and in need of healing. In fact, they have been victimized.

25. As stated earlier, from a critical pedagogical perspective, the idea of a positive self-concept among students is generated by excavation and interrogation of the past, which greatly contributes to a better understanding of the present.

26. The problem with using *Western* when identifying a particular view of the world is that African-Americans and other racially subordinated groups' strug-

gles and resistance are also part of Western history. It is this relational history—a product of colonization and continued imperialism—and its concomitant cultural manifestations and formations that need to be engaged. The use of *Western* in this case creates a reductionistic binarism that obfuscates the complex interrelationships that constitute politics of difference.

27. This pattern also developed in the three-year ethnography that I conducted of a public school district's attempt to infuse multicultural education systemwide.

28. In critical pedagogy it is crucial to define all terms. As language is inherently ideological—that is, arbitrary symbols that are given meaning—semantics should always be a terrain of struggle and understanding.

29. With a long history of global colonization and continued imperialism, the relational aspects of cultural development are also important to recognize. Culture must also be examined as being contingent. That is, cultures emerge out of particular contexts, for example, the culture of the bus, the classroom, the school, the corporation, the nation, and so on. Often, power relations shift in these contexts and resituate social identities and positions of subordination and dominance. From this perspective, power can be understood as much more multifaceted than simply a monolithic binarism of the haves and the have nots. In some contexts we are the oppressors and in others we oppress (Freire, 1970).

30. Often, within mainstream models, whereas Europe is defined by individual countries, Africa is depicted as a single entity bereft of nation-states. There is the racist assumption that the vast continent of Africa consists of one people.

31. As we will see in Chapter 3, ethnicity is a partial product of oppressive ideologies. However, mainstream multicultural education's act of exclusion via race and ethnicity does not take such a connection into consideration, rendering the other interpenetrating markers of the politics of difference culturally invisible. In fact, these mainstream models do not even articulate the direct links between ethnicity and racialization.

32. There is an assumption that if a person does not pass on his or her lived experiences, then he or she is not involved in a cultural process. For example, one often hears that gays do not constitute a culture. However, what is largely missing from this limited understanding of cultural politics is an analysis of the overwhelmingly heterosexist landscape that deals with and situates gay, lesbian, bisexual, and transgendered people in very specific ways—treatment that has historically reproduced patterns of conflict, resistance, and survival. It is also important to note that one need not be homosexual to pass on a more just sense of sexual politics.

33. This disarticulation also serves to disregard the interpenetrating relationship between gender and class—the fact that women make seventy-two cents to a man's dollar.

34. By no means do I want to imply that there is a single working class in the United States. Class cuts across the politics of difference. I am simply using this generalization for the sake of analysis.

35. This position may be interpreted by cultural relativists as an imposition on the worldviews of the Hmong. However, the goal of critical multiculturalism is to provide access if parents/caregivers want/choose to get involved.

36. Part of the problem is that many educators do not actually live in the towns in which they teach. The physical distance between teachers' and students' communities means that educators are probably unaware of parent/student realities (Torres-Guzman, 1995).

37. As a teacher, I constantly hear well-intentioned, progressive students say that, upon completion of graduate school, "I am going to return to 'my community' and work toward change." However, until challenged to develop deeper theory, they never clearly articulate or understand what constitutes "my community."

38. Such communities are often referred to in a negative way as special-interest groups. However, working toward democracy is not a special interest; it should be the central interest of the country. In addition, it is in fact the totality of so-called minority groups that actually represent a majority, and not some esoteric constituency.

39. For example, Fraser (1994) observes how women have historically used the "private idioms of domesticity and motherhood precisely as springboards for public activity" (p. 78).

40. The use of "radical" is problematic when talking about critical pedagogical considerations. It connotes being extreme, ultraistic, fanatical, even rabid. It seems to me that it is far more extreme to not want to change the harsh sociohistorical realities faced by many people than it is to want to work toward democracy and social justice.

41. If all contingencies in the community, such as businesses and houses of faith, also worked to provide forms of public education, they too could participate in rebuilding the local communities. This participation is not meant to imply a move toward the privatization of public education, nor does it support creating public pedagogical spaces where the capitalist story can be beaten into the heads of youth. The idea is to put aside self-interest in the name of public good (Goodlad, 1994).

42. The Fenway Program, at Boston English High in Massachusetts, also shows potential to embody the kinds of outreach that endeavors to rebuild the immediate world in which students live (Bryan, 1993). Boston's Dudley Street Neighborhood Initiative, which has been working toward community development and empowerment from the bottom up, is also a source of insight and inspiration.

43. *Discourse*, taken from Jim Gee's (1996) conception, is defined here as a distinctive and integrated way of thinking, acting, interacting, talking, and valuing connected with a particular social identity or role—academic discourse, legal discourse, and so on.

44. An uncritical use of sublanguages is problematic in that it implies that there is a standard by which other languages can be measured, evaluated, and relegated to a lesser status—that is, *sub* as in "under." This is surely not Gee's intention.

45. I disagree with any use of the descriptor "bicultural" found in a great deal of current multicultural literature. In fact, all people, including those from the dominant powers, are multicultural. In other words, in the ***poststructural*** sense, they occupy and navigate multiple discourses and social identities across a poli-

tics of difference. The cultural complexities of subordinated students should not be reduced to nation and language, abstracted from issues of class, race, gender, sexuality, age, religion, employment, locality, etc.

46. There are many theorists who argue that object association—naming thought with language—is inevitable in any system of communication, and that language has very little, if any, effect on thought. Notwithstanding, it is important to note that object association is not the same as conceptualization, that is, how we come to perceive and understand the object or action. For example, we all have a basic mental association for the word *welfare*. However, language can play a detrimental role in manipulating, distorting, and thus shaping our understanding of the word. Take, for instance, the following descriptors: "welfare queens," "illegal aliens," and "illegitimate children." The ideology strategically embedded in all of these terms effectively functions to taint our thoughts of what constitutes welfare in the first place. Such conventions are strategically used in representational politics, and thus an understanding of the dialectical relationship between language and thought is extremely important.

47. For example, "a more adequate analysis must also take into account gender-based relations, since most parent–teacher contacts, at least in the elementary schools, are between women who hold subordinate positions in patriarchal institutions" (Levin, 1987, p. 270).

2 Presence of Mind in the Process of Learning and Knowing: A Dialogue with Paulo Freire

Paulo Freire has been the most widely recognized and influential theorist and educator of critical pedagogy. He is perhaps best known for his literacy work in the decolonization process in a number of countries in South America and Africa, and for his first book, *Pedagogy of the Oppressed,* published in 1970. While the **theoretical** grounding and implications of Freire's practices are profound, at the foundation of such work is the conviction that a critical, multicultural democracy should be the driving force of the struggle for freedom. For Freire, conscientization, a sense of history, **praxis,** and **dialogue** are central to such a struggle.

Conscientization (i.e., **critical consciousness,** or what I refer to as "presence of mind") is the ability to analyze, **problematize** (pose questions), and affect the sociopolitical, economic, and cultural realities that shape our lives. Such a level of consciousness, according to Freire, requires that people place themselves in history, the assumption being that we are never independent of the social and historical forces that surround us. That is, we all inherit beliefs, values, and thus **ideologies** that need to be critically understood and transformed if necessary. For Freire, this process of transformation requires praxis and dialogue. *Praxis* refers to the ongoing relationship between theoretical understanding and critique of society, and action that seeks to transform individuals and their environments. Arguing that people cannot change a given situation simply through awareness or the best of intentions, or through unguided action, he contends that we, as active **subjects,** must continuously move from action to reflection and from reflection upon action to a new action. Paulo Freire is an **anticolonialist** writer and intellectual, and, as such, any reinvention of his work should never be abstracted from a political project to achieve social justice.

Pepi: Your pedagogy stresses the enormous role of dialogue and speaking from one's **location.** Is there a contradiction in the idea that if a person speaks from his or her location and personal experiences that negotiation, in terms of meaning and direction of the conversation, is not entirely possible? On the other hand, if one speaks from a negotiated place, then **subject position** and **voice** are somehow lost. Could you elaborate on this idea of dialogue, voice, and negotiation in the classroom?

Paulo: First of all, I am convinced that when we talk about dialogue and education we are talking about a way to approach an object of knowledge. Let me make this clear. I think that in an attempt to understand the meaning of the dialogical process we have to put aside any possibility of understanding it as pure tactics or strategy. The dialogue is characterized by epistemological relations, and in this sense, it is a way of knowing and not a tactic to involve. It is also not something that I create to involve the naiveté of the other. At the same time, a dialogue is not simply another word for a mere conversation among people about everyday matters. Dialogue, from an epistemological perspective, requires approaching and examining a certain knowable object.

Pepi: So the exchange of different personal experiences is not in and of itself a dialogue, because the speakers never move beyond descriptive conversation. In other words, such discursive practice is bereft of theorizing, that is, making sense of one's history in relation to an object of knowledge. For example, without an analysis of racism, we cannot explain why it is that something that is potentially race related has happened to us.

In the United States, even educators that appreciate and attempt to articulate forms of practice around the idea of critical dialogue end up using it as a strategy of interaction without realizing that understanding the object, and its relational aspects, is the fundamental goal of the process. I am constantly confronted with educators in graduate courses who attempt, knowingly or not, to disregard the theoretical. When this type of indifference comes from reactionaries, I understand it is a conscious process of deskilling students in the name of conformity—it's a kind of "just do this, do as I say" attitude. Unfortunately, among more progressive educators, this resistance to theory also often occurs. In this case, I don't believe that it's done consciously in the name of conformity, though this is generally the inevitable result. Theory is simply disregarded in the name of descriptive voice. As such, the authority to speak emanates from the personal—"authentic"—experience in which theoretical explanations of the ideological and sociohistorical formations of such incidents and identities are ignored or simply dismissed. There is an erroneous perception that location predisposes presence of mind. However, in reality, this type of interaction is not about conscientization or social agency—it is more like storytelling hour, or a blind form of therapy.

Paulo: By disregarding the object of knowledge, the dialogical process of coming to know becomes an impossibility. You understood it very clearly. Viewing dialogue from this perspective, we have to acknowledge the following, something that is an unconditional requirement, something that without it we can't say that the dialogue actually occurred. This something is the presence of epistemological curiosity among all of those involved in the interaction. Humans are curious beings. In fact, this is an essential element of our existence. So, dialogue presupposes curiosity; it doesn't exist without epistemological curiosity, without the desire to understand the world around us. That is what differentiates dialogue from simple conversation. Such curiosity embodies the conscious willingness to engage in a search for the meaning of an object, to clarify or apprehend the full meaning.

Pepi: Especially when, in many cases, the full meaning of that object exists in a way that has worked to shape identities and experiences. Via critical dialogue we develop a more profound understanding of our place and possibilities in the world. However, critical curiosity is often systematically crushed out of the spirit of learners in educational institutions, even by well-intentioned teachers who unfortunately do not understand the importance of presence of mind in the process of learning and knowing.

Paulo: One of the difficulties that educators have when assuming a dialogical posture is that they often fall into a position that I call bureaucratic—their minds become bureaucratized. The teacher who becomes a bureaucrat turns into a rigid methodologist, a pure repeater, like a machine, a tape recorder. The students become the stimulus that incites the memorized **discourse,** a bureaucratized discourse. The traditional teacher keeps talking, talking, and talking, totally convinced that he or she is teaching a lesson. In a similar fashion, the more progressive educator believes that he or she is engaged in dialogue by allowing students to participate in a mechanical pedagogy of questions and answers. This is not a dialogue because it is empty of any real epistemological curiosity and profound engagement with the material at hand.

The teacher who seeks to dialogue has to be very reflective, constantly refining his or her epistemological curiosity and reflecting on his or her view of the world. Educators can't merely repeat information. For a real dialogue to take place, the teacher also needs to engage the students in epistemological uneasiness in a way that inspires them to revisit the knowledge that they already possess in order to get a better understanding of, expand upon, or rewrite, it. And that is why it is not easy to be dialogical; it requires much work. It is much easier to be descriptive, purely descriptive, without epistemological curiosity. Now, teachers who are really dialogical get tired. They get tired because, as I've said, they first and foremost have to keep themselves epistemologically curious, and then to engage students in that very practice.

Pepi: On the other hand, there are those types of social interaction in the classroom, masquerading as dialogue, in which the rules of discourse inevitably silence all participants. What often happens in these "learning" environments is that a deceitful form of democracy is used in order to make the teacher's interactions with students and the object of knowledge appear dialogical and egalitarian. For example, each person is allocated an obligatory twenty seconds to speak. What I often find in graduate school is that during my twenty seconds, any critical question that I raise is avoided at the level of "Okay, . . . because of the limited time, let's hear from someone else." This superficial affirmation—"Okay . . . "—and apparent emphasis on equal opportunity to participate, strategically disrupts any possibility for profound theoretical engagement and analysis.

Paulo: You can't have a dialogue thinking that it is simply a process of turn-taking and a mechanical back-and-forth!

Pepi: Such a dialogue is not an exploration of the object of knowledge; if anything, it's a distracter. What I often find is that, as a diversionary tactic, this type of pedagogy simply abstracts the learner's curiosity and identities from the institutions and socially sanctioned practices that produce inequality, injustice, and cultural resistance—institutions and practices which ultimately remain in tact.

Paulo: As I've said, this is a product of the bureaucratization of the mind. It happens when the epistemological curiosity is discouraged or deadened, while relegating the object of knowledge to the periphery of the dialogue. We cannot assume that epistemological curiosity is always present, particularly when the forces that work to bureaucratize the mind work very much to kill it. Even graduate students often do not possess the intellectual stimulus of epistemological curiosity, and that is why most of the time they study mechanically. Epistemological curiosity, which allows for discovery and rigorous investigation of the object of knowledge, is rarely evoked. Since students are not asked to participate as such, it comes as no surprise that they have a hard time if and when requested to do so. The obvious consequence is that they develop superficial understandings of the subjects or problems.

Pepi: As Noam Chomsky has argued throughout his work, the more formally educated they are, the more indoctrinated they become. On the other hand, Terry Eagleton is correct in assuming that kids generally make great theorists—they are relentless in their efforts and courage to understand the "whys" of the world. Unfortunately, as a process of **cultural reproduction,** that innate curiosity that you speak of, that can lead to critical consciousness if properly nurtured—via a deep and meaningful examination of the object in relation to the participant—is eliminated. At this point, educators are engaged in a paradox: While they claim to be teaching, they are actually deskilling students. That is, without critical teaching, learners don't acquire the necessary tools to participate in a dialogue that reveals the object of knowledge. They are thus unable to read and reinvent, as you would say, the world around them.

Paulo: Which brings up your original question about location. While it is true that people need to use their historical location as the place to begin to reflect upon the object of knowledge and to create meaning, the problem is that they often neglect to question their own self or others. My locality necessarily conditions me to ask certain questions about an object. However, even within the limits of my position, and under historical and cultural influences, my job as a learner is to connect it to the rest of the world. In other words, I need to be able to make linkages with other historical events so as to gain a greater comprehension of reality. That is why rigor should be viewed as part and parcel of any method of analysis, as well as an indispensable characteristic of any form of dialogue as a way of knowing. As a process of learning, it can't make any concessions that may inhibit a deeper understanding of the object of knowledge.

Take, for example, a classroom in the United States, where the object of knowledge is multiculturalism. Let's say we have a diverse group of participants—a Kenyan, a Dutch, a Norwegian, and so on—and each one of them would look at the issue from the point of view of their own location, their culture. What we aim at is to reach a knowledge that generalizes. That is, while it is very important to use your location as a point of reference to know your world in more depth, and to also use this point of reference to relate to other locations in the world, the challenge is always to transcend without losing touch of that place. By overemphasizing your immediate location without reflection or understanding of other perspectives of the world, you will invariably fall into a form of **essentialism.**

Pepi: You would be limited by the boundaries of your own experience, values, and beliefs. People often misinterpret your work as saying that if personal experiences are not present, then it's a pedagogy of imposition. But realistically we can't always move from direct experience.

On the other hand, there is also the lack of awareness necessary for engaging how certain experiences exist **dialectically** with those of other people; that is, they may exist relationally in terms of institutionally and socially sanctioned practices. However, I would argue that those relationships, because they are not based on face-to-face interactions, are usually unacknowledged. In other words, an affluent white person may never actually interact with a black person in the ghetto, but the white's participation in the status quo that generates those very conditions of poverty is formative and interpenetrating. These relations, which are often antagonistic, play a significant role in shaping cultural realities, identities, and politics.

A deep understanding of one's subject position thus requires engagement with the unknown on a number of levels. Another justifi-

cation for critical dialogue via an object of knowledge, such as capitalist social relations, racism, sexism, homophobia, and classism.

Paulo: Exactly! The way that I conceive of it, we are engaged in a dialogue at this moment. This theme could lead us not to an interview of an hour but a whole semester, discussing points that
would emerge from the dialogue. We have an object of knowledge
and we have come very close to it many times in our discussion.
What I would like is that this conversation that we are having now
be published as a dialogue where the readers could also assume a
dialogical posture.

Pepi: This type of interaction that you call for would lead to unity in
diversity, that is, a level of understanding alternative perspectives
while being able to critically situate ourselves in whatever the debate may be. Unfortunately, many folks misconstrue this idea by
falling into the trap of cultural relativism. In fact, your work is often misinterpreted as embracing all cultures and perceptions of
reality. On the contrary, I have always understood your pedagogy
as calling for the engagement of cultural realities, in terms of a
search for the strengths, weaknesses, and possibilities therein,
and a transformation where need be. Thus, no culture should be
taken at face value, especially considering the fact that all cultures are intimately related to the dynamics of power.

Paulo: First of all, I think that all cultures have their own identity, a
reason of being, and they should undoubtedly struggle to preserve it. This does not mean that cultures don't carry within
themselves weak dimensions. This reminds me of Amilcar Cabral,
the famous African leader who used to talk about the weaknesses
of cultures. One of the weaknesses that I found in Brazil, just to
cite an example, is the "machismo." Machismo is part of our culture, but that doesn't mean that we should preserve it. So, I think
that cultures should struggle to reinforce what is already valid
and to promote what needs to be validated—especially that
which has yet to be recognized—and, obviously, understand and
eradicate what is negative.

Pepi: What about intercultural dialogue?

Paulo: I think that dialogue among cultures should have two dimensions. It should be a spontaneous and loving one—not only
epistemological, when attempting to understand a certain object
or objects from a general perspective of the culture. In other
words, we should embrace an intercultural dialogue moved also

by affect, and not only our rationality. We should use our sensitivity in this task in order to become almost like the artists, to understand and respect the cultures. We should also possess the political quality of tolerance.

Pepi: But tolerance also implies unequal power relations: There are those who have the power to decide who will and will not be "tolerated." Tolerance in your sense of the word, I assume, is not about "putting up with" so-called others!

Paulo: No, in this respect tolerance enables us to open ourselves to other worlds. Prejudices are in part based on an intolerance of differences. What I mean is that people often tend to be more prejudicial when they face the differences with intolerance. For example, when we look at a person from somewhere else, we feel our differences and we tend to find ourselves superior. But differences have nothing to do with superiority or inferiority. The real concern is to identify the differences and to find the similarities within them, to find certain aspects from a perspective of unity in diversity. We should look for unity; we won't get anywhere if we are not united.

Pepi: I agree that an initial level of affirmation is necessary, especially when it comes to schooling and identity; however, those cultural manifestations, such as art, are also embedded with ideologies that express particular visions of the world. As Edward Said's work has pointed out, culture and imperialism have existed in relationship to each other in a way that such expressive bodies as literature, opera, etc., are formative in that they shape "otherness." These distorted **representations** give rise to false justifications for domination.

Difference is the problematic term here. The concept does not exist without a referent. Unfortunately, we often perceive of differences without understanding how our own location in fact shapes those discontinuities. Acknowledging this relationship is especially dangerous for dominant groups; it questions the legitimacy of their privilege in society. For example, in the United States, the dominant referent of white, affluent, heterosexual male is what shapes the margins of society, situating identities hierarchically. And yet this dominant paradigm, even within models of multicultural education, is rarely if ever named. As an object of knowledge it remains invisible.

This particular point brings to mind a criticism that I have heard, here in the United States, of your work. The basic complaint is that your conception of oppressed, which seems to focus on social class, fails to take into account issues of race and gender.

Paulo: This is generally a response to *Pedagogy of the Oppressed,* in which my central point of analysis, which was social class, was a means to understand a more global sense of domination. What I want to make very clear to both women and men in Brazil and North America is that it doesn't matter to me in what geographical or historical site a woman or a black person has been born; I just want to say that I am, and always have been, sympathetic to their causes. I've been expressing solidarity with these causes since I was a boy, and certainly in much of my writing. One needs to simply read more of my work and to explore the struggles that I've wholeheartedly engaged in Africa and South America.

Pepi: If we are to recognize and engage a **politics of identity and difference,** which I think is crucial in order to dismantle all forms of oppression, at what point does transformation begin, and from whom? While *Pedagogy of the Oppressed* speaks of the voices of peasants, the United States, as Brazil, is faced with multiple, shifting, interconnecting, and oftentimes contradicting voices. Whose interests do we begin with in the struggle for change without creating a hierarchy of oppression or false binarisms? And, how do we avoid paralyzing the possibility for agency, which often occurs in an endless relativistic defining of *difference*?

Paulo: The imperative of unity in diversity should bring all the oppressed groups together with the goal of doing away with inequality. Politics is a game of concessions; we need to be essentially critical to understand what is really necessary and what is superficial in my position and in others, and promote unity by bringing together common goals—that is how I see it.

Pepi: How would you deal with the conflict among differences when these differences are rigid and essentialist?

Paulo: I think that it is very important that the leaders of the groups get a better comprehension of what could be conceded. Let's think about this. I am a Brazilian from the Northeast of the country. Let's say that the profile of northeastern culture is not the same as São Paulo or Rio Grande do Sul. What really matters to me as a northerner, or to a southerner, or someone from São Paulo, for example, is to get to know what it is that, within those differences, could bring us together. The idea is not to try to eradicate the differences. There are a lot of people who think that we will have unity in diver-

sity by a reduction of the differences, creating a whole by this reduction. Unity in diversity does not mean homogenization.

Pepi: How do you avoid a false form of assimilation into the dominant group, because, as you know, this is their agenda? We see this
with reactionaries in the United States, such as E. D. Hirsch Jr.,
who call for common cultural literacy. This move to educate the
masses is at best a process of homogenizing, and at worst, a form
of segregation that, via symbolic violence, will ensure that certain
groups, regardless of how hard they try to join the club, will be
marked and excluded.

Paulo: Yes, dominant groups have this type of discourse. But it is
not the vision of those who are discussing unity in diversity. Unity
in diversity can't ask of me to deny of what and who I am. If I am a
northeasterner, I don't have a reason to renounce the beat and
tone of my voice to sound like a southerner, and they don't have
to do the same thing either. I am giving you the simplest possible
example. Now what I would call for, if this were the case of Brazil,
and the fundamental goal was the unity of the country, is that
everyone make concessions in relation to certain demands of our
regional culture in favor of a broader culture that unites and iden-
tifies all of us as part of the Brazilian culture. That may serve as a
glue for a national identity. However, this cultural glue should
never suffocate the multiple cultural manifestations that are part
of the Brazilian reality. Unity in this sense should never constitute
a process of incorporating difference in a manner that leads to
blind assimilation. What I want to make very clear is that I am not
proposing, for example, that women or gays who fight for liberation renounce their role. Unity in diversity would call for their association with other oppressed groups in order to be truly engaged in a fight for freedom.

Pepi: A fight against social injustice, for example. But this would require that the broader culture that you spoke of be about democracy, which is based on participation and dissent, and not coercion and conformity. In other words, democracy and cultural
commonality are contradictions.

Paulo: Exactly, in the end, the political tactic that I support would
lead to liberation via democracy, and not containment in the unjust sense.

Pepi: You spoke earlier of leaders. It seems to me that people, even
many critical pedagogues, are confused about the role of leader-

ship in social movements, as well as in the classroom. There is this notion that leadership is antithetical to social equality and engaged learning.

Paulo: For me, any movement, any pedagogical process, such as education, which has both social and individual dimensions, necessarily implies some leadership. The political process, which is also educational, implies it even stronger. An action aiming at a certain dream—a realization of a utopia—is not possible without leadership. Without leadership, we would fall into the dismantlement of a practice that is characterized purely by spontaneous reactions, and a form of laissez-faire without rigor or goals. What kind of leadership should there be? How does it come to be? What is the nature of the relations with the people who are being led, and who in fact are the ones also commanding the leadership? The origin of authentic leadership is politics, and there is no other place for leadership to be born than within the group that intends to lead. Leadership should not be something or someone coming from outside the group to take charge.

Pepi: It emerges from the group itself, but surely it allows influences from the outside. For example, your literacy work in the decolonization process in a number of African nations. However, there is a big difference between this type of influence and, say, using the voices, that is, the ideologies, of the colonizer to rebuild. This seems to be the case in many countries that have internalized their inferiority after years of subjugation—a great many Cape Verdeans still believe, often unknowingly, that Portuguese is a superior language to their native tongue.

Paulo: Exactly! From a political point of view, you can see the difference between the leadership that denies, that does not recognize the voices of the people, and the kind of leadership that defends its constituents from the bottom up. In short, we have a democratic leadership and an authoritarian leadership. When considering the democratic leadership and its nature, we have to understand that it has obligations that include establishing principles and limits that have to correspond to the goals to be achieved—which have to be shared by the whole group in a general policy.

Pepi: Avoiding a false form of consensus that contradicts the ideals of a participatory democracy.

Paulo: Yes, avoiding a debilitating consensus where principles of social justice are sacrificed so we can "get along." Although it has authority, the democratic leadership should not impose its ideas. It has to know how to deal dialectically and democratically with the freedom and the authority. That is, it needs to establish limits on, or I should say through, its subjects; *through* because I don't believe that these limits should be established exclusively by the leadership. Those in power by consent of the population should set the limits that express the desires, dreams, and history of all the people who are part of a multicultural society. Leadership is only authentic when it is governed by validating the wishes of the people.

Pepi: This is especially important in a country such as the United States—most countries for that matter—in that the tyranny of the majority, inevitable in a majority rules kind of democracy, is problematic in a multicultural society in which the numerical minority is silenced in the process. This appears to be the missing key. However, being united across markers of oppression—women, the racially subordinated, the lower classes, gays and lesbians, the disabled, etc.—and bringing together common goals, as you've said—this makes for very different numbers than implied by the term *minority.* This also takes a great deal of leadership. I would imagine that your philosophy of leadership also pertains to educational institutions and the classroom.

Paulo: Yes, teachers who take ownership of their students' desires and dreams are using their position of authority in an authoritarian manner. Neither in the affective nor epistemological sense is this dialogical. Such a teacher is in the class, but not with the class. He or she might mechanically teach a lot of biology but nothing about making meaning and democracy.

Pepi: Teachers need to be directive, but there is an enormous difference between exposing students to a body of work and imposing a particular view of an object of knowledge. Many teachers and students often misinterpret your ideas as saying that, in order to evoke epistemological curiosity in students, their directive role as teacher should be reduced to that of a facilitator. But this contradicts your call for academic rigor and the responsibility of teachers to teach, to act as learners, and to authentically participate—that is, to express themselves in the classroom dialogue. My understanding of your work is that we are first and foremost teachers, and that our job is to teach to facilitate the process of learning and knowing.

Paulo: There is an enormous difference between facilitating and teaching. When someone calls himself or herself a facilitator and not a teacher, deep inside what they are doing is renouncing the task of teaching, and therefore the task of dialogue. Their job of apprenticing students into a body of knowledge, and ensuring a critical examination of that body, becomes an impossibility. They are renouncing their duty of teaching, the task of placing the object of knowledge as a mediator between himself or herself and the students and then assuming the responsibilities as a dialogical educator—that is, an illuminator of the object, a revealer of the object. The student should also play this role. However, as far as I'm concerned, I am a teacher—I mean, to teach is my duty, and in doing so I seek to facilitate learning. It is exactly as you said.

Pepi: Denouncing their role as a directive teacher is also an inherently political action that is guided by an ideology that works to inhibit presence of mind both for teachers and students.

Paulo: Exactly, and this ideological posture is to be kept hidden. In other words, they create mechanisms that give the illusion that their position in the world is not informed by ideology. Only the other has ideology. Of course, this is not possible—we are all ideological beings.

Pepi: When you spoke earlier of dialoguing among cultural groups, you mentioned the need for love. Both you and Che Guevara have discussed the role of love in leadership, and you have certainly expressed the importance of love in the classroom. In my experiences in classes such as antiracist multicultural education, and education for social and political change, there are a number of people who are not so eager to engage in dialogue from a position of love, and understandably so. There are a great many people who have suffered, and continue to suffer enormously, in this country. Having experienced the oppressive nature of schools and other social institutions, many students carry with them justified anger.

Paulo: First of all, I understand the process of teaching as an act of love. I mean, it is not an act of love in the formal sense, and never in the bureaucratic sense. It is an act of love as an expression of good care, a need to love, first of what you do. Can you imagine how painful it is to do anything without passion, to do everything mechanically? Second, in loving the very teaching process I cannot exclude loving those I work with when teaching, and those whom I teach. Lovingness, however, as part of the process of educational practice, does not exclude moments of anger. I feel this anger exactly because I love. I do not need to hide this anger. But I also need to understand the anger of the students. They also have this very right to be angry. Teachers working in coordination with the ideology of most formal institutions of schooling often forbid the students to expose their anger, frustration, and disappointment with the teacher and the institution itself.

Pepi: In schools in the United States there is this de facto understanding that we are supposed to pry apart our inherently subjective and affective beings from our work, rather than honestly express ourselves. As **modernist** institutions, schools for all ages uphold the idea of a mind/body/heart split which discourages the presence of emotions, passion, and the physical body in the process of learning. As such, students come to believe that they are listening to neutral, objective facts that have nothing to do with the ideology of the teachers, or the institution in which they teach. As bell hooks points out, this constricting, bourgeois **cultural capital,** which reinforces particular kinds of etiquette that shape classroom interactions, undermines a true exchange of ideas, and ultimately works to neutralize any potential critical/challenging exploration of the inherently political nature of education, identity, and difference. In my experiences, being accused of being angry or passionate is used in a way to silence people—as if one is being emotional and thus irrational and unscientific. This has been a classic tactic for silencing women.

Paulo: Both teachers and students have this right. To not be angry when you are a victim of a violent oppression constitutes a form of complicity with the very conditions that oppress you. Love and anger lie behind the fundamental concern of one of the greatest French Marxist philosophers of education in this century, George Signider. He debates the question of joy in almost all of his books. Signider can't understand, nor can he accept, a school that is not full of joy. You can't bring this kind of joy to life and you can't involve yourself with joy if you don't have the possibility of experiencing love and anger.

Pepi: And the struggle to make meaning via real rigor to learn and know is part of that joy, part of that process of liberation, of breaking free. Again, liberal educators often misunderstand such words as *joy* and assume that learning and knowing is only about having fun. If students are not engaged in pleasurable activities, then the pedagogy is dismissed as being harsh and debilitating, or imposing.

Paulo: I think that love, anger, rigor, and struggle are part of the constitution of joy. I would say that this joy that Signider claims for schools should be extended to the whole world, to the whole existence. I think that good politics should be the one that does not close its eyes and ears to the call for joy.

Pepi: Revisiting your past, considering your political and educational position, is there anything that you would have changed about the course of your life?

Paulo: No. My response may sound a little arrogant, but this comes from a man like me who has reached seventy-three years of age and who has been able to confirm and build upon what he said in his twenties. But that's how it has been in terms of my entire experience; I keep adding new knowledge. My curiosity has been working, constantly increasing my knowledge, enlightening myself. I can say that, as an example, this dialogue has challenged me to a point that I ended up saying things that I have said before, but never like this. The readers might not find it anything special, but I think that there is something new in it. In general, I've been the person I always wanted to be. I might have become more radicalized, but I have always fought the temptation of falling into sectarianism.

Pepi: I want to thank you for this time and insight, and for the enormous hope that you have given me and a great many others, in the struggle for social justice and joy.

Paulo: I would say that this has been one of the best dialogues that I have had in the last two years. I like this.

Notes

I would like to express my undying appreciation to Donaldo Macedo for introducing me to Paulo's work and to the person himself. Without Donaldo's exceptional mentoring I would have never been able to participate in such a dialogue. I would also like to thank Adilson Ramos, who translated the sections in which Paulo felt more comfortable expressing himself in his native tongue.

Paulo Freire, Pepi Leistyna, and Donaldo Macedo. (Photo by Susan Kubik)

3

Racenicity: Whitewashing Ethnicity, Education, and the Public Mind

I was having a beer down at the local pub in Boston last Saint Patrick's Day when the inevitable conversation broke out about who was Irish. Making the rounds, the bartender inquired about my ethnic background. Thinking that perhaps he had found some solidarity in the reddish blonde white guy in front of him, he looked somewhat perplexed when I did not instantly and eagerly raise my mug to celebrate the holiday at hand.

In the past, I would have simply replied that I was Austrian on my father's side and French-Canadian on my mother's—leaving out the details of what has historically been a mishmash of who knows how many relationships. It was not that not being Irish (at least not that I know of) resulted in any reluctance to speak up, but rather, I wondered what all of this really meant. Here we were, a bunch of white third- and fourth-generation immigrants who were momentarily, in some ambiguous and seemingly insignificant way, declaring our ethnic identities: "Italian," "Irish," and another "French-Canadian."

Tony assured us that his mother made the best tomato sauce in the world, Donny claimed that he could drink anyone under the table, and Philip raged about the superiority of Canadian hockey players. The irony of this scene was that these three working-class guys, who were raising their family's coat of arms, are the same ones who readily yell at the television that "America is for Americans!" and for "those people" (which always implies Latino/as, Asians, and blacks) to "go back home!" At their most accommodating they shout, "Learn English and get a job!" "If our immigrant grandparents made it, then why can't you!" The blatant contradiction between celebrating and denouncing ethnic roots has always gone unmentioned and thus uncontested.[1]

Having known these guys for years, it is obvious that any authentic connection that we have with our ancestors is superficial at best, a connection that comes to life around such holidays. In fact, there is virtually no trace of my grandparents in my life—no religious affiliation, no common language, values, or social practices, nothing but a name. But then what is in a name?

I looked over at Philip and asked him if he knew the meaning of his family name, to which he immediately responded, "of the wood!"—admittingly the only two words in French that he knew. I then inquired if he was aware of the fact that he had the same last name as one of the most famous African-American intellectuals in U.S. history. With a look of utter disgust and in blatantly racist overtones his earlier cries for American patriotism turned into a fervent denial of any affiliation with a black man.

In Philip's mind, do differences in skin color preclude individuals from any form of ethnic connection, and if so, does being "American" exclude racial groups other than whites from membership?[2] What historical and sociopolitical mechanisms have shaped these white men's ethnic identities and perceptions? And, what in fact are the defining characteristics of being "American"?[3] I would like to explore these questions by examining *racenicity,* the process through which the **sociohistorical** and **ideological** construction of race ("whiteness" in particular) has had a significant impact on defining national identity, ethnicity, and the perception of ethnic differences in the United States.

I fully recognize that there are other factors, such as gender, capitalism, class, health, age, locality, religion, and sexual orientation, that play an important role in the construction of ethnicity/culture, as well as in the multiple social identities, **discourses,** and struggles that we all individually embody. Although the discussion of this paper focuses on the effects of the ideological construction of race, the analytic distinction of *racenicity* should not be abstracted from these and other important defining factors—in fact, we need to develop a more **dialectical** understanding of the multiple and interconnecting relationships that speak to a more profound understanding of the **politics of difference.**[4]

The Fragmentation of Race and Ethnicity

Far too often, mainstream scholars and the general public have differentiated between racial and ethnic lines. Although there is a plethora of publications that list the two terms side by side, such literature fails to adequately articulate their connection. Consider the following definition of *ethnicity* taken from *Sources: Notable Selections in Race and Ethnicity:*

> Ethnicity refers to an affiliation of people who share similar cultural characteristics. Members of ethnic groups share common languages, religious beliefs, cultural traditions and customs, value systems, and normative orientations. They also share a similar world-view, an ethnic consciousness—a peoplehood. Ethnicity is a sociopolitical construct that emerges from collective experiences in a society. That is, ethnic consciousness is a consequence of or a response to the social conditions minority populations encounter once they migrate to a foreign country. (Aguirre & Baker, 1995, p. 24)

This particular definition, while more progressive than most, nonetheless fails to point out that not all ethnic groups have been immigrants, that a great many were victims of slavery, conquest, colonization, and coercion. It also adheres to an ambiguous use of the term *minority:* In the United States, groups such as Dutch-Americans or German-Americans have never been referred to as "minorities," regardless of their population size. In fact, there is rarely the use of hyphenation between the two words with those who are considered "white."[5]

As a marker of low status, the term *minority* has historically been used to categorize racially subordinated groups. The use of this descriptor is also problematic in that, as Lilia Bartolomé (1994) points out, "the term connotes numerical minority rather than the general low status (economic, political, and social) these groups have held" (p. 174).

Although Aguirre and Baker's (1995) definition recognizes ethnicity as a sociopolitical construct and the fact that social conditions shape experience, it neglects to adequately point out how the sociohistorical and ideological construction of race greatly contributes to those social conditions—that is, as this chapter explores, how the **racialization** of identities and the racism therein has played a significant and inextricable role in shaping ethnic identities and perceptions in the United States.

The Racist View of the Relationship Between Race and Ethnicity

Conservatives have historically equated race and ethnicity within unsubstantiated claims that biological characteristics result in predisposed psychological, intellectual, and social behavior. Such propaganda has proved to be more than useful in justifying genocide, slavery, colonization, and segregation. Native Americans—"the red man"—were represented as ignoble savages, "untrustworthy, dishonest, and lazy" (Bowker, 1993, p. 29). Blacks have been portrayed as only partially human, wild, uncontrolled, and deviant.[6] Mexicans, who were also considered part of "the lower races," have been characterized as simple-minded, carefree, and indolent half-breeds who are "somewhere between savagism and civilization" (Menchaca & Vallencia, 1990, p. 228).[7]

Such racist sentiments continued to echo at the turn of the century as social theorists, historians, and scientists insisted that whites were the genetically superior race. IQ testing became one of the predominant methods for "scientifically" arguing that African-, Native, and Mexican-Americans were intellectually inferior to Anglos (Gould, 1981). More recently, Richard Hernstein and Charles Murray's (1994) publication of *The Bell Curve: Intelligence and Class Structure in American Life,* or perhaps more importantly, the popular reaction to the book, continues this ideological onslaught by reasserting that blacks and other subordinated groups are intellectually limited—implying that their learning and earning capabilities are restricted.[8]

Asians—"the yellow man"—have long been victims of this racist equation of biology and ethnicity. Asian immigrants of the late 1800s were portrayed in mainstream U.S. society as inherently "immoral, dangerous, and addicted to drugs" (Knowledge Unlimited, 1987).

> During their entire settlement in California [the Chinese] have never adapted themselves, to our habits, mode of dress, or our educational system, . . . never discovered the difference between right and wrong, or advanced a step beyond the traditions of their native hive. (California State Legislature, 1876)

In 1902, propelled by this concocted fear of the "yellow peril," Congress passed the Oriental Exclusion Act, which virtually eliminated all immigration from the Far East. In order to get a sense of the sociohistorical influences of such legislation on more recent regulations, it is important to note that it was not until changes in the immigration policy of 1965 that race and nationality were removed as criteria for qualifying as an "acceptable" immigrant.

During the World War II, Japanese-Americans would be targeted by this same racist ideology based on inborn cultural traits. Take, for example, General DeWitt's comments in support of what would lead to the theft of their property and their internment in concentration camps:

The Japanese race is an enemy race and while many second and third generation Japanese born on United States soil, possessed of United States citizenship, have become "Americanized," *the racial strains are undiluted.* [emphasis added] (as cited in Yinger, 1994, p. 30)[9]

Today, Asians face a new form of divisive racism embedded in model minority stereotypes that depict the youth of these multifarious populations as predisposed to be "science and math whiz-kids." Such stereotypes also generate the idea that these groups are overwhelmingly reaping economic benefits as owners of corner stores and other small businesses. These **essentializing** images not only monolithically bunch together the enormous complexity of the peoples/cultures that fall into this category but also misrepresent the history of exploitation of Asians in the United States. In addition, such **representations** strategically function to disregard the harsh realities of "the other side of the Asian-American success story" (Walker-Moffat, 1995)—that is, they ignore the great many Hmong, Laotians, and Cambodians, among others, who actually live in abject poverty and readily experience social injustice. The preponderance of these exaggerated "positive images" simply serves to perpetuate intergroup antagonistic relations (e.g., one of the messages being, "Why can't you blacks and Latino/as be like them—so hard-working with such good family values?") and acts as a justification for cutting federal support for the needy.[10]

Although the list of groups that have fallen victim to this type of racist ideology is far more extensive, these examples nonetheless serve the purpose of articulating some important connections between race and ethnicity.[11] However, the connection is not between biology and behavior. As we shall see throughout this chapter, understanding the inextricable relationship between the two categories entails dissecting how racialization/racism affects the patterns of everyday living: language, traditions and customs, values and normative orientations, worldviews, and so forth. In this sense, *race* and *ethnicity* should not be observed as entirely separate entities; thus the concept *racenicity*—a point of analysis that embodies, without conflating, a fusion of these two terms.

What Is Racenicity?

As John Milton Yinger (1994) points out, "Many recent studies of ethnicity have focused much attention on cultural differences and the value of pluralism, and less attention on how ethnic differences are implicated in the distribution of power and privilege" (p. 22). Ethnicity needs to be understood as being shaped by the lived experiences and institutional forms organized around diverse elements of struggle and domination. As argued in Chapter 1 of this book, beyond the limits of traditional anthropological/sociological definitions, ethnicity/culture also embodies the experiences and behaviors that are the result of the asymmetrical distribution of power across such social markers as race, gender, class, health, and sexual orientation—that is, forms of oppression that are lived out. Culture does not take place in a social vacuum, but rather, as people interact with existing groups and institutions, and participate in social practices in which the values, beliefs, bodies of knowledge, representations, and styles of communication of the **dominant culture** are imposed, intergroup tensions inevitably emerge. Within these volatile social relations, groups "may mobilize or invent the rudiments of ethnicity in an effort to oppose discrimination" (Yinger, 1994, p. 22). At the same time, they may also reproduce ethnic patterns that reinforce the status quo.

Racenicity is thus the result of the antagonistic social relations caused by the unequal distribution of power throughout society along racial lines. It is the product and driving force of an ideology in which "whiteness," which I will show has been a sociopolitically and institutionally sanctioned marker of status in the United States, in part shapes ethnic identities.[12] As Peter McLaren (1994) contends, "Whiteness does not exist outside of culture but constitutes the prevailing social **texts** in which social norms are made and remade" (p. 59).

I will argue that as ethnic/cultural differences are purged and social practices are reshaped around this racial identity, a hierarchy emerges that subcategorizes while devaluing groups of people that are designated "racial others" and/or "ethnics." This racist hierarchy has resulted in three general patterns of ethnic/racialized behavior:

1. Most whites uncritically assimilate the cultural criteria of dominant racist values and practices and as a result are unable to historically situate themselves—that is, they are unable to identify the cultural mechanisms that have shaped their ethnic identities.

2. Groups that are racially subordinated, such as blacks, Latino/as, Asians, and Native Americans, develop ethnic/cultural artifacts and practices that function to resist social injustice.

3. Some members of racially subordinated populations come to believe in their imposed inferior status and consequently buy into the dominant paradigm by attempting to change their ethnic and physical beings in order to fit in.

It is important to note here that there is an infinite number of ways in which racenicity manifests itself and that these categories only represent three examples. It is also crucial to recognize that such categories are not fixed in the sense that people either belong to one or the other. Individuals, with their multiple and contingent social identities, may simultaneously participate in liberatory and oppressive social practices.

The point of creating this new analytic category (racenicity) is by no means meant to essentialize race (to imply that racial groups are fixed and exclusive), to assume that all racially subordinated groups/individuals think about is their oppression, or to argue that **resistant/oppositional behavior** or assimilation manifests itself in deterministic or monolithic ways. Contemporary African-American culture, for example, "is radically complex and diverse, marked by an intriguing variety of intellectual reflections, artistic creations, and social practices" (Dyson, 1993, p. xiii)—it is also cut across by such issues as class, gender, and sexuality. In addition, racenicity does not imply that racism is monolithic and unchanging. As Paul Gilroy (1987) argues, "Different patterns of 'racial' activity and political struggle will appear in determinate historical conditions (p. 27) . . . 'race' politics has no givens, no essential meanings or preferred images which establish its continuity beyond the limits of history and struggle" (p. 115).

It is also important to note that this new point of analysis does not imply that the category of *race* is simply a synonym for *ethnicity.* Conservative social and educational theorists have historically attempted to obfuscate the realities of racism by hiding behind so-called ethnic differences—what they have perceived to be deficiencies. However, this cultural deprivation model has merely served the purpose of strategically disguising, while maintaining, the fabricated legacy of genetic inferiority.

Before I discuss the three previously mentioned manifestations of racenicity and illustrate how race, beyond mere skin color, is an important source of meaning, (dis)advantage, and identity, it is crucial to first depict whose perspectives and interests have been defining the national standards of racial/ethnic character.

The Social Construction of Whiteness:
The Yardstick of Ethnicity

> The White economy, polity, society, values, and religion, and even the White self, were constructed and reconstructed with the Black slave—and after emancipation the Black "semi-slave"—as a central point of reference. (Feagin & Vera, 1995, p. xi)[13]

It is only in a race-conscious society that skin color takes on historical, sociocultural, ideological, and political significance. In the seventeenth century the colonial planter class, in what was to become the United States, brought the first enslaved Africans and indentured white servants to the colonies. Facing the realities of labor unrest, interracial marriages, and uprising, this Anglo elite strategically made use of the idea of a white race in order to create racial solidarity among the white classes (Allen, 1994). Providing the disenfranchised and propertyless white workers with racial privileges proved successful in ensuring their disassociation with enslaved blacks and their servitude to the dominant classes.

Laws were passed to maintain this racial hierarchy in which "white" would come to define "American." In 1790, the first Congress demanded that any naturalized citizen of the United States had to be "white." Adhering to such an ambiguous discriminatory category, this racial marker proved to be extremely difficult to interpret. As David Roediger (1994) states, "The legal and social history of immigration often turned on the question 'Who was White?'" (p. 181).[14] Groups such as the Irish, Italians, Hungarians, Jews, and Greeks, through struggle, would eventually become "white," the Chinese and Japanese were relegated to nonwhite status, and groups such as Asian-Indians and Mexican-Americans, who were originally considered "white," were later designated "nonwhite."[15] Roediger elaborates:

> In the mid nineteenth century, the racial status of Catholic Irish incomers became the object of fierce debate, extended debate. The "simian" and "savage" Irish only gradually fought, worked and voted their ways into the white race in the U.S. Well into the twentieth century, Blacks were counted as "smoked Irishmen" in racist and anti-Irish U.S. Slang. . . . The nativist folk wisdom that held that an Irishman was a Black inside out, became transposed to the reckoning that the turning inside out of Jews produced "niggers." Factory managers spoke of employees distinctly as Jews and as white men. (p. 184)[16]

By the late 1850s, Sir Francis Galton, who spearheaded the Eugenics movement, and Herbert Spencer, the father of social Darwinism, set forth what they considered to be historical and scientific evidence for the superiority of Anglo-Saxons. Attributing the dominance of Anglo-Saxons to the purity of their race and culture, Galton and his followers advocated for the sterilization and segregation of racially subordinated groups and poor immigrants (Menchaca & Valencia, 1990).

In the 1870s, the Teutonic origins theory, used to explain the genetic legacy and superiority of Anglos, rapidly spread through U.S. social, religious, labor, media, educational, and political institutions and practices. For most whites, this ideological stronghold instilled strong feelings of allegiance to their race, nationalism, and a firm belief in separate but equal legislation. Needless to say, it was also used to justify the "necessity and right" of Anglo rule. The impact of this racist ideology in the United States was dramatic, for example:

> By 1861, Mexicans were transformed into a landless class, their rancho-pastoral economy destroyed, and by 1878 all traces of their political institutions were dismantled. Moreover, by 1870 the residential segregation of Mexicans became firmly entrenched in California's multiethnic structure and was viewed by Anglo-Americans as the natural division between an inferior and a superior race (Menchaca & Valencia, 1990, p. 229).[17]

This racialized ideology of "whiteness"—a pure race and culture, which has fanned the flames of white supremacy in the United States—set the infernal standards of ethnicity. "They were standards that accepted Anglo-Saxons as the norm, placed all other Whites on what may be called ethnic probation, and excluded from serious consideration the Japanese, Chinese, Mexicans, and Blacks" (Franklin, 1995, p. 27). *Ethnic* became associated with racial otherness, difference, and deviance.

Exploring the Greek roots of the word *ethnic*, and the possibility of its semantic linkages to the term *heathen*, Raymond Williams (1976) argues that "*Ethnics* came to be used in the United States as a polite term for Jews, Italians, and other lesser breeds" (p. 119). Whether or not *ethnic* can be linguistically traced to the word *heathen*, the histories of many groups marked as such have been consistent with this derogatory use.

This ideological stronghold based on whiteness would function to shape perceptions of racial difference and social relations and to significantly influence the formation of ethnic/cultural identities throughout the country. Cornel West (1993) clearly articulates this dynamic:

> European immigrants arrived on American shores perceiving themselves as "Irish," "Sicilian," "Lithuanian," and so forth. They had to learn that they were "white" principally by adopting American discourse of positively val-

ued whiteness and negatively charged blackness. This process by which people define themselves physically, socially, sexually, and even politically in terms of whiteness or blackness has much bearing not only on constructed notions of race and ethnicity but also on how we understand the changing character of U.S. nationalities. (p. 31)[18]

In their struggle to become white—a process that was shrouded in the romanticized guise of becoming American—many immigrants, similar to the indentured servants of the past, identified less with their real roots and further disassociated themselves from any threat of otherness. Consequently, many poor whites, such as Italians and Irish, who had been known to readily mix with blacks and other racially **subordinated** groups, cut virtually all ties after the Civil War—once again, the infused social logic that being white, regardless of the level of poverty and oppression experienced in society, was at least a step up from being black/racially other (Allen, 1994; Feagin & Vera, 1995; Roediger, 1994). As Howard Winant (1995) points out, even during the Civil War, despite Northern white workers' "occasionally enthusiastic support for emancipation," they were nonetheless "determined to maintain the separate and elevated status the designation 'white' bestowed upon them" (p. 33). W.E.B. Du Bois (1935) observed how white workers were willing to sell their labor for less money in order to gain what he referred to as "a sort of public and psychological wage. They were given deference because they were white. They were admitted freely with all classes of white people to public functions, public parks" (p. 700). He also noted that the racial privileges bestowed upon them did little, if anything, to improve their socioeconomic status, pointing out the reality that they were getting used by the powers that be.

Even some of the more progressive social movements, such as the early struggles to form labor unions, gave way to such an ideology in which whiteness split class consciousness, rendering blacks and other nonwhite groups unprotected outcasts (Goldfield, 1992, 1997; Roediger, 1991). As unions adopted racially exclusive forms of organization, the concept of "race was already present in the way *white* workers recognized themselves in the 19th century. Why else would they have been more threatened by emancipated black labor (or conquered Mexican labor or immigrant Asian labor) than by the flood of European immigrants in the later 19th century?" (Winant, 1995, p. 33). The outcome of these social antagonisms was the racialization of working-class identity as white.

This hierarchy of whiteness has also historically created skin tone tensions among racially subordinated groups. Lighter-skinned blacks and Latino/as, within the dominant paradigm, have often been given more prestige (e.g., house slaves in the case of African-Americans). On the other hand, because of the tensions caused by such differentiation, darker-skinned people may not consider those with lighter skin with the same kind of solidarity. Caught in the racial trap—in the struggle over identity and respect—one may hear, as a sign of indigence, that "Latino/as are the next best thing to being white!"

Drawing this historical portrait of the racialization of identities clearly reveals how racism has historically been an important mechanism of **cultural production** and **reproduction** in the United States—that is, how four hundred years of Anglo domination have been a fundamental part (as opposed to an external or separate feature) of most institutional and everyday cultural practices in this society. From this perspective, it is obvious that when we talk about race in the United States, it has nothing to do with the biology of skin pigmentation, but it has everything to do with how we see and act in the world based on the historical construction and social implications of what it means to be associated with a certain color. For the sake of analysis, the complex and contradicting values and beliefs about race should be considered influential factors in defining ethnicity. That is, racist ideologies, like any other values and beliefs, inevitably belong to any group's ethos. With that in mind, the terms *race* and *ethnicity* should not be dealt with in separation in the United States but rather in conjunction with each other—racenicity.

The More Things Change, the More They Remain the Same: Contemporary Ramifications of This Racial Hierarchy

> In U.S. society, race is a fundamental organizing principle, a way of knowing and interpreting the social world. . . . As we watch the videotape of Rodney King being beaten up by Los Angeles police officers; compare real estate prices in different metropolitan area neighborhoods; select a radio channel to enjoy while we drive to work; size up a potential client, customer, neighbor, or teacher; or carry out a thousand other normal tasks, we are compelled to think racially, to use the racial categories and meaning systems into which we have been socialized. . . . (p. 31).

> Racialization organized a basic U.S. social structure: it established the overall contours, as well as the particular political and cultural legacies, of subordination and resistance. (Winant, 1995, p. 36)

As epitomized in the above extract, an essential part of the everyday in the United States remains prisoner to the colonial construction of the white race. Cultural racism and the resultant racialized ethnic/cultural identities (values, beliefs, norms, traditions, language, worldviews, etc.) continue to be advanced intergenerationally through a predominantly white government, Supreme Court, and media, as well as through white schools, business communities, and public opinion (Delgado & Stefancic, 1997; Dyer, 1997; Frankenburg, 1997; Haney Lopez, 1996; Goldfield, 1997; Hill, 1997; McIntyre, 1997; Novick, 1995; Omi & Winant, 1994). As Jessie Daniels (1997) documents in her study *White Lies,* the legacy of white supremacy and the current themes and stereotypes of extremist, white supremacist discourse are very much a part of our actual mainstream society.[19] John Ogbu's (1987) research points out, "Feelings of aversion, revulsion, and disgust they [negative images of other racial groups] evoke come to be incorporated into the culture of the dominant group and children learn them 'naturally' as they learn other aspects of their culture" (p. 260).

I work as a lifeguard in the summer months and this past year I had a young white boy tell me that his father brings him to a country club in the southern states each year to golf. He said that he loves the club because "they try to maintain our history there by having all Black caddies . . . you know, having things the way they were!" In the midst of a soliloquy in which he pretended to be handing a golf club to someone, he then laughed out loud and demanded, "Here darky, spit-shine this!"

A. W. Smith's research (1981) illustrates that even today a person's/group's position on the racial hierarchy in the United States continues to determine how tolerant whites will be toward "other" people. In fact, except for a few superficial and usually exotic aspects such as food, most ethnic differences continue to be looked upon with disdain—as "anti-American." As Lee Mun Wah (1994) states in his video production *The Color of Fear,* "For the Chinese, being American means being white."

Educational institutions continue to perpetuate cultural racism through their curriculum (e.g., what/who's values, beliefs, voices, and representations of history, identity, and difference are included?) (Castenell & Pinar, 1993; McCarthy & Crinchlow, 1993), teacher assumptions and teaching styles (Delpit, 1993; McIntyre, 1997), and de facto segregation of racially subordinated students via tracking (Oakes, 1985).

The white corporate-owned media is deeply implicated in the current perpetuation of cultural racism (Dyer, 1997; Ferrell & Sanders, 1995; Fiske, 1994; Gray, 1995; Hall, 1995; Rhodes, 1995; Seiter, 1995; Sklar, 1993; Squire, 1997). Popular texts, which constitute a wide range of aural, visual, and printed signifiers, are not simply expressive or reflective of social reality but also formative in that they can influence how we see ourselves, others, and the world around us. The struggle over identity and representation (that is, over who has the power to articulate experience, fashion identities, define the nature of problems, and legitimate solutions) greatly contributes to shaping the social relations and ethnic patterns of everyday life—how we look at, feel about, fear, and interact with each other (Carby, 1993; Dyer, 1997; Dyson, 1993; Giroux, 1996; Goldberg, 1993; hooks, 1992; Lott, 1994; McCarthy, 1993; McCarthy, Rodriguez, Meecham, David, Wilson-Brown, Godina, Supryia, & Buendia, 1997; Mercer, 1994; Riggs, 1987; Said, 1993; Sklar, 1993; Squire, 1997).[20]

Studies (Kluegel, 1990; Kluegel & Smith 1982, 1983) have clearly shown how the media plays a crucial role in shaping public opinion about racially subordinated groups. It is thus not surprising to read in a *New York Times* survey about some white people's distorted perceptions of blacks and Latino/as:

> 78 percent of Whites thought Blacks were more likely than Whites to prefer living on welfare, and 74 percent thought Hispanics more likely to prefer welfare. In the same study, 62 percent of Whites thought Blacks were less likely to be hard-working; 56 percent thought that Blacks were more prone to violence; 53 percent of Whites thought Blacks were less intelligent; and 51 percent thought them less patriotic. (as cited in Daniels, 1997, p. 5)

Social institutions in the United States not only maintain racist practices but continue to exploit economically underprivileged whites who are intentionally set up to be, but usually unknowingly, preoccupied with issues of race rather than social class (Kushnick, 1996). As epitomized by the chapter opening story of the barroom, whites continue to buy into images that degrade and demonize blacks, Latino/as, and so-called others. For example, when one of the bar patrons referred to his Irish buddy as a "white nigger," the man replied, "You can call me a dumb Irish Catholic, but don't ever call me that—that's the worst!" In order to abstract his identity away from any notion of blackness (which, as Roediger [1994] stated, Irish were associated with), the customer assertively shared the following "joke": "How do you get a nigger down from a tree? You cut the rope!"

Scapegoats/social outcasts are created and targeted in order to draw attention away from the very real abuses of power that produce and sustain sociocultural and economic inequality, as well as intergroup conflict in the United States. Noam Chomsky (Chomsky, Leistyna, & Sherblom, 1995) elaborates on how discrimination and violence are justified against others, as well as how attention is being diverted from the violence to the general population:

> This building up of scapegoats and fear is standard. If you're stomping on people's faces, you don't want them to notice that; you want them to be afraid of somebody else—Jews, homosexuals, welfare queens, immigrants, whoever it is. That's how Hitler got to power, and in fact he became the most popular leader in German history. People are scared, they're upset, the world isn't working, and they don't like the way things are. You don't want people to look at the actual source of power, that's much too dangerous, so, therefore, you need to have them blame or be frightened of someone else. (p. 117)

Wallace Lambert and Donald Taylor's study (1990) on *Coping with Cultural and Racial Diversity in Urban America,* which examined the attitudes of a diverse sample of people toward multiculturalism, concluded that white Americans, especially the working class, are the least supportive. As Feagin and Vera (1995) state:

> White workers have paid a heavy price for their "White selves." Since the nineteenth century, racist attitudes among White workers have prevented them from seeing clearly their own class exploitation and from organizing effectively with Black and other minority workers. As a result, they have suffered lower wages and poorer working conditions. (p. 15)

As a result of this history of racialization, uncritical whites have lost track of who they are.

White Ethnic Unconsciousness

"The key to understanding White racism is to be found not only in what Whites think of people of color but also in what Whites think of themselves" (Feagin & Vera, 1995, p. xi). As argued earlier, racialized ethnic patterns are embedded in the cultures and institutions of the United States, but few whites recognize the impact that such racism has had on shaping their values, beliefs, personal and social interests, and actions (Terry, 1970, 1981; Wellman, 1977). Nor do most whites question how such identities are passed down from generation to generation. Unfortunately, the United States is plagued by **historical amnesia,** or, at best, the sense of the past that we receive, as personified by the young boy at the country club (mentioned earlier), is limited, often distorted, and uncritically assimilated as fact. As Winant (1995) warns, "Forces at play in the construction of contemporary racial identity are descended from a past that we ignore or misinterpret at our peril" (p. 32). Most whites, even those whose ancestors experienced a great deal of social, cultural, and economic injustice (such as the Irish), have little, if any, critical recollection of the history of the racialization of identities in this country. In fact, the Irish bar patrons (among others) simply perpetuated this socially and self-destructive process.

Having run the racial gauntlet, assimilated/indoctrinated whites, who are the product of the ideological construction of whiteness, have virtually lost their ethnic heritage. Tomato sauce, drinking, sports, and calling oneself Irish, Italian, or French-Canadian certainly do not do justice to a family's history, nor do baseball, hot dogs, apple pie, and Chevrolet define what it means to be American. Many whites have few, if any, signposts to help excavate, so as to develop, their cultural identities to transcend race and as such they have become ignorant of who they are. As Stanley Lieberson and Mary Waters's (1986) studies reveal, "There are a substantial number of people who recognize that they are White, but lack any clear-cut identification with, and/or knowledge of, a specific European origin" (p. 264). Without an understanding of who they are as historical and cultural beings, unable to make linkages to the social and political realities that have shaped their world, they have become vulnerable to ideological manipulation (the cultural criterion that is characteristic of this racist society) that reproduces racist sentiments and thus renders them complicit in the injustices inflicted upon others, as well as upon themselves. As Donaldo Macedo (1994) states in his book *Literacies of Power: What Americans Are Not Allowed to Know,*

> This disarticulation of knowledge anesthetizes consciousness, without which one can never develop clarity of reality. . . . The apprehension of clarity requires a high level of **political clarity,** which can be achieved by sifting through the flux of information and relating each piece to another one so as to gain a global comprehension of the facts and their raison d'etre. (p. 22)

The working-class bar frequenters, victims of such a disarticulation, were unable to see their own **location** as an emergent construct of the relation between race and ethnicity such that they could not make the connection between what happened to their ancestors as well as to them. Although virtually powerless socioeconomically, they nonetheless buy into the illusion of being part of the norm (the model of national identity) with the self-determining power to do as they please with their ethnic heritage. In fact, many believe that they are "making it," even when in many cases they are worse off in terms of material struggle and self-actualization than those who they so readily castigate.

One of the bar patron's comments when black entertainer Will Smith was invited on the *Jay Leno* show clearly illustrates that he has bought into a fictitious self-representation. Seeing Smith enter the scene, he barked out at the TV, "Get *dem dang niggers* off the stage. I'm *not prejudice or nutt'in,* but they're *tak'in* over Hollywood, and if that *ain't the* half of it, they're *mess'in up* our language!" [Emphasis added to point out the speaker's particular discourse style.] Within this statement, Will Smith is not evaluated as an individual artist but rather as a member of a specific group—that is, "dem dang niggers." Thus, regardless of who he is, in the patron's mind race predisposes "them" to be all the same. Realizing that people heard his comment, the white man throws in a disclaimer, insisting that he is "not prejudice or nutt'in." In other words, in his mind, what he is saying has nothing to do with racism; it simply has to do with what he perceives as "the truth"—that is, if what he believes is in fact true, then it is by no means unacceptable thought.

The subsequent comment that, "They're tak'in over Hollywood," implies a feeling of ownership on the bar patron's part. His fear and anger is that blacks are moving in on *his* cultural territory. However, while Hollywood has certainly played a significant role in shaping the racist contours of his identity, it has by no means accurately portrayed the realities of the white working class. Nor has he had the power to shape the representations therein. If anything, Hollywood has worked to exploit the working classes in the United States. For example, the blockbuster film *On the Waterfront* was clearly an attempt to discredit unions, which (regardless of their internal inequities) are the only potentially democratizing force with which workers can struggle (Aronowitz, 1992). Corporations are totalitarian regimes by nature. They are only accountable to their stockholders and profits.

This feeling of ownership/membership is also embedded in the man's comment about "mess'in up our language." The possessive "our" not only erroneously situates the individual within the dominant culture but embodies a misguided belief in a "common culture" and "standard English." However, it is immediately obvious that his use of English—his working-class dialect (also built off of gender relations, locality, etc.)—is by no means in tune with the standard. Having bought into the myth of meritocracy and the American dream, the bar frequenter closed his argument, asserting, "And then they want affirmative action. . . . See [pointing to Smith on TV]—they don't need help. Whatever happened to merit. . . . Pull yourselves up by your own bootstraps!"

A very similar event recently occurred when I attended the Wynonna country music concert in downtown Boston. By happenstance, I was sitting next to this white guy. When the band came on stage, there were eleven musicians, seven of whom were black. Thinking that he could find some solidarity in the white person sitting next to him, he grumbled first to himself and then to me, "Ahhh! . . . Get the spooks off the stage! . . . Why's she gotta have them?" In the tone of his command there was a feeling of ownership of the music and a fear of cultural invasion. He had no recollection that that very art form (a composite of blues, gospel, funk, etc.) is in fact a product of African-American experiences in this country—that Wynonna Judd is the appropriator and reinventor, and that he is the guest. In order to recognize this relationship between struggle and expression, the white man would have to acknowledge the fact that blacks are an essential part of this country's history—the Western world for that matter. But, as we live in a culture of denial, he has the privilege to refuse to accept (even consider) this connection. He is in fact the product of the social construction of not seeing.

Racenicity does not imply that whites are without ethnicity—that is, without values, beliefs, a worldview, cultural practices and traditions, and so on. It simply argues that whites are, for the most part, not only unconscious of the ideologies and power relations that shape and reproduce racialized ethnic patterns but also unable to clearly and profoundly define what those patterns are and why exactly it is that they hold so tightly to them—that is, to articulate the racial categories that "form part of the social blueprint Whites use to orient their actions" (Feagin & Vera, 1995, p. x).[21]

Most whites are imprisoned by an assimilationist ideology that paradoxically has claimed to support them while undermining their very beings. By no means do I intend here to act as an apologist for white racism by placing their current problems on institutions alone—people breathe life into such bodies that function to reproduce oppressive social practices. Any group's uncritical loyalty to this paradigm is especially disconcerting when such allegiance draws attention away from that powerful center—those who are truly profiting from the present sociocultural and economic conditions. My goal is to analyze how this cultural production and reproduction occurs.

It is also important to note that racenicity does not imply that racial attitudes are one-dimensional, but it does argue that they are not completely separate from other attitudes and values. "White identity is his-

toric, but it is also a fluid, living identity that is continuously being constructed and reconstructed" (Bowser & Hunt, 1996, p. xvii). In addition,
the analytic category of racenicity is not meant to infer that all whites
are ethnically the same, or that pockets of white resistance against racial
supremacy are nonexistent. It simply points out the fact that those
whites (across differences of gender, class, language, sexual orientation,
locale, religion, etc.) or any other group, for that matter, who have assimilated the dominant ideology of whiteness (consciously or not), are
complicit in the perpetuation of such a racial hierarchy and its concomitant ethnic realities and injustices.

The Myth of Ethnic Identity
Among Assimilated Whites

The majority of whites in the United States believe that all ethnic immigrant groups have had common histories upon entering this country
(Alba, 1990). Richard Alba's data revealed that whites generally view ethnic identification as an individual choice, a private matter, and otherwise not very important. Many participants in his sample equated it
with their private family history, rather than viewing it as a group's collective experience. As with the men in the barroom, the most frequently
identified markers were the superficial elements of food, festivals, and
holidays—what Alba refers to as "symbolic characteristics."

Some social theorists have argued that assimilation and the retention
of symbolic ethnicity is a conscious choice for ethnic groups in their efforts to become authentic members of the host society (Gans, 1979;
Roberts & Clifton, 1982). Roberts and Clifton (1982) claim that,

> Those who possess a "symbolic ethnicity" command the flexibility neces-
> sary to participate and benefit as members of a complex industrialized so-
> ciety while also feeling that they belong to a smaller community. This flexi-
> bility exists because symbolic ethnicity is a psychological rather than a
> social construct; it services individual rather than community needs, and,
> as such, is less subject to forces beyond an individual's control. (p. 19)

However, after dissecting the historical struggle to survive within the
U.S. racial/ethnic hierarchy, the idea that "ethnicity is a psychological
rather than a social construct," and that one has individual control and
choice to assimilate, constitutes nothing more than a euphemistic and
deceitful portrayal of the harsh sociopolitical realities that have in fact
significantly structured cultural identities and contemporary social rela-

tions. Christine Sleeter (1993) accurately rebuts this selective assimilationist assumption:

> The symbolic meaning Euro-Americans attach to ethnicity today upholds the ideology of individuality and mobility within an open system and the myth that everyone came to the U.S. in search of a better life and had to work equally hard to better themselves. In so doing, this meaning averts a structural analysis of racism and inequality in contemporary U.S. society, implicitly reaffirming the superior position of Euro-Americans. (p. 165)

In fact, there have been a plethora of historical incidents that debunk the myths of selective integration and the American dream. For example, African-Americans have been in the United States far longer than most whites. They have spoken English for centuries and yet still remain in an overwhelming socially, politically, and economically subordinated status. As Benjamin Bowser & Raymond Hunt (1996) ask:

> What are the chances of any of them [racially subordinated populations] being able to step right into the American dream without an equally miraculous transformation in the views, attitudes, behavioral dispositions, and institutional practices of powerful or influential sectors of White America? . . . No miraculous transformation of Africans, Puerto Ricans, and Native Americans (aside, perhaps, from bleaching) would eliminate or even materially reduce racially unequal outcomes. (p. xiv)

Assimilation, let alone selective acculturation, is generally not an option for many groups that are considered nonwhite. Although claiming to embrace the idea that everyone become a contributing member of society, dominant groups have historically imposed ethnic maintenance within these outcast groups (via social, educational, economic, and political segregation) so that they can socially mark, subordinate, and consequently exploit the resources of such people in order to serve their own ideological and economic interests (Spener, 1996). Blacks are the most residentially segregated group in the urban United States, and the dramatic extent of this segregation makes discrimination in other sectors of society, such as the political arena, public education, employment, and public services, easier and more likely (Bowser & Hunt, 1996). As microcosms of the larger society, schools typify this kind of segregation. Martha Menchaca and Richard Valencia (1990) note that, "Over the last twenty years, Chicano and other Latino students as a whole have become more and more isolated from their Anglo peers" (p. 222). The irony in this process of racialization is that by uncritically buying into symbolic ethnicity and the myth of choice whites have actually actively participated in becoming more distanced from themselves.

Racenicity in the Shape of Cultural Resistance

Culture is the central medium of human existence. Within the volatile social relations generated by the history of racialization of identities in the United States—segregation, stereotyping, and concomitant sociopolitical oppression—groups have developed a diversity of cultural artifacts and ethnic patterns to resist/oppose discrimination. To clarify what is meant by resistance, consider Giroux's (1988) explanation:

> Resistance has been defined as a personal space, in which the logic and force of domination is contested by the power of subjective agency to subvert the process of socialization. Seen this way, resistance functions as a type of negation or affirmation placed before ruling discourses and practices. Of course, resistance often lacks an overt political project and frequently reflects social practices that are informal, disorganized, apolitical, and atheoretical in nature. In some instances it can reduce itself to an unreflective and defeatist refusal to acquiesce to different forms of domination, or even naive rejection of oppressive forms of moral and political regulation. (p. 162)[22]

Signithia Fordham (1988) uses the term "fictive kinship" to describe the collective identity that develops among racially subordinated groups that are mistreated and segregated in society. She argues that this kinship is based on more than just skin color in that it also implies "the particular mind-set, or world view, of those persons" (p. 56). G. A. DeVos (1967) refers to this phenomenon as "ethnic consolidation."

John Ogbu (1987) also makes reference to "oppositional identities" and "survival strategies," which he describes as instrumental, expressive, and epistemological responses to cope with subordination and exploitation. He refers to these strategies as "secondary cultural differences," stating that,

> In the case of black Americans, for example, the interlocking of the job ceiling, social, and residential segregation and their lack of political power and influence, created for blacks a special type of physical, sociocultural, and psychological environment. Within this environment blacks developed adaptive lifestyles different in many respects from the adaptive lifestyles of white Americans . . . not that the contents of black culture are derived from African sources . . . black culture is characterized by elements of opposition and ambivalence in its relation to white culture or mainstream culture. (p. 264)[23]

Although Ogbu's basic point supports the idea of racenicity, I nonetheless think that aspects of African and other cultures were brought to these shores and used as tools of resistance; for example, call and response, drumming, and so on (Jones, 1963). I also believe that such ethnic developments are not solely influenced by and restricted to national borders. As Gilroy argues (1987), "Culture does not develop along ethnically absolute lines but in complex, dynamic patterns of syncretism in which new definitions of what it means to be black emerge from raw materials provided by black populations elsewhere in the diaspora" (p. 13).

An example can be seen in the international roots, influence, and transformations of reggae. This music is a hybrid of U.S. rhythm and blues, Mento, and calypso, and its history and transitions have played a significant role in international popular culture and political/cultural struggle. Gilroy (1987) articulates this international connection best when he states that,

> An intricate web of cultural and political connections binds blacks here to blacks elsewhere. At the same time they are linked into the social relations of this country. The social movements which have sprung up in different parts of the world as evidence of African dispersal, imperialism and colonialism have done more than appeal to blacks everywhere in a language which could invite their universal identification. They have communicated directly to blacks and their supporters all over the world asking for concrete help and solidarity in the creation of organizational forms adequate to the pursuit of emancipation, justice and citizenship, internationally as well as within national frameworks. (p. 156)

He also argues that blacks and other racially subordinated groups have actively organized in defense of their communities from the very point of their enslavement, and explains such resistance as the way in which "race and racism articulate various forms of action" (p. 13), described as "politicized roots culture among Black populations" (p. 92) and "racial culture or ethnicity" (p. 101).[24] Both Ogbu (1987) and Fordham (1988) observe that generations pass down this fictive kinship—norms, values, and competencies—and that racially subordinated children thus learn the survival strategies and solidarity from their parents/caregivers and peers.[25]

Looking specifically at one form of cultural resistance, many educators and social theorists (Fine, 1991; Gilroy, 1993; Rampton, 1995; Weis, 1985) argue that in order to maintain their identity, students exposed to racist conditions often create spaces within the school context—language, clothing, style, behavior—that reinforce their solidarity with their communities. In fact, the significance of ritual, style, and dress are often symbolic manifestations that signify a rejection of racial stratification and the **cultural capital** of the dominant society. One of these strategies of resistance entails the "anti-achievement ethic" (Granat, Hathaway, Saleton, & Sansing, 1986), or "low effort syndrome" (Ogbu, 1987). Equating formal education as "acting white" and refusing, consciously or not, to abide by the codes and discourses of the dominant culture are the direct results of racial as well as other forms of subordination (Darder, 1991; Everhart, 1983; Giroux, 1983; Fine, 1991; Fordham, 1988; Fordham & Ogbu, 1986; Freire & Macedo, 1987; MacLeod, 1987; McLaren, 1986; Ogbu, 1987; Solomon, 1992; Weis, 1985; Willis, 1977).[26] When driving by her high school, an African-American woman (a high school dropout and participant in my doctoral research) pointed to the building and exclaimed, "*Anonymous* High, the big white lie!"[27] A Native American woman, also a high school dropout, is clearly opposed to what she considered to be an Anglo political agenda within the schools: "Despite all the intrusions on our culture by white people, we have remained Indians. If we give up our language and culture to the schools, we can kiss that good-bye" (as cited in Bowker, 1993, p. 161).

Conservative interpretations of resistance/oppositional identities, especially the more self-destructive kinds, either psychologize such behavior—equating it with individual forms of pathology, deviance, and **learned helplessness**—or simply attribute it to cultural inadequacies and/or genetic flaws. There is no effort to understand that marginalized students/people reject education/social practices because they represent the oppressive values and racist nature of the dominant society.

As there is an inextricable relationship between language and culture—language being codified culture—inevitably antagonistic social relations not only play a significant role in the structure and use of language and meaning but also lead to the production of languages of resistance. For example, African-Americans, by reinventing the dominant communicative form of English into **counterdiscourses** to fight white supremacy, were able to forge a culture of rebellion out of the oppressive nature of slavery and were thus able to work toward the political solidarity necessary for avoiding total domination. These new languages created the "space for alternative cultural production and alternative epistemologies—different ways of thinking and knowing that were crucial to creating **counter-hegemonic** world views" (hooks, 1994, p. 171).

Toni Morrison (1992), in an attempt to create "an endlessly flexible language" (p. xii), describes her efforts to eradicate semantic and symbolic racial coding in mainstream English:

Neither blackness nor "people of color" stimulates in me notions of excessive, limitless love, anarchy, or routine dread. I cannot rely on these metaphorical shortcuts because I am a black writer struggling with and through a language that can powerfully evoke and enforce hidden signs of racial superiority, cultural hegemony, and dismissive "othering" of people and language. (p. x)

Artist and writer Guillermo Gomez-Pena, referring to the Chicano/a struggle against Anglo domination, states that Chicano/as have a culture of resistance rather than a culture of affirmation, and as such, they have developed "an extremely minimal, direct, and confrontational way of relating intellectually" (as cited in Fusco, 1995, p. 152). When dealing with English, he states:

I am very interested in subverting English structures, infecting English with Spanish, and in finding new possibilities of expression within the English language that English-speaking people don't have. I find myself in kinship with nonwhite English-speaking writers. (as cited in Fusco, 1995, p. 157)

Gloria Anzaldúa (1990) contends that Chicano/as, in the face of colonization, have also developed significant differences in the Spanish they speak.

Ben Rampton's (1995) research around "stylized Asian English," Creole, and Punjabi makes a powerful case that language crossing (i.e., linguistic code switching) among racially subordinated youth contributes to the development of an active sense of community in which groups come together to combat common forms of domination experienced in their everyday lives.[28] He states:

Language crossing foregrounded certain kinds of micro-social relationships and that through processes of symbolic evocation they invited extrapolation to wider fields of political contestation. . . . Interactional code-crossing provides a productive site for the analysis of informal political processes among youth in a multiracial urban setting. (pp. 132–133)

Other expressive cultural forms are also the products of racenicity. James Scott (1990) argues that, "We might interpret the rumors, gossip, folktales, songs, gestures, jokes, and theater of the powerless as vehicles by which, among other things, they insinuate a critique of power" (p. 5). Perhaps the most prevalent ethnic/cultural forms that attempt to rupture the oppressive social order and create a space for rewriting history are found in the arts: music, performance, dance, multimedia, literature, and so forth. In fact, there has been a long history of cultural subversion in music and performance: slave dances, blues, jazz, Mardi Gras parades. Tricia Rose (1994) points out:

These cultural forms are especially rich and pleasurable places where oppositional transcripts, or the "unofficial truths" are developed, refined, and rehearsed . . . these dances, languages, and music produce communal bases of knowledge about social conditions, communal interpretations of them and quite often serve as the cultural glue that fosters communal resistance. (pp. 99–100)[29]

Hip-hop culture/rap music provides a vivid and powerful example of racenicity. Rose (1994) argues that, "A large and significant element in rap's discursive territory is engaged in symbolic and ideological warfare with institutions and groups that symbolically, ideologically, and materially oppress African Americans" (p. 101). Michael Dyson (1993) observes that rap artists "were creating their own aesthetic of survival, generated from the raw material of their immediate reality, the Black ghetto" (p. 191). He contends that rap has made possible alternative cultural identities and thus created a vehicle for personal and cultural agency:

Rap has also created for its participants a way of being in the world, an ontological stance as it were, that joins the best features of street society (savvy about rules of survival, ability to adapt quickly in an environment of constant flux, the development of a language of chic, hip, and cool that has influenced the larger American culture). (p. 277)

The idea here is not to romanticize popular culture and to assume that all of its manifestations are clearly forms of cultural resistance. Inevitably, within the stronghold of white supremacy, capitalist social relations, and corporate directed media, expressive forms such as rap are easily co-opted in ways that are antithetical and destructive of their ostensible purposes. For example, many white youth, caught up in the identity crisis generated by racenicity and the **commodification** of culture and identity, have uncritically appropriated the styles and clothing of black urban culture. Not connecting such phenomena with racenicity, most of these suburban gangstas abstract such cultural formations from their intended **anticolonial** political project. Though singing "fight the power," the majority have little, if any, understanding of the message or intent of the music—that the song, to a certain extent, is about them.[30]

The music industry also thrives on producing shocking videos and songs that glorify violence and misogyny, which serve the purpose of entertaining while misfeeding the minds of youth about what it means to be black/other. As such, they attempt to depoliticize discursive foundations of dissent, and, via spectacle, motivate the sale of a great many records.[31] Dressed up in his gansta garb, a friend of mine's son, whose bedroom walls are covered with fantasy posters of commercial rap artists and pictures of Janet Jackson, was afraid to go out of my Boston apartment—thinking that, as the media has been telling him, he as a white person is under siege. The "cartoonish minstrels that entertain White kids," as David Samuels (1991) refers to them in his article in *The New Republic*—"The Rap on Rap"—suddenly become "real" threats. In any case, the manifestations of ethnic/cultural behavior based on a resistance to racial subordination and the process of defusing counterdiscourses are extremely important in understanding what actually is implied when the word *race* is used in the United States.

Racenicity in the Shape of Internalized Oppression/Cultural Alienation

In developing his ideas about the social determination of mental activity, Lev Vygotsky (1978) argued that humans are internalized culture: The ways in which we think and see the world and ourselves therein are dramatically shaped by our social interactions. When attempting to understand the racialization of cultural identities, one must consider that white supremacy has been historically rooted in the structures of U.S. society, and thus, we must take into account the social psychological effects of this legacy of racist stereotypes, social practices, and institutions that has served to degrade racially subordinated groups.

One result of constant mistreatment and stigmatization is that some oppressed people internalize an inferior view of themselves and their culture, and in turn place faith in the "superiority" of the dominant group. As Paulo Freire (1970) observes:

> For cultural invasion to succeed, it is essential that those invaded become convinced of their intrinsic inferiority. . . . The more invasion is accentuated and those invaded are alienated from the spirit of their own culture and from themselves, the more the latter want to be like the invaders: to walk like them, dress like them, talk like them. (p. 151)

Within such alienating social psychological practices, people may participate in their own oppression. As Herbert Marcuse (1955) states, "The struggle against freedom reproduces itself in the psyche of man, as the self-repression of the repressed individual, and his self-repression in turn sustains his masters and their institutions" (p. 16).[32] Joseph Suina (1988), a Native American, recalls his first experiences in school: "My life was no longer just right. I was ashamed of being who I was and I wanted to change right then and there. . . . I was beginning to take on the white man's ways, the ways that belittle my own" (pp. 298–299).

This discussion of racenicity is not meant to blame victims for their predicament and decisions, but rather, it is intended to help us all, especially educators, understand and work toward eradicating the actual institutional and social causes of such behavior. As witnessed in the work of anticolonial theorists/revolutionaries (Cabral, 1973; Fanon, 1967; Memmi, 1965; Ngugi Wa Thiong'o, 1986), often a crucial first step in the fight against white supremacy has been to decolonize the mind of those who have been indoctrinated to believe that they, by taking on all the ethnic characteristics of the colonizer, could transcend the ideological distortions associated with the color of their skin and ethnic heritage.

Richard Rodriguez, in his autobiography *Hunger of Memory: The Education of Richard Rodriguez* (1982), embodies this particular side of racenicity. Throughout his book, Rodriguez describes the painful tensions that exist between his racial/ethnic reality and what he refers to as the "obedience" required in public life. Having bought into the dominant stigmatized representations of his identity—as witnessed in his embarrassment of his parents, insistence on losing his Spanish accent (which eventually leads to a total loss of his native language), diatribes against bilingual education and affirmative action, and especially in his attempts to actually shave the dark skin from his face with a razor—Rodriguez calls for all members of society to assimilate the dominant norms. In demanding that people alter their habits, he offers the following description:

> Here is a child who cannot forget that his academic success distances him from a life he loved, even from his own memory of himself. The scholarship boy must move between environments, his home and the school classroom, which are cultural extremes, opposed, and eventually go against his family ethos . . . the boy takes his first step toward academic success, away from his family—he has used education to remake himself. (p. 32)

Rodriguez admits that all of his ideas are borrowed, that he lacks self-confidence, that he is a "mimic, a collector of thoughts, not a thinker," and that he has no opinion. However, instead of equating formal education with indoctrination, and condemning the racist, classist, sexist, and heterosexist values that inform and maintain the dominant ideology in the United States—an ideology that has crushed his identity and creativity—he acts as an apologist for the system. Rodriguez insists that education requires radical reformation; however, in his adopted terms, it is the reformation of the self in order to meet the criteria for membership to the dominant society, and not transformation of its discriminatory institutions and social practices. In having transferred his allegiance from his community's struggles to an ideology that serves to exploit him, Richard Rodriguez has in fact lost and remade his ethnic voice.

I am not arguing that as a consequence of his allegiance with the dominant ideology Rodriguez is a welcomed member of the dominant group. It is only as long as he plays the role of the "good minority" (attacking "difference") that he will be rewarded by right-wing think tanks and other reactionary organizations. The interesting contradiction here is although he argues that in order to succeed one must assimilate into the mainstream at all cost, in fact, his work in literary criticism (a field controlled by whites) is not what brought him recognition.

Fordham (1988) argues that blacks and other racially subordinated groups sense that they have to give up aspects of their identities and their fictive kinship if they hope to achieve academically and socially in schools, as well as in the business world. Faced by educators and the general public's deficit view of their realities, Fordham's research reveals that some students and professionals, in an attempt to distance themselves from the stigma imposed on their communities, try to appear to be "raceless" by taking on attitudes and behaviors that are characteristic of the dominant white society:

> Because the high-achieving students believe firmly in the "American dream" they willingly, and in some instances not so willingly, seek to distance themselves from the fictive-kinship system in the Black community. The organizational structure of the school rewards racelessness in students and thus reinforces the notion that it is a quality necessary for success in the larger society. As a result, the students are also led to believe in the view of racism and discrimination as the practices of individuals rather than as part and parcel of institutionally sanctioned social policies. (p. 80)

Although the implications of Fordham's research are important, I do not want to give the impression that one should universally equate high-achieving students with selling out their race/ethnic identity. I am certain of the reality of efforts to become raceless; however, there are nonetheless a multiplicity of successful strategies for dealing with formal schooling among racially subordinated students.

People who uncritically buy into the stigma, and as Fordham states, attempt to be raceless, do feed into a sociopolitical strategy that functions to sweep the realities of racism under the rug. Consequently, whiteness remains elusive, invisible, and uncontested. At the same time, those willing/compelled to try to "fit in," regardless of how hard they try to assimilate, will never be welcomed members of the dominant group. At best, they become bridge people—that is, they connect two conflicting/relational worlds but they belong to neither of them; the first often sees them as breaking the solidarity of the group in struggle, and the other never wanted them in the first place. As Trinh T. Minh-ha (1989) explains, "Being accused of 'ignoring one's own culture' and 'looking whiter than Snow White herself' also means taking a trip to the promise land of White Alienation" (p. 52). James Baldwin (1985) expressed this fear when he stated that, "A child cannot be taught by anyone whose demand, essentially, is that the child repudiate his experience, and all that gives him sustenance, and enter a limbo in which he will no longer be black, and in which he knows that he can never become white. Black people have lost too many black children that way" (p. 652).

The Invisible Ideology

As this chapter has argued, whiteness has played a significant role in shaping ethnic patterns, social identities, and institutions in the United States. However, whiteness has paradoxically been able to mask itself as a category—it is simultaneously "everything and nothing" (Dyer, 1988). The underlying evasive ideology that informs the social construction of whiteness is strategically infused such that those who for whatever reason buy into its logic are unable, or simply unwilling, to see and thus name its oppressive nature.

By not recognizing whiteness as a racial identity, most whites see themselves as race-free and less ethnic than others, and consequently take for granted the privileges they secure by such an ideologically charged racial marker (Frankenburg, 1993, 1994; Hill, 1997; MacCannell, 1989, 1992; McIntosh, 1990; McIntyre, 1997). Frances FitzGerald's (1986) data reveal that white upper-middle-class professionals do not identify themselves as "ethnic, cultural, or powerful" (p. 218). Ruth Frankenburg's research (1993), which consisted of interviews with white women, showed that whiteness is "difficult for White people to name . . . those that are securely housed within its borders usually do not examine it" (pp. 228–229). As Peggy McIntosh (1990) asserts:

> I think that Whites are carefully taught not to recognize White privilege.
> . . . My schooling gave me no training in seeing myself as an oppressor, as

an unfairly advantaged person, or as a participant in a damaged culture . . .
(p. 31)

as a member of the dominant group one is taught not to see. . . . (p. 35)

Obliviousness about White advantage is kept strongly inculturated in the
United States so as to maintain the myth of meritocracy, the myth that
democratic choice is equally available to all. (p. 36)

Within this society's individualistic ideological underpinnings, meritocracy—success merited by virtue of talent—is perceived as the only
active and justified gatekeeping mechanism. This language of individualism and competitiveness functions to render invisible social injustices
such as racism. Racism is psychologized into individual and pathological acts, rather than attributed to public and institutionalized practices,
and as such it is strategically disarticulated from white supremacy—
from whites' responsibility to transform the institutionalized sociocultural inequities from which they "profit."[33] As Russell Ferguson (1990)
points out,

In our society dominant discourse tries never to speak its own name. Its authority is based on absence. The absence is not just that of the various
groups classified as "other," although members of these groups are rou-
tinely denied power. It is also the lack of any overt acknowledgment of the
specificity of the dominant culture, which is simply assumed to be the all-
encompassing norm . . . (p. 11)

the invisible center which claims universality without ever defining itself,
and which exiles to its margins those who cannot or will not pay allegiance
to the standards which it imposes. (p. 13)

For the most part, racism becomes white people's concern only when
it is something they claim to experience rather than perpetuate. This is
evident in an examination of how whiteness as a social force has only recently come to center stage in the national debates over affirmative action. Affirmative action and other such programs are currently under
heavy attack, however, not for their inability to level the social, economic, and political playing field but for their "unfair" treatment of
white men who are convinced that they have unjustly lost their privilege. In this case, the focus is not on how whiteness is implicated in the
subordination of other groups, but, rather, how Otherness is responsible
for "reverse discrimination," as well as its own predicament. One of the

bar patrons asked, "You know why blacks don't like aspirin? Because they're white, they work, and you've gotta pick cotton."

This paradox of racial centrality and invisibility is in part made possible because the ideology that informs white realities is obscured by dominant modes of representation that focus, in a distracting manner, on the other.[34] "As the other becomes more culturally visible the [white] self becomes correspondingly less" (Rosaldo, 1993, p. 202). In fact, efforts by racially subordinated groups to survive within the racial hierarchy in the United States are strategically misinterpreted and misrepresented by conservative educators, politicians, and the popular press. Racially subordinated people's attempts to combat oppression and transform the status quo through group solidarity are summarily dismissed as a form of cultural separatism/anti-Americanism. It is made to appear that the "unwillingness" to join the mainstream is the central reason for their poor living conditions. In this way, otherness is again readily visible and, as such, is often used in a manipulative way to explain this country's social unrest and economic demise—what Schlesinger (1992) and others refer to as "the disuniting of America."

Historians and educators of the likes of Schlesinger reduce the complexity of white supremacy to a simple response: "Why don't you just join us?" However, the call to "Learn English and get a job!" is merely a victim-blaming mechanism that obfuscates the realities of discrimination—especially racism—and those responsible, consciously or not, for its perpetuation. Consequently, "Whiteness has secured universal consent to its hegemony as the norm by masking its coercive force with the invisibility that marks off the other as all too visible—coloured" (Mercer, 1988, as cited in Haymes, 1995, p. 32). As McIntosh (1990) states,

> To redesign social systems we need first to acknowledge their colossal unseen dimensions. The silences and denials surrounding privilege are the key political tool here. They keep the thinking about equality or equity incomplete, protecting unearned advantage and conferred dominance by making these subjects taboo. (p. 36)

As previously mentioned, the media and popular culture are seriously implicated in this process of racialization/color coating and targeting otherness, while not naming whiteness. The images of crime, drug and welfare abuse in the popular press are predominantly of blacks and Latino/as. Violence and moral corruption are thus portrayed as being endemic to such communities—an integral and inherent part of their culture (Dyson, 1994; Giroux, 1996; Sklar, 1993). In fact, violence, urban unrest, street crime, the inner city, welfare, and other such terms are merely code words for racially subordinated groups. The racialization of crime and violence was clearly the case when ex–Los Angeles Police Chief Daryl Gates developed a video game, *Police Quest: Open Season,* which used black suspects who spoke a form of black English taken directly from a rap song (Lott, 1994).[35]

Having bought into such representations, one bar patron, while thumbing through the sports page of the local rag, spotted a series of pictures of black high school track state champions. He publicly commented, "I'm surprised that they don't have numbers across their chests!"—the implication being that the pictures were mug shots. Another white guy, hearing the overtly racial slur, responded, "There's a black and a Puerto Rican in a car. Whose driving? . . . The cops!"

On a separate occasion, a white woman, "well educated" and on her way to the University of Virginia to study criminal law (of all things), stated to me when a young black man drove by in a Jaguar XJ7, "Tell me that's not crack!" Uncritically shaping her perceptions of others with distorted media representations, this woman not only was unwilling to believe that a black person could achieve such class/material status but also that there was a very specific drug that "his community" dealt and consumed (Reeves & Campbell, 1994).

White crime, on the other hand, is generally individualized/psychologized (i.e., it is the fault of the pathological individual with no indication of his or her group orientation), and as such, whiteness remains invisible while the negative images of racially subordinated populations are accentuated. When there is a crime portrayed in the news, there is almost always a racial categorization made when the perpetrator is racially subordinated, for example, "A Hispanic youth killed a seventeen-year-old . . ." We rarely, if ever, hear that, "A white man killed . . ." For whites, the description generally provides only information about the age and the gender of the accused. What comes as no surprise in a racist society is that whiteness appears when the crime committed is against a white person.

Making no effort to identify and challenge the oppressive conditions (severe unemployment and exclusion) within which some crime is inevitable in communities of struggle, such images confirm through the conditioned eyes of the white mainstream that blacks, as well as other "racial" groups, need to be both culturally and physically contained. Instead of implicating white supremacy in the long history of economic and social oppression such as the creation of ghettos, the fingers of guilt are pointed at what is perceived to be a culture of laziness, violence, drugs, and amorality.[36] For example, in the popular press, how often have we heard, "If they only had family values!" Again, the theoretical discussion is halted at the level of the family, with no deeper analysis as to why the family unit—community in general—has been splintered throughout this country.[37] Nor is there recognition of the great many racially subordinated families that are hard-working, loving, and surviving in the face of overbearing and unjust obstacles.

Armed with fictitious justifications for the realities of oppression, many whites sit home and entertain themselves, and ensure their own security by watching a growing number of police shows, such as *Cops*, or *America's Most Wanted*, as many shirtless "dark" people are chased down and locked up; the logic of these images is that "animals"/"savages" do not wear clothes and such dehumanization legitimates violence and mistreatment. Or, comfort is found in the fact that prison construction is a growing private industry.

The "invisibility" of whiteness is not only evident in mainstream social relations but also in more progressive efforts toward change. Take, for example, the descriptor "people of color." As Macedo (1994) argues,

> By calling non-white racial and ethnic groups "people of color," one is proposing that white is not a color, even though colorless white as a proposition is a semantic impossibility. . . . This process facilitates the continued dance with bigotry without having to take responsibility for the poisonous effects of racism. (p. 223)

Anzaldúa (1990) also makes this point about the word *Hispanic*. She argues that,

> Anglos, in order to alleviate their guilt for dispossessing the Chicanos, stressed the Spanish part of us and perpetrated the myth of the Spanish Southwest. We have accepted the fiction that we are Hispanic, that is Spanish, in order to accommodate ourselves to the dominant culture and its abhorrence of Indians. (p. 211)

Many well-intentioned activists and teachers use such language uncritically, not recognizing that the ideology embedded in such terms is in fact the product of racenicity.

It is interesting to note the ways in which language is also used as a marker of racial inferiority by dominant groups. For example, if a white woman meets a man with a Spanish accent and assumes that he is from Spain, she will interact with him as a European—"high culture," flamenco, bullfights, Picasso, and so forth. If that same Spanish-speaking individual informs the other person that he is from Puerto Rico, suddenly the accent (even though he is as white as she is) evokes a racialized social identity that is not looked upon favorably—do you have a knife, are you on welfare, are you going to hurt me . . .

The absence of whiteness is also prevalent in mainstream efforts to infuse multicultural education. Under the rubric of multicultural education, a great deal of research, literature, curricula, and classroom practices presently attempts to address issues of cultural diversity, as well as racial and economic inequalities. However, as argued in Chapter 1 of this book, the majority of this work, which endeavors simply to affirm diversity and identities through positive images of subordinated groups, does so in a limited fashion, focusing on color coordination, food festivals, cut-and-paste add-ons to the existing canon, and group-based methodologies. These efforts, by abstracting particular groups' similarities from an understanding of their various complexities (such as differences among them in terms of gender, class, language, locality, age, health, and sexual orientation), often fall into the trap of essentializing (e.g., perceiving all Latinos/as to be the same), objectifying (i.e., seeing people as objects of educational policies and practices, rather than as self-determining subjects with a say in their education), or even romanticizing the lives of those on the margins. Within such limited models that focus exclusively on the other, the concept of difference is often not taken up in terms of recognizing and critically engaging the dominant referent group—the norm of white, upper-middle-class, heterosexual male by which all others are measured.

Even the very realities of white supremacy disappear behind terms such as *multiculturalism* and *racism*. Consequently, these all too common depoliticized and ahistorical approaches to multicultural education fail to adequately examine the ideologies that inform unequal power relations and social stratification along such lines as race, and to name white supremacy as a cultural foundation in the United States. Such mainstream endeavors can invite surface reforms, but merely recognizing our differences will not lead to a transformation of the exclusionary ideological and structural patterns of our unequal society. Coco Fusco (1988) warns, "To ignore white ethnicity is to redouble its hegemony by naturalizing it. Without specifically addressing white ethnicity, there can be no critical evaluation of the construction of the other" (p. 9).

In the courses I teach that deal with issues of whiteness and other forms of oppression, there are always teachers who argue against drawing attention to racial and cultural differences. "I see my kids as individuals; I don't see color," is a common response. However, as well intentioned as they may be, this lack of acknowledging and engaging such ideological markers has negative consequences. As Sonia Nieto (1992) asserts, "To see differences, in this line of reasoning, is to see defects and inferiority. Thus, to be color-blind may result in *refusing to accept difference* and therefore accepting the dominant culture as the norm. It may result in denying the very identity of our students" (p. 109).

By no means is Nieto implying that skin color predisposes behavior, but rather, she is emphasizing that in this society the sociohistorical and ideological construction of race dramatically impacts cultural practices and experience. It is thus theoretically insufficient and dangerous to simply psychologize experience via the notion of individuality, abstracting it from the realities of social and institutional practices. "Despite exhortations both sincere and hypocritical, it is not possible to be 'color-blind,' for race is a basic element of our identity" (Winant, 1995, p. 31).

A public elementary school teacher in my graduate course, Cross-Cultural Perspectives, recounts the following story. She observed a group of thirteen children between the ages of three and five, who were asked to describe themselves. The children, looking at pictures taken of themselves, responded, "happy, angry, sad, bored, and so on." They then began describing their clothing. The final angle of inquiry pertained to skin color. When it was the African-American girl's turn to describe herself, "She became suddenly and unusually troubled and very apprehensive. At first she hesitated, then without conviction, described herself as 'white.' A Euro-American child shouted at the top of his lungs, 'Black, black, you are black!' With lots of embarrassment she brought herself to say 'brown.'"[38]

The young girl from India also identified herself as being white, even though her skin tone was darker than the African-American girl. The Mexican child "simply said 'blanco' and then withdrew from the group." The teacher comments:

> It's important to note that none of the students, although very young, have problems distinguishing between the seven basic colors. The difficulties started when the children were to describe their own skin color. When it was my turn to describe myself, the students volunteered to identify my skin color. Out of the entire group, only two Euro-American children labeled me, hesitatingly at that, as "brown." It was not until I described myself as brown that the Mexican child consented to rejoin the group with a big smile. In subsequent descriptions, I noticed a propensity for all non-white children to describe themselves as brown.

It is clear from this anecdote that the process of racialization/racenicity, regardless of whether we choose to recognize and address it, begins at an early age. The children not only reveal an internalized stigma about color but also how whiteness has come to signify the norm, intelligence, beauty, and so on. It seemed normal to them that the Dominican woman could only be a teacher if she were white. When the positive attributes of intelligence and power were then identified as belonging to a "brown" person, the children found comfort and solidarity in their actual identities. The Mexican child's initial resistance and subsequent rejoining of the group is symbolic of this process of rupturing racialization and cross-cultural ambivalence.

As previously stated, the point of creating this new analytic category (racenicity) is not meant to essentialize race, to assume that all oppressed groups/individuals think about is their oppression, or to argue that resistant/oppositional behavior or assimilation manifests itself in deterministic or monolithic ways. The purpose of racenicity as a point of analysis is to examine how race, beyond biology, is a social and historical construction that in part shapes ethnic identities, representations, perceptions, and social relations and practices, as well as what it means to be American. Proper exploration of the social construction of whiteness as an ideological category and ethnic identity demands that we as educators reconceptualize our inadequate notions of education, especially multicultural education.

Racenicity and Education

Unfortunately, even within the more progressive mainstream multicultural education movement, categories such as race and ethnicity remain fragmented (which disregards their interrelationship), and thus, so do the possibilities for excavating, understanding, and transforming our cultural identities. Educators and citizens need to interrogate the unspoken centrality of white, male, affluent, heterosexual identity. Schools should embrace critical pedagogy as a point of departure from the confines of the dominant social and educational paradigms.[39]

As argued in Chapter 1 of this book, critical pedagogy can create the self-empowering pedagogical conditions within which both teachers and students can better make sense of the world and their interactions therein—to engage and thus interact as participants (shapers) of history, rather than as simply **objects** (passive recipients) to be acted upon, manipulated, and controlled. Emphasizing the need for political awareness, critical work is enormously important for developing a theoretical framework that historically and socially situates the deeply embedded roots of racism, discrimination, violence, and disempowerment in the United States. Instead of perpetuating the assumption that such realities are inevitable, critical pedagogy should invite the participant to explore the relationship between these larger historic, economic, and social constructs and their inextricable connection to ideology, power, and identity.

The initial step toward developing presence of mind is the critical recognition of one's own location in history, society, and privilege. As Frankenburg (1994) contends,

> Rehistoricizing whiteness and Americanness as locations of cultural practice entails learning more about the multiple histories of assimilation, appropriation, and exclusion that shape the cultural field(s) that White Americans now inhabit. Rehistoricizing also requires engagement with whiteness and Americanness as culturally specific spaces rather than as cultureless, culturally neutral, or culturally generic terrain . . . whiteness and Americanness are like other cultural assemblages . . . that generate norms, ways of understanding history, ways of thinking about self and other. (p. 75)

White educators, students, and citizens need to seriously interrogate collective whiteness—racenicity—by challenging the narratives of national identity and culture. As James Baldwin (1985) eloquently states, "A price is demanded to liberate all those white children—some of them near forty—who have never grown up, and who never will grow up, because they have no sense of their identity" (p. 320). Identity needs to be understood as a place of struggle, a space of self-definition and representation. Otherwise, we will remain in a state similar to what Anzaldua (1990) describes in the following passage: "An Indian mask in an American museum is transported into an alien aesthetic system where what is missing is the presence of power invoked through performance ritual. It has become a conquered thing, a dead 'thing' separated from nature and, therefore, its power" (p. 32).

Tragically, so many Whites buy into the illusion that their turf is being invaded by immigrants, "aliens," and "illegals." Such propaganda, which works toward an uncritical allegiance to whiteness, draws attention away from the powerful center—those who are truly profiting from the present social and economic paradigm. Instead, the media, politicians, and other **cultural workers** create a trumped-up nostalgia to go back to some "golden age" when supposedly "things were good." These illusions of a golden age need to be ruptured because that very past was when most of us were the ones being exploited, as we lost our roots and became imprisoned by assimilationist ideologies that paradoxically have claimed to support us while, in the form of ignorance, fear, and support of an unjust and undemocratic society, they have actually undermined our very beings.

This anesthetizing racial consciousness—whiteness, which subdues and consequently subverts any chance of a cultural democracy—urgently needs to be confronted and transformed. It is in fact democracy (which thrives on difference, participation, and dissent), and not race, that is supposed to unite us as a nation. Wake up white America and name yourself!

Notes

1. Although I often use the analytic distinction "working class" to emphasize my points throughout this paper, by no means am I implying that they are the core source of white supremacy in the United States. As my argument unravels, my intention is to show how the white working class, to a great extent, has been diverted away from the sources of power that instill racism and shape their everyday realities. This point of analysis is also not meant to essentialize working class into some mythical homogeneous group. My hope is that schools (and other public spheres) can embrace political consciousness as a fundamental part of the educational process so that the great many people who are socially, politically, and economically disenfranchised can work to challenge and change, rather than participate in, the reproduction of the present social order.

2. This also begs the question of whether or not there is an "American" ethnicity.

3. The use of the term *American* is problematic. Its appropriation by the United States is a symbolic example of U.S. imperialism in North, South, and Central America. Because of the limits of language and the historical use, the reader will find that I contradict myself throughout this chapter by using *American*. I realize this and am working toward a new descriptor.

4. For a discussion of these other issues, see P. Leistyna; A. Woodrum; & S. Sherblom (1996). *Breaking Free: The Transformative Power of Critical Pedagogy.* Cambridge, MA: Harvard Educational Review Press.

5. "It seems much more democratic to affirm that nobody—or everybody—is a hyphenated American" (Yinger, 1994, p. 7). With a resurgence of ethnic pride in the 1960s, self-employed hyphenations have taken on a positive political connotation, one of solidarity, for example, African-American.

6. These distorted representations historically have shifted with changing social relations. For example, images of enslaved blacks portrayed them as being ignorant, servile, and in desperate need of guidance. After Emancipation, their image was reshaped by the dominant ideology as being violent and dangerous, in need of control (Riggs, 1987).

7. These derogatory images of Mexicans would eventually serve to represent all Latino/a groups.

8. For an extensive discussion of the issues raised in the *Bell Curve*, see *Measured Lies: The Bell Curve Examined,* edited by Joe Kincheloe, Shirley Steinberg, and Aaron Gresson, 1996. New York: Saint Martin's Press.

9. It is important to note here that German- and Italian-Americans during this same period were not interned. Race and European origin certainly played a significant role in this decision.

10. A common criticism toward such a critique of white racism is that all groups can be racist. I would argue that there are antagonistic relations among racially subordinated groups. However, I believe that such tensions in the United States are the product of the racialization of identities and the struggle over crumbs at the bottom. This does not imply that all groups are incapable of being racist. But within the unequal power relation in the United States, it is only whites who have the power to institutionalize and socially sanction their racist ethos. All others can only discriminate against each other.

11. Puerto Ricans, Native Hawaiians, Filipinos, and so on. See Joel Spring (1994). *Deculturalization and the Struggle for Equality: A Brief History of the Education of Dominated Cultures in the United States.* New York: McGraw-Hill. For an in-depth discussion of the mistreatment of Mexicans, see *Occupied America: A History of Chicanos,* by Rodolfo Acuna. New York: Harper & Row, 1988.

12. As previously mentioned, capitalism is a major factor in the production of American identity. As a result, social class is also a significant factor in cultural practices. However, socioeconomic status is not simply about money. More importantly, class, which cuts across difference, shapes our physical being, values, attitudes, social relations, and ways in which we exchange knowledge. Perhaps we should refer to this phenomenon as "classnicity." In this way, we can understand how race can be cut across by class such that there is also a diversity of experiences within a single racial category—that is, the identity of an upper-class Puerto Rican is usually significantly different from that of a poor Puerto Rican living in the ghetto. Although the discussion of this chapter focuses on the effects of the ideological construction of race, the analytic distinction of racenicity should not be abstracted from other important factors. We need to develop a more dialectical understanding of the multiple and interconnecting relationships, along such lines as race, class, gender, and sexual orientation, that speak to a more profound understanding of the politics of identity and difference.

13. Although I have used this quote to initiate my argument and I talk about enslaved Africans being part of the plot to divide and conquer, I recognize that "whiteness" was also historically shaped around Native American, Mexican, and other racialized identities.

14. For an elaboration on how a person gets socially and legally defined as "black" in the United States, see F. J. Davis (1991). *Who Is Black: One Natisn's Definition.* University Park, PA: Pennsylvania State University Press. See also T. Allen (1994). *The Invention of the White Race.* London: Verso; I. F. Haney Lopez (1996). *White by Law: The Legal Construction of Race.* New York: New York University Press; C. Mills (1997). *The Racial Contract.* London: Cornell University Press.

15. The use of "nonwhite" is also problematic in that it situates "white" as the referent. Although this is important for naming racism, it symbolically limits the process of decentering its hold as the norm.

16. For an in-depth look at this process, see Noel Ignatiev's book *How the Irish Became White* (1995). New York: Routledge.

17. The impact of slavery and the colonization of Native Americans should be blatantly obvious. The impact on Puerto Ricans, Native Hawaiians, and Filipinos (among others) has also been devastating, though inadequately discussed in national history.

18. It is important to note that many newly arrived immigrants in the United States continue to uncritically adopt negative images and feelings toward racially subordinated populations, especially toward blacks. Feagin and Vera (1995) argue that some of the nonblack immigrant groups "have been able to improve their racialized status within the White dominated society, but only because Whites have come to see them as 'better' in cultural or visual-racial terms than African Americans. Even so, 'better' has never meant full social, economic, and political equality with Euro-Americans" (p. xii).

19. See also R. Bellant (1991). *Old Nazis, the New Right, and the Republican Party: Domestic Fascist Networks and Their Effects on U.S. Cold War Politics.* Boston: South End Press.

20. Toni Morrison (1992) provides an interesting discussion of how the author's assumption that the readers of fiction are "positioned as white" has affected his or her literary approach. See *Playing in the Dark: Whiteness and the Literary Imagination* (1992). New York: Vintage. See also the work of Edward Said, especially *Culture and Imperialism* (1993). New York: Knopf. Henry Giroux offers a great deal of insight on this issue in *Disturbing Pleasures: Learning Popular Culture* (1994). New York: Routledge; and in *Fugitive Cultures: Race, Violence, and Youth* (1996). New York: Routledge. Other important contributions on this topic are *Cultural Studies* (1992). L. Grossberg, C. Nelson, and P. Treichler (Eds.). New York: Routledge; R. Dyer, *The Matter of Images: Essays on Representation* (1993). New York: Routledge; and D. Strinati, *An Introduction to Theories of Popular Culture* (1995). New York: Routledge.

21. For a discussion of the psychological development of racial identities, see B. Tatum (1992). "Talking About Race, Learning About Racism: The Application of Racial Identity Development Theory in the Classroom." *Harvard Educational Review.* Vol. 62, No. 1. See also J. Katz (1978). *White Awareness: A Handbook for Anti-Racism Training.* London: University of Oklahoma Press.

22. Hechter (1974) refers to this as "reactive-ethnicity." Bowser and Hunt (1996) identify this phenomenon as a "reactive role."

23. Ogbu's model is problematic in that race is not the central factor in his categorization of voluntary and involuntary or castelike immigrants. African-Americans, or blacks, in his model are defined by their history of slavery, rather than by their race. As such, a black person who has recently come from Jamaica falls into Ogbu's "voluntary immigrant" status. However, it is the color of his or her skin that predominantly predetermines the treatment that he or she will face in this country. In addition, Ogbu's assumption that many of these immigrants are "voluntary" is an ahistorical analysis of U.S. foreign policy. In other words, to

assume that our involvement in such countries as Guatemala, El Salvador, Nicaragua, and Panama did not lead to violence and upheaval, forcing people from their homelands, is a radical distortion. But Ogbu's position comes as no surprise considering that he has a "blame the victim" tone throughout his work, a kind of "if you just didn't have those oppositional identities" attitude.

24. Houston Baker Jr. (1991) frames this manifestation of cultural opposition in terms of "racial" or "racialized resistance" (p. 5).

25. John Ogbu (1987) also makes reference to "survival strategies," which he describes as "instrumental and expressive responses to cope with their subordination and exploitation" (p. 261). He insists that these survival strategies develop into norms, values, and competencies.

26. I do not want to imply that cultural practices and identities are necessarily defined in direct opposition to the dominant values—that is, you do this, so we will do the opposite. Counterdiscourses and subversive identities also take their own independent forms.

27. The use of "Anonymous" was my choice. As promised in the contract with my research site, this descriptor protects the school's identity.

28. Although Rampton's research was conducted in England, the significance of his findings certainly translates to the U.S. setting.

29. In the social struggles in Detroit in the 1970s and 1980s, in what he describes as "blacktown surrounded by a white noose" (p. 174), Kofi Natambu (1992) attributes the plethora of cultural activities in the city to insurgent political resistance. Winant (1995) argues that, "In the post–civil rights period, what constituted a 'true' black identity expanded vigorously into every area of social and cultural life: language, skin color, taste, family life, and patterns of consumption all became testing grounds for blackness" (p. 41).

30. Nor do they understand that baggy clothes are the product of sanctioned prison life. They certainly do not question why blacks represent a disproportionate amount of inmates across the country.

31. For a more in-depth discussion of the white cultural forms that produce and perpetuate racism in everyday life, see the video *Ethnic Notions: Black People in White Minds* (1987), by Marlin Riggs (California Newsreel).

32. I'd like to thank Antonia Darder (1991) for putting these two quotes together in her book.

33. The term *profit* is in quotes because I want to make clear that my idea of profit and success is by no means the same as the commodified mainstream version. "Profit" in their sense of the word implies material wealth and the enjoyment of power over others. However, I believe that in the process of dehumanizing other people, they have in fact dehumanized themselves; therefore, in my estimation, they have actually lost out—what greater cost is there than one's humanity.

34. This centrality and invisibility can be seen in such descriptors as WASP. When the Jutes, the Angles, and the Saxons emigrated from Germany to England in the fourth and fifth century, only later to become Protestants in the 1500s, they were inevitably white. The question then presents itself: Why be redundant and call yourselves white Anglo-Saxon Protestants? The use of *white* is surely a marker of separation from racial otherness.

35. Beyond the racial hegemony that is maintained by such cultural representations, as Tommy Lott (1994) argues, there is also "a strong market incentive to exploit mass media constructions of hip-hop culture as a criminal underclass" (p. 241).

36. Those in power use such misrepresentations to their advantage. These negative images can instantly become positive ones if need be. We have seen this phenomenon in the social construction of Asians, and more recently of Cubans. However, the "positive" images also function to perpetuate racism and antagonistic social relations.

37. I do not want to imply here that there is a universal notion of "family," as the Republican onslaught would have us believe. In fact, their model of the family is one that is fundamentally exclusionary and authoritarian. Simply ask Newt Gingrich why he chooses to deface his lesbian half-sister in public. Ask the Republicans why domestic abuse against women and children and alcoholism are so prevalent among mainstream families; ask why they blame working women for the extremely high divorce rates.

38. This quote was taken from the observing teacher. The identification with whiteness recalls the research conducted by Kenneth Clark, a professor of psychology at City College of New York, in which the black children involved in the study chose to identify with the white dolls over the black dolls. See K. Clark (1955). *Prejudice and Your Child.* Boston: Beacon Press. This incident also recalls the central theme of Toni Morrison's *The Bluest Eye* (1970). New York: Washington Square Press.

39. This discussion of the educational implications of racenicity does not imply that schools alone can eradicate racism. Society as a whole must work toward the kinds of social agency that can transform any and all unjust and undemocratic practices and institutions.

4 Demystifying Democracy: A Dialogue with Noam Chomsky

*The following dialogue took place between Noam Chomsky and Pepi Leistyna and Stephen Sherblom in the fall of 1994, at Chomsky's office at the Massachusetts Institute of Technology. The purpose of the conversation was to frame the lives of youth in the United States and the culture of violence that permeates much of U.S. society within an interdisciplinary perspective that explores the historical, sociopolitical, economic, and cultural conditions of this country, laying bare the **ideologies** that drive such conditions. Although Chomsky's prolific work has accomplished this goal in many important respects, his political critiques and insights have been almost entirely excluded from national efforts to understand community disintegration and address issues of youth violence. By bringing Chomsky's critical perspectives, concerns, and outlooks to the center of educational debates, it is our belief that educators can better understand the complex roots and history of inequality and violence in this country, and thus better inform themselves of the current social context in which children live, as well as the tools they will need to become active, aware, critical, and responsible citizens.*

Chomsky focuses on how capitalism, as it has been practiced in the United States, has produced a set of social values and a culture that prioritizes, at great social cost, individualism, the production and accumulation of wealth and material goods, and the wielding of power over others. Some of the effects of these cultural values are a lack of political

---

This dialogue originally appeared in the *Harvard Educational Review.* Vol. 56, No. 4, Summer 1995 (pp. 127–144).

awareness, community, caring, and democratic struggle. In fact, throughout the dialogue, Chomsky vividly illustrates how we, as a society, often work against the values that we publicly profess, such as the growth and health of children, the social and economic well-being of all people, and the basic tenets of democracy.

The **dialogue** dissects the relationship between the state and the business sector and exposes the ways in which the poor and middle class in the United States subsidize the wealthy. Chomsky discusses how the media and public institutions often function (through the use of scapegoats, distortions of history, and propaganda) to **manufacture consent**— that is, to lead the public to internalize values and beliefs that result in the unequal distribution of privilege, wealth, and power. He shows this has happened with media coverage of the problem of violence by divorcing it from larger social causes and portraying it as a problem of inner cities, minority communities, and poor families.

This dialogue's interdisciplinary treatment of violence provides a concrete example of the power of critical pedagogy to help us see beyond the confines of what information we are fed. Chomsky concludes with a discussion of the possibilities for radical social change.

While the media portray violence as if it's a new epidemic in this country, your work has shown that historically the United States has been based on a culture of violence. Could you elaborate as to what you feel are the actual ideological and systemic elements that inform the history of violence in our society?

The entire history of this country has been driven by violence. The whole power structure and economic system was based essentially on the extermination of the native populations and the bringing of slaves. The Industrial Revolution was based on cheap cotton, which wasn't kept cheap by market principles but by conquest. It was kept cheap by the use of land stolen from the indigenous populations and then by the cheap labor of those exploited in slavery. The subsequent conquest of the West was also very brutal. After reaching the end of the frontier, we just went on conquering more and more—the Philippines, Hawaii, Latin America, and so on. In fact, there is a continuous strain of violence in U.S. military history from "Indian fighting" right up through the war in Vietnam. The guys who were involved in Indian fighting are the guys who went to the Philippines, where they carried out another slaughter. This goes right on up through Vietnam. If you look at the popular literature on Vietnam, it's full of "We're chasing Indians." But that's only one strain of the institutionalized brutality in our history.

Internally, American society has also been very violent. Take the labor history. U.S. workers were very late in getting the kind of rights that were achieved in other industrial societies. It wasn't until the 1930s that the U.S. workers got minimal rights that were more or less standard in Europe decades earlier. But that period of development in the United States was also much more violent than Europe's. If I remember the numbers correctly, about seven hundred American workers were killed by security forces in the early part of this century. And even into the late 1930s, workers were still getting killed by the police and by the security forces during strikes. Nothing like that was happening in Europe; even the right-wing British press was appalled by the brutal treatment of American strikers.

There have been other sources of violence as well, for example, the ways that a large part of the population is systematically **marginalized** in this society. We're again different from other industrial societies in that we don't have much of a social contract. So if you compare us even with, say, Canada, Europe, or Japan, there is a kind of social contract that was achieved in these industrial societies concerning public welfare, such as health care. European societies grew out of a social framework that included feudal structures, church structures, as well as all sorts of other things. And the business classes in Europe, as they came along, made various accommodations with these exiting structures, resulting in a more complex society than we have here in the United States, where the business class just took over. It was kind of like we started afresh, creating a new society, and the only organized force was a very highly class-conscious business community. Because the United States is essentially a business-run society, much more so than others, we're the only industrial nation that doesn't have some sort of guaranteed health insurance. In many respects we're just off the spectrum, which is pretty striking considering we're also the richest society by far. Despite being the richest society, we have twice the poverty rate of any other industrial nation, and much higher rates of incarceration. In fact, we're the highest in the world and both will continue to worsen in light of the Gingrich "Contract with America" and the new crime bill. Out of these sociohistorical and economic structures, which embrace conquest and an indifference to public welfare, comes a streak of violence.

From the very roots of this country we see that capitalism and so-called free-market practices have worked to benefit the prosperous few who manage the economy and dictate social policy. In your estimation, where on the spectrum of capitalist practices is the United States presently situated?

In a real capitalist society, the only rights you have would be the rights you get on the labor market. There are no other rights, certainly no human rights. In fact, it's classical economics, but no society could realistically survive that way, though we're closer to that than most others. However, in our system, there is a double standard. The poor, more than anyone, get the rights they can achieve on the labor market, but for the rich, there's powerful state protection. They've never been willing to accept market discipline. The United States has, from its origins, been a highly protectionist society with very high tariffs and massive subsidies for the rich. It's a huge welfare state for the rich, and society ends up being very polarized. Despite the New Deal, and the Great Society measures in the 1960s, which attempted to move the United States toward the social contracts of the other industrial nations, we still have the highest social and economic inequality, and such polarization is increasing very sharply. These factors—high polarization, a welfare state for the rich, and marginalization of parts of the population—have their effects.

One effect is a lot of crime. You have people who are cooped up in urban slums, which are basically concentration camps, while the rich protect themselves in affluent areas, which are often, in fact, subsidized by the poor. In the 1980s and the 1990s, it's been quite striking how much the polarization has increased. A symbol of this is Newt Gingrich, who now is spearheading the "get the government off our backs" campaign. If you look carefully, it again is a double standard. He wants the government "on our backs" when its policies assist the poor, but he wants the government "off our backs" if it's benefiting rich people. In fact, his district, a very wealthy suburb of Atlanta, gets more federal subsidies—taxpayers' money—than any suburban county in the country, outside the federal system itself. This rich suburb is carefully insulated from the downtown, so you don't get any poor blacks coming in there. And here's Gingrich saying, "Get the government off our backs." Well, that tells you exactly what it's all about. You get the government out of the business of helping poor people, but make sure it's in the business of helping the rich. And, in fact, once again, if you look at the Republican Contract with America, that's exactly what it says. It's cutting social spending for the poor but increasing welfare for the rich. That's inevitably going to lead to increased polarization, resentment, brutality, and violence.

How does the money flow from the poor to the rich?

Here we are at MIT, which is part of the system whereby the poor people fund high-technology industries. We have offices and things because the whole system of public funding, meaning taxpayers, ends up supporting research and development. If it's profitable, the technology goes right off to the big corporations.

There sure are a lot of government license plates out in the parking lots.

Yeah, but it isn't just government license plates; they're simply part of the whole system by which the poor subsidize the rich. And, in fact, it was perfectly, consciously designed that way. If you look back to the business press in the late 1940s, they are absolutely frank about it. They said, "Look, advanced industry can't survive in an unsubsidized, competitive free-enterprise economy, in a true market"—the government has to be the savior. And how do they do it? Well, they talked about various methods, but the obvious method was the Pentagon system, which largely functions as a way of subsidizing the rich. That's why it hasn't declined substantially with the end of the Cold War. There was all this talk about defending ourselves from the Russians. Okay, now that the Russians are no longer a threat, has the Pentagon system gone? No, the United States is still spending almost as much on the military as the rest of the world combined. And anyone in industry knows why. There's no other way to force people to pay the costs of high-tech industry.

Take Newt Gingrich, for example. The biggest employer in his district happens to be Lockheed. Well, what's Lockheed? That's a publicly subsidized corporation. Lockheed wouldn't exist for five minutes if it wasn't for the public subsidy under the pretext of defense, but that's just a joke. The United States hasn't faced a threat probably since the War of 1812. Certainly there's no threat now. We're not as threatened as the rest of the world combined. In fact, an awful lot of the production of arms is sold to other countries. If anything, that increases any threat. So the whole thing has nothing to do with threats and security; it's a joke. In fact, that was always known. If you go back to the late 1940s, the first secretary of the Air Force, Stuart Symington, said publicly, I think in Congress, "Look, the word to use is not *subsidy;* the word to use is *security.* That's the way we'll make sure that the advanced industry gets going." That's how the aircraft industry works; that's how the computer and electronics industries work also. About 85 percent of research and development in electronics was funded by the government in the 1950s.

Take, as another example, the research and development of automation. The apologists for our system say that the creation of automation is the result of market principles. That's just baloney. Automation was so inefficient that it had to be developed by the Air Force. The same holds true for containerization; trade looks efficient because we have container ships. How were container ships developed? Not through the market; they were developed by the Navy, through public subsidy. They don't have to worry about the costs, because the public's paying. Now that it's profitable it's turned over to "private enterprise" and is used to undermine working people who funded it. Automation is now putting people out of work.

That's the irony of the military recruitment poster we saw here in this building. Its slogan is, "Born to lead," and it depicts soldiers on a mission. Through the Pentagon system you describe, the military does lead in the sense of developing this technology and using high-tech weaponry to control by force. But in reality, the military ends up being driven by big business interests and becomes nothing more than mercenaries for the rich, as they so blatantly did in the Gulf War, for oil. Even Eisenhower, when leaving the presidency, warned of the power of the military industrial complex and the potential danger to the possibilities of democracy—not that he was a proponent of democratic practices.[1]

Can you elaborate on other ways that the privileged benefit from this enormous system of subsidies?

On top of the Pentagon system there are the straight welfare payments. If you have a home mortgage, you get a tax rebate. A tax rebate is exactly equivalent to a welfare payment. It's exactly the same if I don't give the government $100 or if the government does give me $100. Well, who do home mortgage loans go to? These go overwhelmingly to the privileged. In fact, about 80 percent of them go to people with incomes over $50,000, and as you go into the higher tax brackets, it's skewed even more. Or take business expenses as tax write-offs, for example. If you take your friends out to a ballgame or something like that, for so-called business purposes, that's paid for by the taxpayer. If you look at the whole range of expenditures, which are the exact equivalent of welfare payments, they far outweigh welfare payments to the poor. And these expenditures are going to be increased, because the Republican Contract with America will increase military spending, and increase the regressive fiscal measures that amount to welfare for the rich. They want to give subsidies for business investment and cut back capital gains taxes. Those are subsidies to the wealthy.

So, as the society gets more polarized and more people are marginalized, and people are working harder just to stay where they are, social relations further crumble to a point where you get a lot of violence. Actually, it's amazing that despite all this, if you look at, say, the FBI statistics, the level of violence hasn't changed very much. There's probably more violence among eleven-year-olds than there was, but there's less violence in other places. And the violence among eleven-year-olds is the result of the Reagan and Gingrich war on families.

What are some of the central ways that these social and economic policies and practices affect the lives of youth in this country?

One aspect of this, specifically with regard to children, is something that isn't discussed here in the United States. There's been a war against children and families for the last fifteen years, a real war. There's an interesting study of this by UNICEF, completed about a year ago, called *Child Neglect in Rich Societies,* written by a well-known American economist, Sylvia Ann Hewlett. She compares what has happened to children and families in the last fifteen years in rich societies, and she finds that the results break pretty sharply into two models. The European/Japanese model was supportive of families, with day care systems and prenatal care, and other such benefits, whereas the Reagan/Thatcher model, which extended to some extent to the other English-speaking societies, tended to force families into using privatized child care without other support systems.

One of the reasons child care was impossible to afford was because wages were being driven down. That means that there are plenty of families where you have to have a husband and a wife working for fifty or sixty hours a week just to provide necessities. Perhaps much of one person's salary is going to pay day care. With very little in the way of a public support system, they can't get such things as health insurance because it costs too much. Well, the effect of this, which Hewlett describes in this study, is quite obvious—kids are left on their own, unsupervised and unprotected much more in the Anglo-American model than in the European/Japanese model. There are a lot more latch-key children, TV as baby-sitter, and that sort of thing going on here in the United States. Actually, she reports that contact hours between parents and children in the United States decreased by about 40 percent since about 1960. High-quality contact, where you really pay attention to each other, has declined very, very sharply. The effects of all that are completely obvious—you get violence against children and violence by children. You also get substance abuse. All of these are obvious consequences of that social policy. If kids are neglected, with no care and guidance, they're going to be either watching television or wandering around the streets.

When you put that together with the effects of poverty, discrimination, and racism, and all the other unmet social needs such as quality schooling and economic opportunity, the violence being done to children will inevitably be a catalyst for a rise in violence by children. It's clear that this kind of monopolistic capitalism that you're talking about destroys community even at its most basic level—the family. Despite all the national attention on violence and youth, and a growing body of literature in the social sciences documenting the unmet needs of so many youth in this country, it is amazing how few links are made in the national debates, including those in the academy, between government policies that hurt children and families and the increasing violence involving youth. And we've only just started to see the beginning of it.

Oh yeah! It's going to get worse because now they want to extend the war against families in the name of family values, and they will get away with it, just as Newt Gingrich got away with representing the most subsidized district in the country while he was claiming "we don't want federal subsidies." Now, how do they get away with it? Well, I think the explanation is pretty simple. The political opposition, though they could have made hay out of Gingrich or out of family values, basically agrees with him. There's a class interest in common. They don't want to expose the fact that there are public subsidies for the rich because they're in favor of them. And they don't want to expose the fact that there's a war against families and children because they agree with it. So they're not exposing it. The Gingrich case is particularly interesting, because he is slaughtering the Democrats, but even their interest in political survival didn't override their class interest in not exposing what was going on. The two political parties are more or less united in subsidizing the rich.

The political right seeks to distract the public from these issues by preaching that a stimulated market will be the answer to our social problems. How could the state of the market possibly resolve the violence of racism, illiteracy, and poverty? It certainly didn't in the "prosperous" years following World War II. How can the market solve what in fact it creates?

Maybe people talk themselves into believing that the market is the solution, but the reason they believe it is because the actual system is going to enrich them. They refuse to accept market discipline for themselves, though they insist on imposing it on others. There's almost nobody who advocates market discipline for themselves; it's always for someone else. And that's not because they've figured out that the market is going to solve the problems; it's because that double-edged policy is going to enrich them. Adam Smith talks about this; these are truisms.

One major detrimental result of capitalist social relations, which emphasizes money and acquisition over caring for people's basic needs and fostering community, is that it works to fashion children's identities, and the ways in which they interact socially, around the excesses of marketing and consumption.

One of the things that is indeed fostered, and has been for centuries, is mindless consumerism. It was understood a long time ago that you can't force people to work unless you trap them into wanting commodities. That goes right through the Industrial Revolution—from early England right up to today. So you have to put enormous amounts of effort into atomizing people, breaking down social relations, making sure there aren't other ways of realizing their interests and concerns, and optimally turning them into atoms of consumption and tools of production. That would be the perfect thing, and an enormous amount of effort goes into that. Take, for example, the information highway; it's probably going to end up being a home shopping service because that's a terrific way to atomize people and make them consume more. Therefore, consumers have got to work more, while they are making less pay, and for the business class trying to enrich themselves, this is perfect. And the propaganda that goes into this is extreme. The public relations industry spends billions of dollars a year essentially trying to convince people that they need things that they don't want. Those things are part of the technique of breaking down social relations, making people feel that the only thing that matters is getting more than your neighbor. This diminishes social interaction, feelings of solidarity, sympathy, and support. And, in fact, that provides a backdrop for violence.

Which most people don't seem to understand. If you are taught to believe that the meaning in life resides in getting status, power, and money, and not in the development of quality relationships with others, you're likely to hurt people to get what you want. When an eleven-year-old kills an-

other kid for a pair of sneakers, people generally respond, "I can't imagine how this could happen."

Why not? We're telling this eleven-year-old through television, "You're not a real man unless you wear the sneakers that some basketball hero wears." And you also look around you and see who gets ahead—the guys who play by the rules of "get for yourself as much as you can"—so, here's the easy way to do it. Kids notice everybody else is robbing too, including the guys in the rich penthouses, so why shouldn't they? The rich guys do it their way and the eleven-year-old does it his way.

Well, look what they are telling the rest of the population! They're telling them that someone else, other than the rich, is responsible for the social demise. In fact, conservative mainstream arguments contend that violence and drug abuse are simply the result of the lack of family values. Such arguments contend that women working outside the home are responsible for the breakdown of families. Oppressed groups, portrayed as "lazy freeloaders," and those disgracefully referred to as "illegal aliens" are also targeted. Would you comment on the ability and purpose of those in power to create and punish scapegoats in this fashion?

Those are indeed the arguments, but every single one of them is utterly ludicrous. For instance, if women who want to stay at home and take care of their children are being forced into the marketplace, that's because the Republicans' social policies drive down wages, so you can only survive by having two members of the family work. As I mentioned before, if there's no care for children, that's because we don't provide child support.

This building up of scapegoats and fear is standard. If you're stomping on people's faces, you don't want them to notice that; you want them to be afraid of somebody else—Jews, homosexuals, welfare queens, immigrants, whoever it is. That's how Hitler got to power, and in fact he became the most popular leader in German history. People are scared, they're upset, the world isn't working, and they don't like the way things are. You don't want people to look at the actual source of power—that's much too dangerous—so, therefore, you need to have them blame or be frightened of someone else.

So it not only justifies the violence against the scapegoats but diverts attention from the other violence being done to the general population.

Diverts attention, sure. In fact, you can see this very clearly in polls. People have repeatedly been asked to estimate how they think the federal budget is spent. In fact, of the discretionary funds, over half is military spending. But under a third of the population knows that. Many pick foreign aid—which is undetectable. And they very much overestimate the welfare that goes to, say, "black mothers with Cadillacs." These are the things that people believe. They believe that they're working hard, and that their money is being taken and given to poor people overseas, and to black women who refuse to work and just keep "breeding." The fact is that their money is going to Newt Gingrich's constituents through the Pentagon system. Scapegoating certainly serves that purpose.

It's just amazing how something like California Proposition 187 is so openly racist and, in a time of so-called family values, actually contributes to the disintegration of families. While the cheap labor of illegal immigrants is a staple of the California economy, the state doesn't want to provide much-needed social services to that labor force, such as education and health care for children. Pete Wilson's entire political platform was based on this scapegoating. Conservative media **representations** *of illegal aliens continually work to convince the general public that they are somehow responsible for this country's multi-trillion-dollar debt.*

Which Reagan and Reaganites created. And did on purpose, because they wanted to cut back social spending.

Which is something we never hear from the Democrats.

Rarely, because they agree. Look, there was a Democratic Congress—they basically went along with the policies because they more or less agreed with them. And they all represent more or less the same class. There are, to be sure, important differences: Ted Kennedy isn't the same as Newt Gingrich. But there's enough commonality of interests that they're not going to expose each other very much, any more than they exposed Gingrich this time around. I mean, he was wiping them out on this big government business. I never saw one person point out, "You're the biggest exponent of the welfare state!"

One consequence of this unwillingness to speak the truth is that the present Republican emphasis on creating prisons and employing more police is falsely legitimated. You mentioned earlier the dramatic increase in incarceration. According to the U.S. Justice Department, there are well over a million people presently in prison. Increasing the number of prisons and police are certainly only short-term solutions that serve to divert attention from the real causes of drug abuse, crime, and violence. People being "criminalized" are being scapegoated and incarceration becomes the big business solution to "the problem."

Exactly, for example, the drug war, which was almost completely phony, was simply used as a technique of incarceration. There was a huge increase in imprisonment during the Reagan years, and some enormous percentage of it, like two-thirds, was for drug use. And most of it isn't even crime—it's victimless crime, like catching somebody with a joint in their pocket. In fact, if you look in the federal prisons, you don't find many bankers and chemical corporation executives and so on, although they're involved in the drug racket. Banks are involved in money laundering, and government agencies pointed out years ago that the big chemical corporations are exporting chemicals to Latin America way beyond any industrial use. What they're exporting, in fact, is what's used for commercial production of drugs. But the idea is to go after the black kid on the corner in the ghetto, because he's the one you want to get rid of. For example, take cocaine. The drug most often used in the ghettos is crack; in the white suburbs it's powder. Well, you know, the way the laws are crafted, powdered cocaine gets much less of a sentence than crack cocaine. That's social policy. It's part of criminalizing the "irrelevant" population; even drugs are used for that purpose. Thus, incarceration is a technique for social control. It's the counterpart in a rich society of the death squads in a poor society. You throw them in jail if you can't figure out what else to do with them.

Wouldn't you say that the same is true of the war on drugs abroad?

Yes, it has little effect on the production and sale of drugs but has lots of effect on controlling people. So, in Colombia, the counterinsurgency war has had no effect on drug production; it's had a huge effect on slaughter and controlling the population. In fact, Colombia's now the biggest human rights violator in the hemisphere, with a hideous record of atrocities. And it's also the biggest recipient of U.S. military aid, more than half for the entire hemisphere. Has that stopped the flow of drugs? Of course not. Although it's kind of interesting what has happened, if you look at the details. There were two big drug cartels in Colombia—the Medellin and Cali cartels. In this so-called war on drugs, the Medellin cartel was more or less wiped out. The Cali cartel, however, was untouched, and in fact, much enriched. There was a recent report by a Jesuit-based peace and justice group in Colombia about this matter. They point out that the Medellin cartel was kind of precapitalist. It's similar to the Mafia in Sicily. It had partially lower-class origins, and the guys who were running it were like the city boss type. For example, Pablo Escobar, the head of the Medellin cartel, would build a soccer stadium for the poor people. In fact, they were very popular because of their social roots and because there was something of a Robin Hood quality to them. Not that they were nice guys or anything, but that was the kind of crime it was. Now Cali is different; that's just rich business—bankers, industrialists, and big business enterprises. So while the Medellin cartel was being wiped out, the Cali cartel was untouched and their power was increased.

Just to give you an example of what a joke the drug war is: In the mid-1980s, Colombia requested from the Reagan administration technical aid for a radar station to detect low-flying planes that were coming in from the Andean region, bringing in coca leaves, which were then processed. The Reagan administration agreed, and they built a radar station, but they built in on the part of Colombian territory that is as remote as possible from the drug routes. Namely, they built it out on an island, called San Andres, which happens to be off the coast of Nicaragua. If you think about the map, that's the opposite place from where the drug flights are coming. But it is very useful for surveillance of Nicaragua, and for sending terrorist forces to destroy health clinics and so forth. So that's the way they fought the drug war. And it just works across the board. It's an absolute farce, except that it's serving its purpose. Its purpose in this country is to criminalize blacks and other marginalized groups, to treat them like a population under military occupation, to lock them up, in effect without constitutional rights, and race and class are closely enough correlated in the United States so that this is also part of the class war.

*A great deal of your work, including Media Propaganda, Necessary Illusions, Thought Control in Democratic Societies, and Manufacturing Consent, discusses the role of the media in colonizing the psyche and the social relations of the larger **public sphere,** in terms of getting people to buy into some of the malignant myths we've discussed. You state in your book,* What Uncle Sam Really Wants, *that,*

the sectors of the doctrinal system serve to divert the unwashed masses and reinforce the basic social values—passivity, submissiveness to authority, the overriding virtue of greed and personal gain, lack of concern for others, fear of real or imagined enemies, etc. The goal is to keep the bewildered herd bewildered. It's unnecessary for them to trouble themselves with what's happening in the world. In fact, it's undesirable. If they see too much of reality, they may set themselves to change it.

The Gulf War is a perfect illustration of how the state and the media worked to divert the masses. The strategy was to demonize and thus dehumanize the Iraqis in order to mobilize the U.S. population in support of what really were foreign economic adventures, shrouded in the idealistic rhetoric of defending democracy.

The public relations industry—a U.S. creation—is very aware that their job is controlling the population. But we shouldn't overestimate its success. This is a very heavily polled society, and most of the polls are done for business because the public relations industry wants to know how to craft the propaganda. There's a ton of information on public attitudes. Take the Gulf War, for example. The polls that were taken two or three days before the bombing found the population to be two to one in favor of a negotiated settlement. Those two-thirds who came out in favor of negotiating a settlement did not, when they described their position, know that was also Iraq's position. Iraq had, in fact, put that position on the table, and the United States had simply rebuffed it because they didn't want to negotiate a withdrawal. If the population had known those facts, which were carefully concealed—I believe they only appeared in one newspaper in the United States—the results wouldn't have been two to one; they probably would have been twenty to one. And the same is true on other issues. Take, say, the economic system. Over 80 percent of the population regard it as inherently unfair. In addition, the political system—everyone knows it's regarded as a joke. On issue after issue, the public is not in line with elite opinion, but the public is marginalized.

This business about "the bewildered herd"—I didn't make that phrase up—that's Walter Lippmann, the dean of American journalists, in his "progressive" essays on "democracy." He said that we have to protect ourselves from "the trampling and the roar of the bewildered herd," "we" being the smart guys who are supposed to run things; we've got to make sure the bewildered herd doesn't get in our way. Perhaps 90 percent of the population, "they're bewildered," and we're going to keep them bewildered because, as he put it pretty frankly, in a democracy the public has the role of spectators but not participants. We, the elite 10 percent or so, are the participants. We are the "responsible men." And that's the "progressive" fringe; reactionaries are even worse. And that's understandable, because if people knew what was going on and they acted on their own motives, that would dismantle the system of privilege. Not many people would be happy to know that they're paying taxes so that the people in Newt Gingrich's rich suburb can get even richer. If they found that out, there would be changes.

How do schools and institutions of education—which play a significant role in the ongoing formative nature of culture, identity, and social relations by directly influencing children's ways of seeing themselves and others in the world—contribute to this colonizing of people's minds?

Well, every possible way. It starts in kindergarten: The school system tries to repress independence; it tries to teach obedience. Kids and other people are not induced to challenge and question, but the contrary. If you start questioning, you're a behavioral problem or something like that; you've got to be disciplined. You're supposed to repeat, obey, follow orders, and so on. When you get over to the more totalitarian end, like the Newt Gingriches, they actually want to do things like coerce kids into praying, and they call it voluntary. But you know, you have a six-year-old kid who's got a choice of praying like everyone else or walking out of the room—it's not voluntary and those demanding school prayer know it. Such forms of state coercion and imposing discipline would absolutely horrify the "founding fathers," not that Gingrich cares one way or the other.

How does this manufacturing of consent happen in the larger social and political spheres, and in business and corporate sectors?

When you talk about the state and the business community in the United States, it's extremely hard to separate them. The state is overwhelmingly penetrated and dominated by the corporate sector; the financial and corporate institutions have most of the top decision-making positions, so it's very hard to disentangle the corporate sector and the state. They're different manifestations of very closely related things. The media are another part of this. The media are big corporations that sell audiences to other businesses. An example of this manufacturing of consent was in yesterday's paper, where you'll find Elaine Sciolino, chief intellectual in the *New York Times,* describing Clinton's Indonesia trip, and she describes how his big achievement there was that he was able to get jobs for Americans. How did he get jobs for Americans? Well, by implementing a $35 billion deal whereby Exxon Corporation develops natural gas fields in Indonesia. Is that going to be jobs for Americans? A couple of American executives and some public relations firms, and maybe some corporate law firms, but it's going to give jobs to very few Americans. On the other hand, it's going to give profits to quite a lot of rich Americans, but you're not allowed to mention the word *profits*. That's a dirty word. So, it can't be that Clinton was over there to get profits for rich Americans; it's got to be that he's getting jobs for poor Americans. The discipline on that topic approaches 100 percent. You just can't find the word *profits*—it's always *jobs* in the media and the political rhetoric.

Remember when Bush went to Japan with a bevy of auto executives a couple of years ago? The big slogan was "Jobs, Jobs, Jobs." General Motors is trying to get jobs for Americans? Is that why they're closing down twenty-four plants here and have become the biggest employer in Mexico and are now moving to Poland—because they want jobs for Americans? No, they want profits for rich Americans, but you can't say that. And if you tried to say that, first of all, in elite circles, you probably wouldn't be understood.

What's amazing is that companies like General Motors will strategically shroud themselves in the American flag, and in a kind of baseball, hot-dogs, and apple pie patriotism. And people generally buy into such representations.

Because there is so much indoctrination that many people can't even understand the word *profits*. If you try using the word *profits* around Harvard, for example, in the Kennedy School of Government, if you say "Clinton's out there getting profits for rich Americans," then people would be appalled—"Is this some kind of conspiracy theorist? Marxist? Anti-American? Or crazed radical?" Even elementary truisms like this, which to someone like Adam Smith are so obvious he scarcely even bothered to talk about them, are completely beaten out of the heads of educated people. In fact, I think it's worse among the educated sectors than among the uneducated.

I've talked to all sorts of people, and it would be harder to convince Harvard graduates that this deal with Exxon was for profits than it would be to convince guys on the street. They'd say, "Yeah, obviously." And the reason is, if you've been really well educated, meaning well indoctrinated, you can't even think rational thoughts any longer. They can't come to you; the words can't come to you. So, I don't think Elaine Sciolino is lying; it's just that the conception of the state working to increase profits for wealthy Americans is inconceivable. You can't think that thought. If it's ever expressed, you have to designate it unthinkable, with scare words like *conspiracy theory.* And that's the process of "good education." People who don't internalize those values are weeded out along the way. By the time you get to the top, you've internalized them.

This phenomenon certainly carries over in the teaching of history, especially U.S. history. The possibility of thinking about the history of this country in terms of profit and greed, and the resulting violence and even genocide, is eliminated. Those words are seldom even in the textbooks.

Well, it's a little better than it used to be, but not much. Much of history is just wiped out. We just went through a war in Central America in which hundreds of thousands of people were slaughtered, and countries destroyed—huge terror. U.S. operations were condemned by the World Court as international terrorism. It's nevertheless described in this country as an effort to bring democracy to Central America. How do they get away with that? If you have a deeply indoctrinated educated sector, as we do, you're not going to get any dissent there, and among the general population who may not be so deeply indoctrinated, they're marginal. They're supposed to be afraid of welfare mothers and people coming to attack us, and busy watching football games and so on, so it doesn't matter what they think. And that's pretty much the way the educational system and the media work. So the *New York Times* and the *Washington Post,* they're for educated folk, and they sort of beat them on the head with the right ideology. Most of the rest of the media are there just to keep people's minds on something else.

This practice of constricting what's acceptable to think and to consider in the academy and public debate is certainly evident in your experiences as a social theorist. Your work has been recognized globally and you're seen historically as one of the world's most brilliant intellectuals. However, at the same time, your political critique and insights have been for the most part marginalized, if not ridiculed, in the United States.

True, but respectable intellectual culture is not so dramatically different in most countries.

The idea of public intellectual in present-day politics is a contradiction. If people are honest in their critique of the system in the United States, they are either declared nonintellectual, or, as you state, derided as "anti-American, Marxist, or conspiracy theorists," and removed from the public media.

It's not really a contradiction; it's perfectly normal under this system of control. For one thing, I'm on the radio and television and writing articles all over the world—not here. And that's to be expected. If I started getting public media exposure here, I'd think I were doing something wrong. Why should a system of power offer opportunities to people who are trying to undermine it? That would be crazy. It's not that this is something new. The people who are called intellectuals are those who pretty much serve power. Others may be equally intellectual, but they're not called intellectuals. And that goes all the way back to the origins of recorded history. Go back to the Bible; who were the people who were respected, and who were the people who were reviled and jailed and beaten and so on—they're the ones who years later were called prophets. And it goes right up until today.

In the United States, people respected Soviet dissidents, but they weren't respected in Soviet society. There, they respected the commissars. So you are a respected intellectual if you do your job as a part of the system of doctrinal control. Raise questions about it and you're just not acceptable—you're anti-American or some sort of shrill and strident something or other. Why was Walter Lippmann one of the responsible men, whereas Eugene Debs was in jail? Was it that Walter Lippmann was smarter than Eugene Debs? Not that I can see. Eugene Debs was just an American working-class leader who raised unacceptable questions, so he was in jail. And Walter Lippmann was a servant of the major powers, so he was respected. And it would be amazing if it was anything else.

*But then what is the role of intellectuals, in terms of offering a public counterdiscourse that links violence and social decay to structural flaws and undemocratic practices? And, in light of the recent Republican repositioning of power, what are the possibilities of such **counterdiscourses**?*

The job of the honest intellectual is to help out people who need help; to be part of the people who are struggling for rights and justice. That's what you should be doing. But, of course, you don't expect to be rewarded for that.

In terms of teachers in this country who express the desire to work toward more democratic social change, what do you think they could do?

It's easy for me to talk, but the fact is, if you're in a classroom and you try to act like an honest, independent person, you'd probably be thrown out. The school board won't like it—especially if it's made up of wealthy parents, they're not going to like it. I remember in the 1960s when the student ferment began, we lived in Lexington, a professional, upper-middle-class suburb of Boston. The parents wanted the school to be run like the Marine Corps. They wanted their kids controlled. They didn't want them to think. Well, there were in those days, maybe more than now, young people coming out of the universities who believed in teaching kids to think, as a means of social transformation. They would do things like elementary school teaching, and some of them tried and they were very good. My son had one of these teachers for a while in elementary school. But it's very hard to live in the system and survive it. It's clear what you ought to do, but whether you can survive it is another question.

*This question of teaching children to **think critically,** to better understand and participate in the transformation of the violence, racism, social control, and social disintegration around them, is taken up in critical pedagogy. While you certainly embrace critical education, what do you think are its realistic possibilities here in the United States?*

It's just not going to be allowed, because it's too subversive. You can teach students to think for themselves in the sciences because you want people to be independent and creative; otherwise, you don't have science. But science and engineering students are not encouraged to be critical in terms of the political and social implications of their work. In most other fields you want students to be obedient and submissive, and that starts from childhood. Now, teachers can try, and do, break out of that, but they will surely find if they go too far that as soon as it gets noticed there'll be pressures to stop them.

*There is a problem with this fragmentation of knowledge into separate disciplines in the academy—this is science, that's politics, this is psychology. Even the word discipline is so ironic, alluding to constraint. When I try in graduate school to talk about moral development and its inherent connection with the **sociohistorical** and political structures that we've been speaking about, then some people immediately react by saying, "You're not talking about moral development anymore; now you're talking about politics, or some other discipline, and we don't deal with that." How can you talk about moral development and violence without talking about the larger social, cultural, and economic environments in which people live and develop?*

You can't! On the other hand, if you simply talk about the world in the accepted ways, that would not be called politics; that would be being reasonable. It becomes ideological or extremist when it deviates from the accepted patterns. The term *ideological* is an interesting one. If you repeat the clichés of the propaganda system, that's not ideological. On the other hand, if you question them, that's ideological and very strident or anti-American. Anti-American is an interesting expression, because the accusation of being antination is used typically in totalitarian societies, for example, the former Soviet Union accused dissidents of being anti-Soviet. But try anti-Italian or anti-Belgian—people in Milan or Brussels would laugh.

The term propaganda is used in neither the media nor the academy in reference to this country's practices—as if propaganda only functions in places like the former soviet Union or Nazi Germany.

Yeah, like the invasion of Haiti, or whatever you want to call that thing. The big thinkers in the press presented what they called historical background. R. W. Apple over at the *New York Times* wrote an article on perspectives and explained that for hundreds of years the benevolent Westerners have been trying to bring some order to Haitian society, where groups with homicidal tendencies are attacking each other and are heavily armed, like right now. So you've got two homicidal gangs attacking each other—the people who are getting murdered in the slums, and the troops whom we trained and armed who were killing them. Then he goes on about how, at different periods in history, both Napoleon and Woodrow Wilson tried to do "good things" for the Haitian, which didn't work.

We are used to the fact that the Wilson intervention, which was murderous and brutal, was regarded as sweet charity, but Napoleon? That was one of the most murderous invasions of a period that was not known for its gentility, but it must be that "good" Westerners were trying to bring order to this society. And David Broder of the *Washington Post* wrote the same thing. That's history—the idealistic Americans are trying to help out. But they're baffled by the violence of the society that has no experience with democracy, and so on and so forth. I mean the relation of that to history—it's 180 degrees off. But if you repeat that stuff, that's not being ideological; that's being "responsible."

David Landes, a well-known Harvard historian, wrote an article on Haiti some years back, in which he described the Marine invasion—the Wilson intervention—as very beneficial to Haiti. In fact, it had a devastating effect on the society, dismantling the Parliamentary system and killing thousands of people, forcing them to accept laws that let U.S. corporations buy up the land and turn it into plantations, reintroducing virtual slavery. It also left a military force to attack the people—it was monstrous! This from a leading historian—but that's not ideological. On the other hand, if you tell the truth, that's ideological. That makes sense, in some strange way.

*Fostering **historical amnesia** and refusing to acknowledge the violent and **hegemonic** nature of their own ideology allow those who have historically run this country to perpetuate the myth that this is a democratic society. Your work has shown that the U.S. international political and economic practices have actually destroyed what you refer to as "good examples—prospects for real progress toward meaningful democracy and meeting human needs" in "third world" countries. Such examples are falsely represented to the American public as posing a threat to our security and well-being, and people generally buy into that. They actually believe that they live in a truly democratic society.*

I suppose that around Harvard they do! But if you look at the polls, half the population thinks that both political parties should be dismantled. Is that living in democracy? What you get in off-year elections is about a third of the population voting—this year, around 39 percent. That's because people just regard the whole electoral process as a farce. In fact, there are regular Gallup polls in which people are asked, "Who do you think runs the government?" And about 50 percent regularly say that the government is run by a few big interests looking out for themselves. Try that in the Harvard Faculty Club. The official story is that the political system is pluralistic; everyone's part of some different interest or pressure group. It's not a few big interests looking out for themselves. You have to be uneducated to be able to see that.

*Given the implications of your work and what we've said in the last hour, what are the possibilities for fulfilling a progressive vision of a future social order—one that actively incorporates the majority of the population in nonviolent political struggle, **resistance,** and social transformation?*

As everyone has always known, the best way to defend civil liberties is to collectively build a movement for social change that has broad-based appeal, that encourages free and open discussion, and offers a wide range of possibilities for social agency. The potential for such a movement surely exists. Many positive changes have taken place in the last thirty years as the result of popular movements organized around such issues as civil rights, peace, feminism, and the environment. If this struggle ever becomes a mass movement of the oppressed and exploited on an international level, the impulse to contribute to it may intensify, growing both from moral pressure and the desire for self-fulfillment in a decent and humane society. One immediate concern of industrial democracies is the rational and humane use of the Earth's resources, on which the United States continues to do very poorly, and which, as exploitation, is another form of violence. "Broad-based" also implies that along with the general public, scientists, engineers, technicians, and skilled workers, educators, writers, and artists also need to be deeply involved in the development of the intellectual resources necessary for providing plausible, concrete, short- and long-term solutions to the problems of our advanced industrial society.

You have stated in the past that any system of power, even a fascist dictatorship, is responsive to public dissidence. In the context of everyday life in this country, where does such dissension begin when the deck is so clearly stacked against popular struggle?

The general population has lots of cards. People can organize, initiate demonstrations, write letters, and vote. They can form unions and other grassroots organizations, political clubs, even an opposition political party so that we'll at least have a two-party system. Citizens can organize to press a position and pressure their representatives about it. Elections can also matter. The systems of private tyranny—totalitarian in character—are also not there by natural law but by human decisions. They can be dismantled and democratized. What concentrated privilege can't live with is sustained pressure that keeps building, organizations that keep doing things, people who keep learning a lesson from the last time and doing it better the next time. Students and others with similar privilege—and it is privilege—can also do their own research by going back to original sources in public libraries. Real research and inquiry is always a collective activity. Such efforts can make a large contribution to changing consciousness, increasing insight and understanding, and leading to constructive action.

Well, as you conclude in What Uncle Sam Really Wants, *"We don't know that honest and dedicated effort will be enough to solve or even mitigate our problems; however, we can be quite confident that the lack of such efforts will spell disaster."*

Notes

I would like to thank Steve Sherblom for all of his support, wisdom, and humor. His friendship kept me going in the face of adversity at the Harvard Graduate School of Education.

1. This comment was excluded from the original publication in the *Harvard Educational Review*. Some members of the student board were adamantly against publishing this dialogue. Although Steve and I, after extensive meetings, were eventually able to argue the manuscript through to publication in virtually its original form, our punishment was to exclude this one comment. I chose to include it here not only for its insight but also to maintain the integrity of the original dialogue.

5 Veritas: The Fortunes of My Miseducation at Harvard

David Landes, a well-known Harvard historian, wrote an article on Haiti some years back, in which he described the Marine invasion—the Wilson intervention—as very beneficial to Haiti. In fact, it had a devastating effect on the society, dismantling the Parliamentary system, and killing thousands of people, forcing them to accept laws that let U.S. corporations buy up the land and turn it into plantations, reintroducing virtual slavery. It also left a military force to attack the people—it was monstrous! This from a leading historian—but that's not ideological. On the other hand, if you tell the truth, that's ideological.

—Noam Chomsky

This quote by Noam Chomsky, taken from the dialogue in the previous chapter of this book, points to the fact that no history is innocent of the intents of its authors. As there is this inextricable relationship between **ideology** and truth, the real battle is over who has the authority to determine which bodies of knowledge, values, experiences, and interests are to be legitimated in mainstream **sociohistorical** narratives and practices.

As a private corporation and educational institution, with a multibillion-dollar endowment, Harvard (which I refer to as "the pillars of the republic") represents a very selective form of truth, and those who have maintained the institution have managed to obfuscate its exclusionary practices by promoting and defending a belief in objectivity, certainty, and a scientific basis for the study of social reality. From this perspective, knowledge and reason are interpreted as neutral and universal, rather than the products of particular ideologies and interests.

Positivism is so embedded in the Harvard Graduate School of Education (HGSE) that its constricting theoretical tenets strategically work to homogenize difference in the guise of science. Within these **modernist** clutches,

127

multiple **voices** cannot be heard because the notion of objective truth implies that only one voice and one view of social reality exists and thus merits legitimacy. On the surface, the Graduate School of Education appears to be one that affirms and embraces diversity. For example, course catalogues present an array of diverse racial portraits. However, deep down, beyond mere color coordination and window dressing, ideological differences that inform cultural identities and political dissent are virtually eliminated.

Refuting this prevailing paradigm, my academic work for the past six years at Harvard has been informed by the idea that any examination of social reality, culture, and educational practices is inherently **subjective,** that is, determined by one's own experiences, beliefs, values, and interests. Because of the overtly political nature of my work (no less political than those who hide behind notions of objectivity), throughout my career as a master's and doctoral student, my insights and concerns have been constantly subjected to abrasive and cutting-floor-type treatment in both classroom discussions and written work.

Within these antagonistic academic conditions I have tried to **theorize,** that is, to make sense of my situation at Harvard. Chomsky's work has proved to be extremely beneficial in this endeavor. I would like to use portions of his theoretical perspectives and critique of status quo institutions that surfaced during our discussion together, in order to cast light on my experiences. In doing so, I will depict the ways in which many professors and students at Harvard make a claim to scientific objectivity as a means to discourage substantive debates over such pressing issues as race, ideology, class, capitalist social relations, gender, sexual orientation, and language.[1]

The Confines of Language

If you simply talk about the world in the accepted ways, that would not be called politics, that would be being reasonable. It becomes "ideological," or "extremist" when it deviates from the accepted patterns. . . . If you repeat the clichés of the propaganda system, that's not ideological. On the other hand, if you question them, that's ideological and very strident.

—Noam Chomsky

The most frequent assault on my work has come in the form of criticisms toward the complexity of language that I have created to express my worldview. For example, in a doctoral seminar a member of the senior faculty (ironically, a major figure in the area of literacy development), after reading only three paragraphs, wrote on my paper:

> When I read another sermon expressed in such abstract terminology—
> whether Giroux's or yours—my mind shuts down. This is a lot of big words
> and clichés. Hard words, I know, but you've been here a year and must have
> written stronger, clearer papers last year and in your personal statement . . .
> revise and resubmit.

From that point on, the professor simply stopped reading. Obviously an issue of ideology rather than a sincere problem with the language ("Hard words, I know"), this attitude not only represents a form of anti-intellectualism ("my mind shuts down") but also the practice of academic censorship. By equating the worldview that informs how I approach research and practice (my **subject position**) with a "sermon," this educator was able to excuse herself from reading what she considered inappropriate academic work. She was also in a position of power to silence the concerns raised therein. I was thus presented with two options: revise the paper to her liking, which entails stripping the work of any critical and substantive content and analysis, or fail. The last sentence in her response seems to be saying, "How did you get into this institution," and, "Why hasn't a year of work here ideologically shaped you to my liking?" It is interesting to note that this same paper, with some minor copy editing, was later published in a reputable journal.

One member of the senior faculty altogether dismissed critical work (in front of the class) as "not worth engaging because it is opaque and incomprehensible." Another professor, who considers himself to be progressive, attacked one of my papers, claiming that, "This is a lot of big words! The use of 'deconstruction,' sounds like a lot of masturbation to me." This type of arrogance (what I refer to as "the arrogance of ignorance," which Harvard breeds) engenders the ultimate form of **stupidification.** With a single statement this professor negates, without ever having engaged the strengths and weaknesses therein, one of the twentieth century's most important movements in literary criticism—Jacques Derrida's work in **deconstructionism.** Not only does this response attempt to dismiss the significance of such work but it also functions to deter students from developing a more interdisciplinary approach to education—that is, from critically appropriating and reinventing educational insights from across the social sciences. This same professor argued,

> The assumption that ideological sophistication is a sign of cultural progress
> ignores the fact that many people just don't give a damn about this kind of
> complex verbalization. They may be temperamentally bent toward build-

ing, or singing, or hoeing corn. So the problem for me is to prevent the *over-interpretive egghead* from claiming a special corner on sacred (significant) knowledge—but still get his or her due. It always makes me a little wary about the extent to which the critical theorists (Freire, Giroux, etc.) appreciate the great range of talents of people who are not so much deluded by all this professional garbage as they are bent toward other enterprises that have little to do with complex elaboration of language. So they often cannot protect themselves, either from specialized professors of literacy or specialized professors of critical literacy.

The constant dismissal of work as being "jargonesque" and "inaccessible" has always greatly troubled me. Inherent in such notions of "unintelligible" is the assumption that there is a universal language and a medium of clarity that *we* all understand. The question is: Who is the inferred *we*? When I say I believe in good education and John Silber says the exact same thing, we are in fact talking about two extremely different conceptions of the world. On the surface, the words that we use are apparently simple, but upon deeper ideological analysis they are worlds apart.

This alluding to clarity, to some mythical objectively verifiable reality, ignores the inherent relationship among language, power, and experience. That is, it ignores the way that systems of communication, which are all social and historical constructions informed by particular ideologies, play a significant role in shaping human subjectivities, literacies, cognitive styles, and cultural identities, and can (and often do) work to either confirm or deny the life histories and experiences of the people who use them.

As accessibility is not a natural and self-evident state of language, the call for plain prose can be interpreted one of two ways: Either people are sincerely seeking to understand, or they are consciously refusing to acknowledge the inherently cultural and thus ideological nature of language. The latter is exemplified by a professor of literacy who responded to a paper that I wrote about the social construction of cognition and literacy: "I worry about the extreme 'embedded' notion so popular today, e.g., when watching Malcolm X working hard on his oral and written discourse by copying the dictionary."

This educator seems to believe that the dictionary is a universal, neutral body of information, and that the context of a prison library and cell is somehow not culturally connected in terms of shaping Malcolm's experience and knowledge. But then again, this is a school of education that uses the standardized TOEFL exam (the test for evaluating international students who do not speak English as their primary language), which has no oral component, to determine whether a student can cope with the linguistic and communicative demands of graduate school in a second language. It is thus not surprising that in my doctoral cohort a young Korean woman found herself without the necessary communicative competence to easily adapt to her new surroundings. Instead of creating supportive structures to help the student begin and complete her doctoral work, the professor in charge, a language specialist, not only publicly humiliated the individual by drawing attention to her inability to communicate but also recommended that she return home immediately—which she did.

The callousness toward reading the world in ways that are different from the norm at Harvard is epitomized in the following situation. A Taiwanese student/friend approached me midway through the second semester of her master's career in order to share with me that she was dropping out of school. As we talked about her experiences that had led up to this final decision, she confided in me: "To stay would leave scars on my spirit . . . they are trying to mold me into something that I am not, something that I don't believe in!"

There is a strong anti-intellectual unwillingness to cross cultural borders at HGSE (e.g., **discourse,** theoretical, ideological) and to embrace the possibility for ongoing **dialogue** among colleagues, and between teachers and learners. The paradox about the positions of many conservative educators (even those who may consider themselves progressive) is that in claiming to promote literacy they are in fact complicit in promoting new forms of illiteracy among students and teachers—the illiteracy of clarity or simplistic thought. Instead of emphasizing the need to be literate in multiple languages and discourses, these educators dismiss work in the name of jargon, and in doing so, they infantilize readers by deterring them, as if they are not intelligent enough, from struggling through and critically appropriating/reinventing diverse languages and theoretical and political positions—ways of defining the world. The basic assumption is that readers simply will not understand. Such educators **objectify** the reader in that they ignore how multiple audiences read and comprehend differently.

It is interesting to note that many of my English as a second language students from Europe, who have experienced systems of public education that explore, to some extent, the critical traditions throughout their studies in secondary and certainly higher education, generally have no trouble engaging the complexity of critical social theories. When some of my colleagues at Harvard discovered that I was planning to use Henry Giroux's book *Disturbing Pleasures: Learning Popular Culture* (1994b) in an adult

English as a second language class, they overwhelmingly responded, "They will never be able to understand that!" Later, when I told them that the students were in fact enjoying the material and were enthusiastically engaged in the discussions, one white person, who originally framed her objection to the use of Giroux in terms of the language he used, revealed her true colors in stating that, "Oh that's just another form of indoctrination anyway!" I responded by asking her if there were materials that were not. She simply turned her back and walked away. In such a case, the issue of clarity is simply used to dismiss politically centered work and reinforce particular forms of authority, intolerance, and thus the status quo.

There is no question that educators need to **problematize** the basis of their own linguistic privilege; however, whereas a scientist may reduce her or his work for a children's science museum exhibit, as "established" educators it is our responsibility to keep up to speed as to the cutting edge of educational/social theory, research, and practice across the ideological and disciplinary spectrum. As **public intellectuals,** it is not as though we need to agree with any particular position, but rather, working from a privileged institutional space, we need to engage the plurality of discourses not effortlessly but struggling as responsible readers to make sense of and subsequently dispute or reinvent them. This is not an argument for a particular ideology. It is rather a depiction of what is fundamental for generating those conditions in which language provides a vehicle for opening up different spaces to allow people to speak to, and be aware of, multiple voices and audiences.

As argued in Chapter 1 of this book, theory and practice in this sense work actively through, and not on, students by helping both teachers and students to reflect on how domination works, and consequently to develop, as they interact with each other, their own transformative practices. Thus, the Harvard professor's assumption that students "cannot protect themselves, either from specialized professors of literacy or specialized professors of critical literacy" is a blatant misreading of the intents of critical pedagogy, and is also a radical distortion of the important contributions and sacrifices that Paulo Freire has made globally to the poor and oppressed peoples of Latin America and Africa.

From his privileged and safe office at Harvard, this professor's romanticized view, of "building, singing, and hoeing corn," recalls images of slavery in this country, a state from which African-Americans have yet to, in the professor's own words, "get their due." In fact, the complexity and difference of black English is a direct result of **resistance** to racial domination. Do we simply dismiss the intricacies of this language as ideological sophistication or complex verbalization!

When any students at Harvard complain about the density of the language of critical social theory, I often turn the argument around by asking them why they think that after more than eighteen years of formal education they have never been exposed to such work. For those who are sincerely interested in expanding their horizons, I always offer a number of introductory books that can help to scaffold the reader into the ongoing discussions and debates around these complex educational and social issues. The following are just a few suggestions from an enormous body of work:

1. *The Concise Oxford Dictionary of Sociology* (1994)
2. *The Blackwell Dictionary of Twentieth-Century Social Thought* (1993)
3. *Keywords: A Vocabulary of Culture and Society* (1976)
4. *The Blackwell Companion to Social Theory* (1996)
5. *Studying Culture: An Introductory Reader* (1993)
6. *Culture: Key Ideas* (1993)
7. *An Introductory Guide to Post-Structuralism and Post-modernism* (1993)
8. *Modernity: An Introduction to Modern Societies* (1996)
9. *Postmodern Theory: Critical Interrogations* (1991)
10. *An Introduction to Theories of Popular Culture* (1995)
11. *Breaking Free: The Transformative Power of Critical Pedagogy* (1996)

The critical appropriation of different discourses has enormous implications for educational theory and practice. Without such an effort, we are certain to become semiliterate—that is, only able to deal with the simple language that masks the intricacies of the reality being examined, thus absolving the examiner from the need to engage the resultant multiple perspectives. If the United States is ever to achieve a critical, pluralistic democracy, then it is essential that all society's members possess a clear understanding of difference. In order to develop such clarity, people need to be both aware and critical of their own location, and literate in multiple ways of perceiving and speaking about reality.

The Price You Pay

The job of the honest intellectual is to help out people who need help; to be part of the people who are struggling for rights and justice. That's what you should be doing. But of course, you don't expect to be rewarded for that.

—**Noam Chomsky**

There is no question that it is a great risk to reveal one's critical posture in an environment such as Harvard's Graduate School of Education. One professor, slapping me with a low grade, exclaimed, "I know you are quite capable of producing critical responses, but I encourage you to remain more faithful to the spirit of the assignment!" Another, in an attempt to shape the way that I would approach a question about "the culture of schools," wrote, "You do a bit better this time, but your particular political agenda has lowered the quality of this paper." Yet another faculty member, on my assigned critique of the cuts in social spending of the 1980s and the recommendations of the *1993 National Assessment of Chapter One,* scribbled (as I began to provide a more in-depth analysis that moved beyond mere description and surface critique), "You have already passed the specific limit!" and penned in a large red "X" over the remaining pages.

As a doctoral student, not only was I shocked to discover that a professor was unwilling to read beyond a certain number of pages but even more devastating was the fact that someone, residing in the comforts of the ivory tower, would be threatened by ideological differences with a student. bell hooks (1994) explains this phenomenon: "If professors are wounded, damaged individuals, people who are not self-actualized, then they will seek asylum in the academy rather than seek to make the academy a place of challenge, **dialectical** interchange, and growth" (p. 165). Such educators fear making paradigmatic shifts, losing control of the classroom, accepting criticism, and learning from their students. Their utter lack of openness, awareness, and willingness to create a space for spontaneity, invention, and change greatly inhibits any real democratic exchange of ideas.

The final paper for a course in language acquisition asked the students to respond to the following question: "After reading the article by Rosalie Pedalino Porter, write an analysis of it, or some part of it, which you make clear your position of agreement or disagreement, and support it with references to the literature."

Porter, author of *Forked Tongue: The Politics of Bilingual Education* (1990), was appointed to the National Advisory and Coordinating Council on Bilingual Education by the former secretary of education of the Reagan administration, William Bennett—a leading opponent of bilingual education. Porter's book, in which she gives credit for its publication to the resources of Harvard College, the Mary Bunting Institute of Radcliff College, the Rockefeller Study Center, and a number of reactionary educators (including the professor who gave me this particular assignment), is essentially a diatribe against bilingual education.

After a great deal of research and writing, which resulted in a comprehensive critique of Porter's work, I submitted my paper, arguing that the book has absolutely no intellectual depth or research sophistication as compared to the major scholars of the field. My extensive efforts were reduced to the following response by the professor: "These [my conclusions] are unsupported politically motivated claims!"

Even when confronted with substantive findings by major researchers and educators in the field, such as Kenji Hakuta, William Lambert, Jim Cummins, and Barry McLaughlin, among others, this professor arrogantly dismissed my work altogether. She rejected my political posture by calling for "a more linguistic analysis" (i.e., "science"). It is interesting that Kenji Hakuta's book *Mirror of Language* (1986) is not only illuminating for its political insights but is based on mainstream research paradigms that this same professor, as well as Porter, often makes claims to. This rejection of my interpretations and ideas comes from a person who is obviously using science as an excuse to not overtly engage ideological differences and dissent.

Later, I had to meet with this same professor because I had received a Title VII Multicultural/Bilingual Fellowship from Washington, D.C., and she was in charge of the Title VII students. In a condescending tone, she snidely remarked in my direction, "I hope you have been reading some hard science." Such educators/power brokers should be more honest with themselves and with their students by simply stating, "I hope that you have been reading 'my science.'" When I turned in a paper (in the same department) on Chomsky's principles of universal grammar as seen through the recent research on pidgin and Creole development, the only response that I received was, "Oh, you belong to that camp!" As Barry McLaughlin (1987) suggests:

> Disciplines tend to become fragmented into "schools," whose members are loath to accept, and are even hostile to the views of other schools using different methods and reaching different conclusions. Each group becomes convinced that it has a corner on "truth" . . . it is counterproductive to believe that there is a single truth that can be known directly and objectively by the application of scientific methods. (p. 5)

Within the contract of the Title VII Fellowship, it is stipulated that students are to receive funding throughout their doctoral career. It is interesting to note that all the bilingual/multicultural fellowship recipients' funding was cut after the first year by this very same person who castigated me for my critique of Porter. Although she informed us that we would be compensated for the loss, this empty promise merely translated into access to more student loans. If not for the incredible compassion and generosity of the people in the financial aid office, I would have been forced to leave school.[2]

When it came time to get letters of recommendation, I knew that my chances of finding someone at Harvard to support my work were slim. The only letter that proved to be at all useful came from a well-known linguist outside of the School of Education. Here again, although the letter was supportive of my abilities, he nonetheless wrote:

> His papers have all been at least excellent, and several have been superlative. The most recent one set out to reconcile Chomsky's language module with a relativistic stance on language and thought, and it was a well-though-out, richly informed try. Pepi's only weakness as a scholar, if it is a weakness, is to become so exercised about matters of social justice that analysis threatens to turn to rhetoric.

This comment comes from a man whose sexuality has been stigmatized throughout his career, an experience that he writes about in his new book now that he has retired from the academy. Although one can sense in his words about me the struggle within him to fight what has in fact contained his identity—"if it is a weakness"—this is nonetheless a perfect example of how the **dominant ideology** always works through people in an attempt to neutralize any **counterdiscourse**—in this case, while acknowledging the academic research and rigor, the work (by virtue of including my own conclusions) is nonetheless reduced to political rhetoric. In fact, Chomsky, who is considered one of the most important intellectuals alive today and has revolutionized linguistic theory a number of times, is often a victim of such facile dismissals because of his political posture. Making the gay professor believe that it is in his own best interest to remain politically neutral/scientific in his analysis plays out perfectly since he actively participated in his own political paralysis and exploitation. This is a perfect example of how **hegemony** works.

As discussed in Chapter 2 in the dialogue with Paulo Freire, as researchers and educators we are somehow supposed to abstract our inherently subjective and affective beings from our work, rather than simply be honest about our positions. That is, modernist institutions such as Harvard uphold the idea of a mind/body/heart split in which emotions, passion, and the physical body are to be eliminated in educational settings. This erasure works to make students believe that they are listening to neutral, objective facts that have nothing to do with the subjective reality of the distributor of such information. Not only does this falsely promote scientism but it acts as a de facto gatekeeping mechanism.

At HGSE there is a politeness paradigm in place that greatly inhibits challenging debate and critical interrogation. In other words, there are only a few acceptable ways of interacting in which fear, anger, and passion are greatly discouraged and even punished. This constricting, bourgeois **cultural capital,** which reinforces particular kinds of etiquette that shape classroom interactions, undermines a true exchange of ideas and ultimately works to neutralize any potential critical/challenging exploration of the inherently political nature of education and difference.

After paying the price a number of times for engaging the classroom and professors in my own way, I was grateful to bell hooks, the author of *Talking Back: Thinking Feminist, Thinking Black* (1989), for breaking the rules on campus. hooks was invited to speak in Lilia Bartolomé's Antiracist Multicultural Education class, in which I was a teaching assistant.[3] In a talk that we opened to the School of Education at large, hooks defended herself for not entirely supporting Anita Hill—stating that, "Hill has been sucking white cocks for years." The look of utter shock on the predominantly white faces in the audience, juxtaposed to the smiles and laughs of a few, generally black students, embodied a subversive and liberating moment.

There was additional fallout from hooks's talk. In the class that followed the presentation, many white students complained that, "She paid no attention to us, and she always looked to a group of blacks that sat to the left of the room." "I wasn't comfortable!" exclaimed another person. It is interesting to note that when whites are no longer in the front row—the center of attention—instead of learning from the feeling of **marginalization** (whether it was a conscious decision of hooks's or not) and listening to learn, the experience is dismissed.

This issue of comfort zone is prevalent among most white students at HGSE. In that same Antiracist Multicultural Education course (different semester), in which I was a teaching assistant for Donaldo Macedo,[4] a group of white women asked him, "Could we wait to get to know and be more comfortable with each other before we deal with the difficult issues such as racism?" Before Macedo or I could respond, a black Puerto Rican woman jumped in, and with a great deal of passion and anger stated, "You have been stomping on my neck for years. This time you're not going to tell me when and how I can speak!" As Macedo left the space open for **subordinated** populations to speak their minds (ostensibly one of the main purposes of such a class), rumors began to circulate among students and faculty outside of the class that he was "aggressive toward whites, and a sexist." Such rumors, which made their way up to the dean's office, as opposed to glowing student evaluations of the course, proved to be the necessary ammunition for the senior faculty to eliminate both Macedo's presence and the course. The use of rumors over hard data (student evaluations) presents an ironic contradiction in Harvard's ubiquitous call for science over subjectivity. Once again, diversity is okay as long as it is on their terms.

The Social Construction of Not Seeing

Even elementary truisms . . . are completely beaten out of the heads of educated people. In fact, I think it's worse among the educated sectors than among the uneducated . . . there are regular Gallup polls in which people are asked, "Who do you think runs the government?" And about 50 percent regularly say that the government is run by a few big interests looking out for themselves. Try that in the Harvard Faculty Club. The official story is that the political system is pluralistic; everyone's part of some different interest or pressure group. It's not a few big interests looking out for themselves. You have to be uneducated to be able to see that.

—**Noam Chomsky**

Do you really see conflict between what parents want/need for their kids and what government (federal, state, local) want/need for their citizens?

—**A Harvard faculty response on one of my papers**

Mainstream educational psychology, in its various forms, has generally focused on what is perceived as a unitary and self-contained individual. From this perspective, it is as if the cognitive and psychological makeup of each person were somehow formulated outside of history and politics, and thus unaffected by ideology, power relations, and such socially constructed categories as capitalism, race, class, gender, and sexual orientation. In fact, this myopic point of analysis systematically ignores the reality that the personal world is, in large part, an intersubjective cultural form.[5] Unfortunately, formal pedagogy and curricula are largely the products of mainstream psychology's structuralist and positivist stranglehold on conceptions of the mind.

The clinical research course that I was required to take as a doctoral candidate was taught by a person whose work is grounded in Piagetian theories around the nature and development of intelligence. The class was designed as an attempt to recognize the multiple perspectives of "our" students and ways of understanding them as individuals. The professor introduced the course with the following statement:

Textbooks, standardized tests, many teacher education programs, and many curriculum programs feed into the belief that there is one best way of understanding. And this is linked with another pervasive, pernicious belief—that students who do not understand it in our way are not smart enough to understand it at all. This course explores the diverse ways that people come to their understanding. What kind of experiences affect a learner's construction of knowledge, and what, then, can be a teacher's role? (*Harvard University Graduate School of Education Course Catalogue, 1993–94*, p. 118)

As I was looking for additional insight into the complexities of multicultural education, this particular class, at least in description, was promising—it implied a rupturing of positivism and the modernist conceptions of the individual.[6] I was especially intrigued to learn how a person who embraced Piaget's structuralist approach to cognitive development would deal with the implications of social interactionism. That is, how she would address the **postmodern** realities of diversity, contingency, and difference.

The course was centered around having the whole class observe the moon for the entire semester. As such, each and every day was dedicated to a discussion of what different people saw in the night skies. Another typical classroom exercise consisted of attaching a string to our nose, with the opposite end fixed to a mirror on the ceiling, so we could see each other from various angles. There were also show-and-tell sessions in which some students presented their own personal crayon drawings to the entire class. This was all done in the name of "understanding individual differences and alternative perspectives."

As these inane exercises continued week after week, I could not understand how this type of pedagogy would help develop self-reflective, multilensed, and critical researchers and practitioners. In addition, I could not help but wonder what any of this had to do with the fact that schools and the streets are virtual war zones where drug abuse, teenage pregnancy, school dropouts, illiteracy, and a long list of oppressive practices and social injustices that directly affect the educational process are running rampant. How would the methodology of this particular graduate course help teachers to understand the dialectical relationship between intergroup strife and struggle and individual psychology?

At one point during the semester, the class participated in observing two young blacks girls engage in a cognitive exercise of solving puzzles. In light of the current debates and conflicts concerning poverty, racism, sexism, and other forms of discrimination, especially the media blitz around the release of Richard Hernstein and Charles Murray's *The Bell Curve* (1994), a book that makes claims to the genetic inferiority of blacks and other groups, I was extremely uncomfortable with a room full of privileged white people (only one black male) hanging over two black girls for the sake of clinical observation.[7] This was especially diffi-cult for me in the sense that we as a group did not problematize the real-ities that have led these two individuals (members of a collective that continues to experience a great deal of oppression in this country) to at-tend by choice an African-American private school. The fact that in or-der to maintain their own cultural capital and avoid total domination they self-segregated themselves to an environment that nurtures and re-spects them was ignored by the room full of budding researchers.[8]

Finding this radical omission disconcerting, to say the least, I openly expressed to the class the importance of context in understanding the multiple and contingent social identities of people, and how such social identities within unequal relations of power invoke particular kinds of behavior and interaction. When I asked why, as a group, we had ne-glected to make the connections between the current national debates of what Harvard represents as an "elite," predominantly white institu-tion, the sociopolitical realities of these young, low-socioeconomic-status black girls, and the contingent nature of cognition, the professor responded, "This is one important and complex set of questions to look at. I think that one can also look at other things."

With one swift and empty statement these "important and complex" issues were simply dismissed. The professor further defended her re-fusal to analyze group experience, insisting that, "There are the risks of stereotyping." In the name of observing "the individual," she simply psy-chologized experience so as to depoliticize the social reality in which these girls live on a daily basis—that is, the realities of the multiple and interconnecting relationships of race, capitalism, class, gender, and so on, which speak to a more dialectical understanding of the **politics of identity and difference,** as well as to the social influences on cognition, psychology, and performance.[9]

This statement about "the risks of stereotyping" epitomizes the resis-tance prevalent in many graduate schools of education to theoretically engage the social. In fact, theory itself is often completely ignored. Even those "liberal" classrooms dealing with educational psychology and hu-man development, which break with traditional methodological re-straints and pedagogical absolutes—such as the one I experienced at

Harvard—are usually mutated into feel-good therapy sessions in which theory is stifled at the level of description.[10] In other words, students and teachers share life stories as if they haphazardly fell out of the sky, but they are rarely encouraged to engage, so as to understand, the historical and sociopolitical realities that in fact have shaped such experiences.

Theory constitutes the ways in which we make sense of the world around us, that is, how we interpret, critique, and draw generalizations (hooks, 1994; McLaughlin, 1987). Generalizations that are not constantly problematized do risk stereotyping and objectifying, and therefore theories should always be flexible heuristics prone to change. As critical educators, we need to keep a healthy tension in our understanding of the dialectical relationship between the individual and society, so as to never **essentialize** and objectify the individual (e.g., to assume that all Puerto Ricans are the same), but to also not disregard group experience—what it means to be marked by race, class, nation, and so on.

The reality of walking the fine line between analytic distinctions and stereotypes should never inhibit educators from attempting to develop a critical understanding of what we observe. As argued in Chapter 3, the point of using analytic categories such as race is by no means meant to essentialize—to imply that racial groups are fixed and exclusive, to assume that all racially subordinated groups/individuals think about is their oppression, or to argue that behavior manifests itself in deterministic or monolithic ways. Contemporary African-American culture, for example, "is radically complex and diverse, marked by an intriguing variety of intellectual reflections, artistic creations, and social practices" (Dyson, 1993, p. xiii). However, race—implying racism and racialization (along with a long list of other significant points of analysis)—is a significant shaper of culture and identity. A more sociocognitive approach to clinical research and practice would require the exploration of the ideological construction of such categories and their implications and possibilities. There is a great deal of critical literature and research, none of which was presented to the class at Harvard, that explores the effects of racism and **racialization,** sexism, classism, and other forms of exclusion on students' reactions to schooling. In fact, terminology such as **internalized oppression, learned helplessness,** and **resistance** are frequently used in the literature to refer to the relationship between the social and the psychological.

If fear of stereotyping and objectifying the research participants in the clinical research course at Harvard was really the issue at hand, then why hadn't the class discussed the realities of **representational politics,** the malleability of theory, and the ideological foundation of each person's particular point of view as a researcher? Why hadn't we discussed the sociohistorically and ideologically constructed (and relational) conceptions of blackness and whiteness, capitalism, gender, or class in the United States, and how they work to shape our perspectives? None of these categories that define a politics of identity and difference showed up in any of the readings. The index of the professor's own well-received book, which was used as the course's main text, did not have a single mention of these crucial points of analysis.

In addition, if understanding alternative perspectives were really the goal of such a methodology, then why hadn't we discussed in depth (i.e., beyond the rhetoric of the course description) the social construction of cognition and literacy, and how schools reinforce only certain kinds of language use, values, beliefs, bodies of knowledge, and learning styles—white, affluent, heterosexual, male ways of knowing? These issues were clearly avoided. The end result was that the professor simply imported black students from the ghetto for clinical observation only to send them back.

Legitimating this vampire style of pedagogy, and contradicting her reluctance to engage the social via issues such as race, gender, and class, the professor stated that, "It is good for these children to be around Harvard; it builds their self-confidence." When I asked, "What has led to a lack of self-confidence, and how have such affective dispositions impacted educational attitudes and cognitive performance?" I was completely ignored. It comes as no surprise that the professor, who discouraged critical reflexivity among her students, never questioned her own assumption that the children lacked self-confidence. In fact, such a disposition was never voiced by the girls themselves, nor was it apparent in their performance during the exercise.

Instead of perceiving my questions as potentially edifying, I was getting the feeling that, in the eyes of the group, I was being disruptive—a pain in the ass of sorts. What often happens in these "learning" environments is that a deceitful form of democracy is used in order to make the teacher's interactions with students' ideas appear just. For example, a critical question is avoided at the level of "Okay, . . . because of the limited time let's hear from someone else" (a common response to my questions during the semester). The apparent emphasis on equal opportunity to participate strategically disrupts any possibility for profound theoretical engagement and analysis among classroom participants. Such limiting practices are carefully used in public institutions as mechanisms of ideological control that work to privilege and exclude particular perspectives, voices, authorities, and representations.[11]

A major role of critical research/interpretation should be to expose and transform inequities of power. However, educational psychology, and its concomitant pedagogical practices, for the most part, completely sidestep such an ethical dimension. As Joe Kincheloe and Shirley Steinberg (1996) observe, "This is the great paradox of contemporary schooling and teacher education: educators speak of empowerment as a central goal, but often ignore the way power operates to subvert the empowerment of teachers and students" (p. 191).

For the next assignment, we were asked to do field work that entailed having random people read and interpret Audre Lorde's poem "Progress Report." The professor, when I asked in class if we should get any background information about our participants, responded, "No! We cannot draw conclusions about a particular group from one person's response." Again, any effort to get inside ideological formations that shape the structures of meaning, forms of life, and norms and social practices, in order to make sense of them through and beyond the individual, were thrown out the window. From this perspective, Audre Lorde's subject position as a black lesbian woman (among other defining characteristics) would also have to be considered irrelevant to understanding her expressive work. Any theoretical inquest was reduced and dismissed by the professor as, "We can never really know the person." This particular stance, which categorically precludes the social, serves to reinforce the myth of individualism in the United States. It also minimizes the interpretive role and ideological lens of the researcher, to say nothing of contradicting the ostensible purpose of the course itself.

Psychological development and the production of knowledge are sociocognitive processes, and socialization thus plays a significant role in shaping the individual. This shaping process was evident in watching the professor's own ideology about individualism growing in the minds of her students. For example, on one occasion, a white woman was asked to participate in a math experiment in front of the class. She told the group, in no uncertain terms, that she had been treated poorly by her male math teachers and that she had ultimately done poorly in this subject area. Approaching the task, the participant was clearly nervous and sweating in anticipation. These important social-psychological manifestations and insights, even after I raised some concerns about sexism and cognitive performance, went untouched. Not a sound was heard from the forty other students who, following the professor's logic, made no connection from the personal to the social, let alone to the political.

Instead, I heard students describe the personality of the woman as introverted or extroverted, inhibited or uninhibited, field dependent or field independent. Not once did I hear people interrogate the history of the participant, or the immediate context of the classroom and the task, in order to address why it is that a learner may sometimes be motivated, extroverted, and confident, and other times unmotivated, introverted, and anxious. Nor was there a discussion of why in one set of circumstances there may be social distance and antagonisms (whether we are conscious of them or not) between a specific group of learners, and less in others.

Educational psychology is certainly concerned with issues of affect, including the learner's motivation, self-confidence, and level of anxiety. But, as illustrated in this clinical research class, all of these variables are far too often relegated to the confines of the individual and abstracted from the social context. It is absolutely ridiculous to assume that stress in working on particular assignments is simply the result of interpsychic factors. As Bonny Norton Pierce (1995) argues, "We need a theory of social identity that integrates the learner and the learning context, and how relations of power in the social world affect social interaction between learners and teachers and among peers" (p. 7).

On a similar occasion, a black male student was asked by his peers in the class, who were in the process of celebrating their personal stories, to share his experiences growing up. He replied, "How can you ask me to speak when for so many years of my life, my voice, my people's voice, has been taken away?" Regardless of the blatantly obvious overtones of this powerful statement, the conceptual understanding of racism in this classroom was reduced to the individual's world of experience. In other words, caught in the paradigm of individualism, acts of racism were not interpreted by the white students "listening" as social and institutional. Racism was psychologized into individual and pathological behavior. As such, any oppression along racial lines was disarticulated from white supremacy. Consequently, the black student was met with sympathy for having to face such harsh treatment from "those people," but was never rewarded with the anticipated self-critical and social reflection that he was looking for from his immediate white colleagues—with recognition that it is whites' responsibility to transform such institutionalized sociocultural inequities. He never again contributed to the class discussions.[12]

As argued in Chapter 3, "whiteness" has been a sociopolitically and institutionally sanctioned marker of status in the United States. Racialized cultural patterns are embedded in the practices and institutions of white America. As John Ogbu (1987) points out, "Feelings of aversion, revulsion, and disgust they [negative images of other racial groups] evoke come to be incorporated into the culture of the dominant group and children learn them 'naturally' as they learn other aspects of their culture" (p. 260).

Educational institutions continue to perpetuate cultural racism through their curriculum (e.g., What/whose values, beliefs, voices, and representations of history, identity, and difference are included?), teacher assumptions and teaching styles, and de facto segregation of racially subordinated students via tracking. But few whites recognize the impact that such racism has had on shaping our own values, beliefs, personal and social interests, and actions. With the help of the professor, the students did not see themselves as white, privileged, and perpetuators, whether consciously or not, of racism and other forms of discrimination. They were never encouraged to explore the history of the racialization of identities, which clearly reveals how white supremacy has historically been an important mechanism of **cultural production** and **reproduction** in the United States—that is, how hundreds of years of Anglo domination have been a fundamental part (as opposed to an external or separate feature) of most institutional and everyday cultural practices in this society. The classroom participants did not understand how the psychological makeup of individuals—the vehicle through which researchers and practitioners see and interpret the world—is, among other things, racially driven.

It has been my experience that the type of pedagogy based on psychological models of the unified individual leads to future teachers who actually believe that they can be bias-free in their classrooms. By not recognizing whiteness as a racial identity, most whites see themselves as race-free and less ethnic than others, and consequently take for granted the privileges they secure by such an ideologically charged racial marker. It is thus essential that educators and citizens interrogate the unspoken centrality of white male, affluent, heterosexual identity. As Peter McLaren (1994) insists,

> Unless we give white students a sense of their own identity as an emergent ethnicity, we naturalize whiteness as a cultural marker against which Otherness is defined. . . . White groups need to examine their own ethnic histories so that they are less likely to judge their own cultural norms as neutral and universal. (p. 59)

The clinical research course that I have been describing at Harvard does absolutely nothing to prepare educators for critical analysis, self-reflection, and awareness. It does not help them develop the interpretive tools to understand and engage the realities of racism and whiteness—any form of exclusion for that matter. Such graduate courses provide no opportunity for students to develop the presence of mind (i.e., critical awareness) necessary to understand what constitutes difference and how the dominant referent shapes otherness. In most cases, deskilled teachers simply sweep such forms of discrimination under the rug with the false hope that they will simply go away.

Within the uncritical and abstract environment of this research course, students came to believe that individual others' minds were simply different, and that diversity of this sort was okay. The central problem as I saw it was that the participants in this class could clearly articulate their own perspectives, but they had no idea from where these thoughts were generated nor were they encouraged to explore such avenues. As such, the referent that they were using to define difference—what the professor loosely described as "our ways of understanding"—went uncontested. Who is the "our," how has it become the norm at the exclusion of "others," why are some cultural portraits deemed more valuable than "others," and how have the antagonistic relations that have emerged over the struggle for a place in these exclusionary practices and institutions led to certain attitudes toward "different" worldviews, literacies, education, and learning styles? If educational psychology is really "a scientific discipline that is concerned with producing general knowledge about how the educational process affects students" (Royer & Feldman, 1984, p. 6), then we are compelled to address such crucial questions, especially if we are to ever really engage what the professor described as "the diverse ways that people come to their understanding" and how the "kinds of experiences affect a learner's construction of knowledge." Unfortunately, this type of inquiry was discouraged in this graduate classroom.

A classroom discussion about the politics of identity and difference would surely beg dangerous questions about the relationship among power, capitalism, language, race, gender, class, sexual orientation, identity, and exclusion. However, such critical questions in this country are for the most part, with the help of mainstream discourses of psychology, avoided at all cost. As a diversionary tactic, mainstream pedagogy simply abstracts the learner's identity from the institutions and socially sanctioned practices that produce inequality, injustice, and cultural resistance—institutions and practices that ultimately remain intact.

The unwillingness to engage the complex interrelationships that constitute identity and social reality only serves to fragment and disarticulate experience from its sociohistorical construction. In fact, fragmentation of knowledge is largely the norm at the Harvard Graduate School of Education. A prevailing rebuttal among faculty to critical and interdisciplinary comments is "That's not *blank* [a particular field of study], that's politics." As Noam Chomsky (1995) states when asked, "How can you talk about moral development and violence without talking about the larger social, cultural, and economic environments in which people live and develop?":

> You can't! On the other hand, if you simply talk about the world in the accepted ways, that would not be called politics, that would be being reasonable. It becomes "ideological" or extremist when it deviates from the accepted patterns. (p. 125)

This disarticulation of knowledge, via the fragmentation of disciplines, serves to obscure political awareness, a clarity that can only be achieved through an interdisciplinary view of the world—what C. Wright Mills (1959) refers to as "the sociological imagination." However, such disarticulation is not surprising in a school of education that houses its courses in literacy and language acquisition in the Department of Human Development and Psychology, with very little connection to the Department of Learning and Teaching—as if the reason that millions of people in this country are illiterate has predominantly to do with cognitive, internal processes rather than the sociopolitical climate of the classroom and the greater society. As Jim Gee (1990) argues when discussing the so-called failure problem, "we need to question several 'commonsense' assumptions inherited from the discipline of psychology":

1. Thinking and speaking are functions of individual minds.
2. Literacy is an individual mental skill involving the ability to read and write.
3. Intelligence, knowledge, and aptitude are states of individual minds. (p. 6)

Within this closed world, the responsibility for success, or lack thereof, resides within the individual. Accordingly, approaching a problem is individualized away from the social conditions within which the learning process is taking place. At best, this leads to a mean-spirited, victim-blaming meritocracy that demands everyone pull themselves up by their bootstraps. At worst, it supports the idea that the reason disproportionate amounts of certain groups are not succeeding in schools and the workplace is that, as argued in *The Bell Curve,* these people are categorically and biologically inferior to the white mainstream.

Discarding these two fundamentally racist and oppressive conclusions, educators need to understand that thinking, speaking, knowing, and literacy are functions of social groups, and that "intelligence and aptitude, as measured by tests, are artificially constructed measures of aspects of social practices taken out of context and attributed to individuals" (Gee, 1990, p. 7). Critical educators need to stress the social nature of the mind, the ideological nature of perception, and the fact that the way in which we learn to think and feel is the product of the groups we belong to and value. If any educational course truly hopes to "explore the diverse ways that people come to their understanding," and "the kinds of experiences that affect a learner's construction of knowledge," as the Harvard professor claimed in her clinical research course, then we urgently need to move away from the personality vacuum. Within this abstract space, the psychological realities of such oppressive institutions as white supremacy go unseen and thus untouched.

When the complex topics of race and class do surface at HGSE in programs such as Risk and Prevention, oppressive social practices are again reduced to the microanalysis of simply finding the right methods to "fix" the kids. Within these **deficit models,** which also psychologize experience along the lines of the individual, the critical yet unasked question is: Who is putting these kids at risk?

Sure, the Harvard Graduate School of Education offers a few courses that deal with the social nature of learning. However, in these particular cases theory is limited to a superficial understanding of cultural similarities and differences. The basic idea in such classrooms is that if we could only recognize and be sensitive to cognitive, cultural, and communicative differences, everything would be okay. There is no attempt to develop the necessary **presence of mind** to understand what constitutes difference and how the dominant referent that shapes otherness is the white, upper-middle-class, heterosexual male. Within this paradigm of cultural similarities and differences, the dominant group in society is perceived as the norm, and its plethora of inherent inequalities and injustices are uncontested. As such, even if educators were able to successfully teach other people's children (assuming that they are willing to do so) by recognizing and building on what they bring to the classroom, there is no guarantee that as soon as those children leave the safety of the classroom they will not face socially and institutionally sanctioned forms of exclusion and abuse. If we are to truly understand the process of schooling, it can never be disarticulated from the larger sociohistorical and political landscape that gives rise to such institutions in the first place.

Becoming a Gatekeeper

If you've been really well educated, meaning well indoctrinated, you can't even think rational thoughts any longer. They can't come to you, the words can't come to you . . . and that's the process of "good education." People who don't internalize those values are weeded out along the way. By the time you get to the top, you've internalized them.

—**Noam Chomsky**

Many of the students who prosper in such a depoliticized, ahistorical environment of graduate schools such as Harvard's are as Chomsky described them: "the more educated, the more indoctrinated." In fact, many students at HGSE are so **domesticated** that they uncritically worship the professors. Concerned with careerism and networking through big names, they play the role of being good little boys and girls and end up eagerly collecting data for faculty and accepting at face-value what they hear.

A white woman, who was the teaching assistant in a course I was taking, attempted to ruin my chances of being selected for the editorial board of the *Harvard Educational Review*. As I challenged the professor of the class in which she was an assistant by asking very critical and difficult questions, the student interpreted my behavior as "irreverent." At the board selection meeting, in which I was not present and thus unable to defend myself, the student-teacher openly slammed me, stating to the other members of the board that I was "disrespectful" and that she was "not impressed with my work." Needless to say, I was denied an invitation to join.

Most revealing about this particular situation with the teaching assistant was the about-face that she took toward my work. Of the first six papers that she had read of mine, her comments were the following:

- "A thoughtful paper."
- "I have enjoyed reading your summaries, all of which are excellent."
- "What you have produced here is thoughtful and comprehensive."

- "This is a nice review of the studies on bilingualism in childhood development."
- "Nice job!"
- "A thoughtful, theory-laden discussion. I found it well-informed and engaging. Well done!"

There are two critical elements at play in her shift of attitude toward me: ideological differences and the process of domestication. These six papers were descriptive in nature (as seen in such comments as "review" and "summaries") and not critical in terms of analysis and implications. However, the final project—my critique on Porter's antibilingual education stance—was overtly political in that I made clear my position on the issues at hand. Up until that point, the teaching assistant stated that she was in fact impressed with my work. Perhaps our ideological differences changed her mind about the quality of my scholarship when she spoke "on my behalf" at the board selection meeting.

On the other hand, could it have been the professor's distaste for my critical questions in class discussions and my stance on bilingual education that led to the teaching assistant's disparaging comments about my personality and work! In other words, the professor's power and prestige functioned in a way that deskilled the teaching assistant through a process of ideological domestication.

Shortly after I received my rejection notice to be a member of the editorial board of the *Harvard Educational Review,* the only two other board members who knew me and came to my defense during the teaching assistant's character assassination resigned over this and other irreconcilable disputes. Ironically, six months later, as the last remaining alternate, I was offered an editor's position.

For the conservative members of the board, their worst nightmare had come true. With the encouragement, passion, and incredible insight of the women who work in the office, in my eighteen-month membership I was able to solicit and publish the work of such critical educators as Paulo Freire, Henry Giroux, Noam Chomsky, Nel Noddings, and Sonia Nieto; I wrote and published twenty reviews of books that dealt with critical issues in education and cultural studies; and I conceptualized and spearheaded the publication of *Breaking Free: The Transformative Power of Critical Pedagogy.* This book was designed to help scaffold educators into the complexity of critical social theories and was described by Freire as "the best introductory text to critical pedagogy that I have ever read." It has become the *Review*'s best-seller—it went into reprint seven months after its release, netting huge profits.[13]

Having looked over a rough draft of the book, one of the most politically influential faculty members on the School of Education campus stated, "I finally understand what those people are talking about." However, when it was suggested that she write a blurb for the back of the book, the suggestion was met with laughter—the implication being that there was no way that this individual would put her stamp of approval on such critical material.

A number of students on the board attempted to reject the proposal for the book project. In fact, some students tried to block the Chomsky dialogue from being published in the *Harvard Educational Review's Special Issue on Youth and Violence*. In an attempt to disguise their ideological discrepancies with Chomsky, they used a specific form of questioning and critique to sabotage the publication. First, they argued against the title of the article—that Steve Sherblom and I "were supposed to interview Chomsky, and not have a dialogue with him." In other words, in the name of objectivity, neutrality, and science, we were supposed to disengage our subject positions from the discussion and create as much of a monologue as possible—as if Chomsky were talking to himself. Antithetical to the basic tenets of true dialogue (in Paulo Freire's sense of the word) and engagement, we refused to artificially eliminate (edit out) our "selves" from the discussion.

After seemingly endless debate, board members gave in to calling the manuscript a dialogue. Their real concern was about what was being said. In fact, they were so disturbed by the content that they immediately met and formally established strict protocol for future interviews. Editors now interested in such a project will have to formally submit a proposal along with the exact questions that are to be asked. This will ensure that the board can control the direction of the conversation.

The board's new angle of attack on Chomsky's words was twofold: First, they felt that because Newt Gingrich was mentioned so many times (what is in fact a scathing critique of the Republican Contract with America), "We are giving him too much attention and dating the piece." Their second major concern was simply that, "There are too many unnecessary criticisms of Harvard." When Steve and I started talking about the immorality of censoring a guaranteed publication, the tides turned and the manuscript was eventually published in virtually its original form. However, those students most opposed to this work also attempted to keep it from being, as originally planned, the opening chapter in the special issue. This effort, because of the committee's voting format, was also defeated. Only one former board member was honest about his position in stating that as far as he was concerned, "It was all a bunch of Chomsky babble."

A very similar scene was recently enacted in a trip down the school's library elevator. A young white woman dressed in very expensive clothing saw that I had a copy of something from the *Harvard Educational Review*—she recognized the *Review*'s insignia and was eager to talk about the publication. However, when she read the title *Breaking Free: The Transformative Power of Critical Pedagogy*, and assumed what the book was about, her smile immediately turned to scorn. She bitterly exclaimed, "Nothing but Freire babble, and I know what tricks he and Giroux are up to!" I asked her if she had read the book, knowing that she had not since the book had just been released and the copy in my hand was one of the first. The elevator door opened and she walked away without a word.

Many students at Harvard are readily complicit in their own deskilling. I think that Chomsky is correct in arguing that, "If you've been really well educated, meaning well indoctrinated, you can't even think rational thoughts any longer." I was hanging posters in the school's Gutman library and a student stopped to inquire about its contents. When I told him that it was a conference on Values and Ideology in Education, he responded, "Oh, I thought that it was something important!" and continued on his way.

The following anecdote epitomizes the tragic levels of domestication that can manifest within such an environment. A critical manuscript had been solicited by the *Harvard Educational Review* from Spain. The author, unaware of the proper procedure for submitting an article, sent only one copy instead of three. I turned the single copy in, thinking that it was no big deal. A week later, a colleague walked up to me and told me that according to policy we needed three copies and that I was to inform the author that two additional copies were required. I looked at the person, looked over at the photocopy machine, looked back in her direction, and seeing that she was not making the connection—glued to policy—I took the manuscript and later made two more copies.[14]

This type of domestication and consequential unwillingness to see Harvard in a critical way was also the case in my attempt to get a book review past the two students in charge of the *Harvard Educational Review*'s book review section. The book that I had written about was Russ Bellant's (1991) *Old Nazis, the New Right, and the Republican Party: Domestic Fascist Networks and Their Effects on U.S. Cold War Politics*. I started the review by telling the following story (taken verbatim from the original draft):

Some weeks before the most recent national Congressional elections, Donaldo Macedo and I (as teaching assistant) decided to read to the group of students at the Harvard Graduate School of Education, who were participating in our anti-racist multicultural education course, some of the basic tenets of a political platform from an anonymous politician. Asking the students if the general ideas of the platform reminded them of anything they had previously heard, the majority pointed to the plethora of Republican rhetoric that was flooding the media. The "liberal," upper-middle-class, White students (which made up the majority of the class) were generally shocked to learn that the platform was in fact that which Adolf Hitler used to rise to power. For many of the racially subordinated students, this revelation came as no surprise.

While the "Reagan Revolution" made it popular in the United States to once again be openly discriminatory, neo-fascist thinking is presently burgeoning among the political right in this country.

I thought that this opening to the book review would be a great way to show how ideology is embedded in language, often in a coded way that creates the social construction of not seeing. Bellant's entire message is that these are not simply right-wing agendas with Nazi-esque potential but they are actually old Nazis actively participating in the political process. Their messages, not unlike Hitler's own words, have drastic implications if we do not have the necessary presence of mind to read between the lines. Nonetheless, the connections that I made to privileged students and indoctrination (as Chomsky would say—to not be able to see what's right in front of their nose) led to the deletion of this entire passage/incident before the review was published.

On another occasion, I was invited to be the teaching assistant for a course entitled Education for Social and Political Change. The syllabus was designed to expose students to various perspectives about institutional structures and agency across the political spectrum. One white student's final remarks about the semester were that the professor and I were "a couple of Communists!" Around Harvard—the United States in general—this practice of dismissing critical cultural workers as being "Marxists," "anti-Americans," or "crazed radicals" is in fact a regular occurrence. As Chomsky states,

> If you repeat the clichés of the propaganda system, that's not ideological. On the other hand, if you question them, that's ideological and very strident or anti-American. Anti-American is an interesting expression, because the accusation of being anti-nation is used typically in totalitarian societies, for example, the former Soviet Union accused dissidents of being

anti-Soviet. But try "anti-Italian" or "anti-Belgian," people in Milan or Brussels would laugh.

Markers such as *Marxist* are not used as intellectual categories. This type of analytic distinction is impossible given that most graduate students have never read Karl Marx. If they had, they would understand that critical courses such as Education for Social and Political Change have moved way beyond the confines of Marx's **reductionistic** and deterministic view of history based on material/class struggle (historical/dialectical materialism). Rather, the use of *Marxist* by reactionary educators and students simply acts as a shock word, playing off of paranoia and misinformation, to justify the rejection of any counterdiscourse. The same goes for the use of *radical.* Defined as being on a particular side of the ideological/political spectrum, radical is used in the sense of implying extreme. However, it seems more extreme to me to accept the present state of oppressive and undemocratic conditions in this country than it is to work for change.

A note on the bright side: A year later this same student approached me on campus and asked if I was still assisting in teaching the course. Anticipating a harsh response, I nonetheless answered yes. To my great surprise, the student graciously thanked me for helping her "confront issues that as a white woman I was unwilling to face." She continued, "The readings and discussions helped me a great deal in the Teaching and Certification Program's summer component in which I was a group leader." We agreed that the issues that we had discussed in class were fundamentally about democracy.

If democracy, which entails participation and dissent, is what binds us as a nation, then the accusation that being critical and aware is anti-American represents a contradiction in terms—those who so readily use it (anti-American) to dismiss ideological differences are themselves against the basic tenets that they vociferously claim to defend.

Anti-Intellectualism as the Norm

Why should any system of power offer the opportunities to people who are trying to undermine it? . . . The people who are called "intellectuals" are those that pretty much serve power. . . . So you are a respected intellectual if you do your job as a part of the system of doctrinal control.

—Noam Chomsky

The lack of critique among many graduate students at the Harvard Graduate School of Education is not surprising considering that many of the faculty members themselves regard critical material with disdain. For example, the *Harvard Educational Review* is largely a mainstream journal, and it is diverse in its board membership, publications, and subscribers. However, when the School of Education faculty was invited to meet with the *Review*'s chairpeople to encourage their submission of work, the group berated the editorial board for publishing "party-line material" (i.e., the critical material that had made it through the gates) and insisted that, "The journal is politically correct and has lost all credibility." Notice how work that is overtly political is targeted as being politically correct and thus not worthy of engaging. There is an interesting contradiction playing out here: While they use the notion of PC to imply that the critical work is containing, that is, unwelcoming, of other perspectives, in fact what they are doing is trying to eliminate ideological positions in the name of objectivity that do not coincide with their own. On the contrary, critical pedagogues who have published in the *Harvard Educational Review*, though few and far between, are more than willing to debate any and all issues.

A major proponent of multiple intelligences, the vanguard of this assault on the *Harvard Educational Review* is also caught up in this contradiction. Although this individual embraces multiple intelligences, such differences are only acceptable within certain ideological constraints. Difference in this sense is abstracted from the real social conditions (including unequal power relations) and experience that shape identity, literacy, discourse, and cognitive styles. In the name of diversity we end up with a perverse form of structuralism: Although the universal structure of cognition is contested, all forms of divergent thinking nonetheless reside within the individual's mind—abstracted from social reality and all of its inequities (again, the personality vacuum).

The following year, the faculty actually intervened in the student board's selection of its new members for the *Harvard Educational Review*. Part of the selection process of the student editorial board is that faculty can have a final say in who is chosen to participate. The argument has been that if a candidate is not completing his or her coursework, then faculty can step in and suggest that he or she not be invited. This is ostensibly in the student's better interest. However, such coded language is left open to interpretation so that such an ideological intervention is possible.

Word had it that the new democratically chosen board was "too brown and too critical," and did not include those student candidates recommended by the faculty. Before board selection, the faculty submit letters of recommendation for particular students who they feel would be "good" editors. The *Review* then sends letters to these students to invite them to apply. Nonetheless, the application process is also open to all doctoral students in the School of Education. When one of the resisting faculty was asked if she felt that "critical material was not worth engaging," she replied that, "It's crap!" As a result, there was talk around campus of the faculty taking over the editorial board. There was also a memo circulated that suggested creating a special section in the *Harvard Educational Review* exclusively for Harvard faculty. So much for meritocracy! If they cannot get in the journal on their own merits, then they will create an alternative advantage.[15]

In a course I took that was supposedly going to deal with the issues of race, education, and policy, I gave the professor (an African-American) a list of critical work that I thought could greatly improve his syllabus. Bumping into him a semester later, he stated in a condescending manner, "I gave the students a piece of that postmodern stuff, but it was at the end of the semester and they didn't have time for it." In another course that dealt with the plight of African-American college students, the black professor took the position (supporting his recent publication) that mediocrity in terms of students' talents and success was good enough and should be embraced.

Such incidents not only illustrate how anti-intellectualism and academic censorship play out but also point out the importance of moving beyond the confines of color coordination and into the realm of ideological diversity and the politics of difference.[16] The Harvard Graduate School of Education is perhaps more than willing to have diversity in terms of different-looking people (not that it has many), but when it comes to those who confront the traditional mold, who can think for themselves, the doors are closed. Sure, the bigwigs will hold a special dinner for Dinesh D'Souza, the author of *The End of Racism* (1995), an openly racist person from a racially subordinated population, who, supported by right-wing think tanks, ardently argues that the legacy of racism in the United States has come to a close. Needless to say, there was no special dinner for bell hooks when she came to campus. As Noam Chomsky said in the dialogue in Chapter 4 of this book:

> Its very hard to live in the system and survive it. It's clear what you ought to do, but whether you can survive it is another question. . . . Now, teachers can try, and do, break out of that [teaching students to be obedient and submissive], but they will surely find that if they go too far, that as soon as it gets noticed there'll be pressure to stop them.

Even among the more progressive faculty, there is resistance to engage critical work. In response to my statement that, "The educator's job is simply to help the learner, through dialogue, reach a better point of being critical, of being conscious such that they are better able to understand the sociopolitical reality that shapes their lives and their capacity to transform that reality," a professor who I thought was aware replied: "I don't want help. I want my friends, some land, a way to make a living on the land, and to be rid of the landlord, the banks, the interest payments, and the yoke of do-gooder liberal educators. Multiculturalism is a bunch of misguided people with good hearts."

This reductionistic perspective of intellectual pursuits as a form of careerism is extremely problematic. More importantly, how does this professor propose that the oppressed negotiate a system that has in fact led to their landlessness and indentured servant status? Without a critical reading of the word and the world, human agency and the transformation of social, economic, and political inequities through democratic practices are virtually impossible.

If graduate students at the Harvard Graduate School of Education want access to critical educators, they either have to scour the yard for marginal programs such as the African-American Department or the Divinity School, or they simply have to go off campus as I did. The Divinity School at Harvard offers a course on liberation theology that includes the work of Paulo Freire. In fact, the Divinity School library carries a significant portion of Freire's books. In the HGSE library, students only have access to *Pedagogy of the Oppressed* (1970). This is interesting when you consider the fact that there is a course at the School of Education entitled The Politics of Literacy. However, this course altogether ignores Freire's monumental contributions, even when a section of the syllabus claims to deal with Latin American issues. To me, this is like talking about physics and leaving out Albert Einstein. However, this rejection of Freire comes as no surprise considering that one of the professors who teaches the class publicly declared, "I can't read Freire. He makes me clam!" This same individual showed up to hear bell hooks when she spoke on campus and walked out partway through her talk.

Freire's name did come up in a positive light in one course that I took at HGSE. On the first day of class a professor mentioned the "incredible importance of *Pedagogy of the Oppressed*." Ironically, there was not a single piece of his work (any critical work for that matter) in the syllabus, and his name was never again mentioned.

Although Paulo's fame is well recognized at Harvard, a profound understanding of his work within the ideological confines of the School of Education is virtually nonexistent. This ignorance became blatantly obvious when the Office of International Education brought him to campus in 1994 to give a talk. The dean of the School of Education introduced Freire as a distinguished teacher, claiming that,

> A half century ago, Freire published his prescriptions for liberation education. His ideas are now in many ways at the heart of school reform in America: ideas such as decentralizing power, active learning, the development of critical thinking, and making schools into neighborhood resources.

During the question-and-answer session that followed Paulo's talk, the first speaker, who identified herself as a "Puertoriquena," stated that, "Oppression is very much alive. . . . Anyone who has the color of your coffee [the dean] as I do understands that." She then exclaimed:

> I get terrified when I hear the dean say that school reform [in the United States] is based on Paulo Freire's ideas. That's not true . . . excuse me, Dean . . . I should not apologize . . . I will because you are here. I truly think that Paulo Freire's ideas are not in the mainstream of education as we know it!

At Harvard, Freire's work is reduced to buzzwords—decentralizing power, active learning, the development of critical thinking—and his ideological stance as an **anticolonialist,** a person who takes head-on the complexities of oppression, is excluded. It is in this way that the institution reinforces itself as an agency of domestication and not liberation.

To state that, "A half century ago, Freire published his *prescriptions* for liberation education," immediately shows that the speaker has no knowledge and understanding of his work—Freire is diametrically opposed to any form of prescriptions, which by their very nature render those involved objects rather than active participants of learning, history, and social transformation. Along these same lines, decentralized power, and critical thinking are very much in the vocabulary of conservatives in the United States. However, the political implications of such concepts are neutralized—for example, critical thinking is equated with higher-order thinking skills (abstracted from any political project), and decentralizing power plays out in the calls to downsize government, provide vouchers that serve to benefit middle-class kids, and privatize public education.

Even if and when Freire's actual political posture is better understood at Harvard, the fact that he is Brazilian and talks about oppressed people outside of the United States makes him much more palatable. In this same vein, Neville Alexander can come to the School of Education to talk about racism in South Africa. These contexts, being far removed geographically from the United States, are exoticized and acceptable. However, if it is an educator talking about our own backyard, it ends up being someone of the likes of D'Souza who argues that racism is over in this country. It is interesting to note that when Alexander, who was basically on a fund-raising mission, was asked by a Haitian student about the inevitable problems of uncritically embracing capitalism in the restructuring process in South Africa, he avoided responding in any depth so as not to disturb his potential benefactors.

Unfortunately, the only three critical courses offered at HGSE are not required: Antiracist Multicultural Education (which has been eliminated), Bilingualism and Literacy (which is no longer taught in its critical form because the Chicana professor left the School of Education), and Education for Social and Political Change. They are also taught by either visiting or junior faculty who will never be accepted by the institution beyond the confines of a semester or a three-year contract. It is interesting that these courses are always packed with students—from sixty to ninety enrollments (still a vast minority of the student body). Some students are so hungry for this type of alternative discourse that they are willing to sit on the floor and in the hallways in order to participate. It becomes obvious for many of these students that the theoretical and pedagogical implications of strings, mirrors, and looking at the moon as in my required clinical research class will not prepare them for the kinds of self-reflection and political awareness necessary to make sense of the teaching environments that they will face.

Many of the students in these critical courses find it extremely difficult in the beginning of the semester to take ownership of their own theories around these issues. Theory is something that has always been handed down to them in the form of methods and prepackaged curricula that objectify both the teacher and the learners. However, in these courses they are expected to generate their own interpretations, criticisms, and generalizations to inform their practice as educators. In this way, they produce, rather than merely reproduce meaning.

It is important to note that the course Education for Social and Political Change was originally student generated. Two years before it officially became an elective, a few students demanded that it be offered. Without faculty support, and the fact that the school would not offer official credits for completion of the class, the formal idea was back-

burnered. Those interested individuals nonetheless held their own seminar. With enough student pressure and the addition of a Puerto Rican
visiting lecturer to the faculty, the course became a reality.

There was also a movement by a few of us to create a course in critical
pedagogy. A formal proposal was written and submitted to the department chair, but it was never responded to, let alone implemented. It was
only after the total success of the Office of International Education's
hosting Paulo (filling the auditorium with community activists and critical educators, as well as the library basement where the talk was transmitted by video) that the School of Education decided to bring him back
to teach a course. Upon Paulo's insistence (threatening not to come),
Donaldo Macedo was also invited to co-teach the class. However, I
strongly believe that it was the fame and attention that Paulo deservedly
carries with him that Harvard desired, and not the content of the political project—a project that interrogates institutions such as Harvard.
This was evident in the fact that when Paulo unfortunately died, the
course was tossed out the window. Macedo offered to develop a forum
in which he would invite major scholars in critical pedagogy to come
and speak on campus (people such as bell hooks, Stanley Aronowitz,
Henry Giroux, etc.), but his proposal was denied.

Breaking Free

*Teaching critical thinking is just not going to be allowed, because it's too subversive.
. . . In most other fields you want students to be obedient and submissive, and that
starts from childhood.*

—Noam Chomsky

The only place where I thought that my voice and the dissatisfaction and
dissent of others could make a stand was in the student course evaluations, which are supposed to be placed on file at the library so that people
can get an idea about a class and a professor before they actually register.
However, when I went to locate the evaluations of a number of senior faculty with whom I had been disappointed, I was not the least bit surprised
to discover that my comments were nowhere to be found. Once again, the
inherent relationship between knowledge, truth, and power!

When asked to write this piece on my experiences at Harvard, to let
my version of the truth be known, I must admit that there were moments of hesitation. With my history at this school I have some serious
fears of not getting work passed through the Committee on Degrees and
graduating. As one of my colleagues stated before this paper was even

written, "You've burned your bridges." In fact, when preparing my thesis proposals for the Committee on Degrees, I was specifically told on a number of occasions by certain faculty to exclude any mention of critical theory. It was only after my sanitized proposal was accepted that I was able to reinsert my intended analysis section based on critical multicultural theory.

Walking up the sidewalk, I bumped into an African-American critical colleague of mine (who I later learned was kicked out of the School of Education). She looked at me and with a concerned tone said, "They're getting to you, aren't they? Your eyes show it." She was right, but what was more important for me, working from the privileged position that I have of being a white, educated male, was that as an "elite" graduate school of education they are getting to the kids by helping, whether consciously or not, to reproduce a body of educators and a system of pedagogical practices that have played a significant role in the perpetuation of educational failure across the board.

Conclusion

During graduation, a feeling of shock ran through me the entire day—it was hard for me to believe that they were actually letting me out with the degree. While in the Harvard Yard I looked around at the other schools standing up to be officially graduated. The Business School was to my right. They were waving one-hundred-dollar bills in the air. The Law School was directly behind them. They were all waving plastic handcuffs—as if their job now was to punish and lock people up, rather than uphold the law and the rights of people. I found this bizarre conclusion to my graduate school experience fitting, in that Harvard is not about critical education; it is really about cash and containment. Although I no doubt feel somewhat beaten down from this seven-year experience, in retrospect the truth is, because of the fact that such education is as Chomsky stated a form of indoctrination, I am grateful for the fortunes of my miseducation at Harvard. I present my story with hope for change.

Notes

1. The following anecdotes occurred between 1991 and 1996. I have purposefully concentrated on my own personal experience at the Harvard Graduate School of Education. I have for the most part avoided co-opting the abundance of others' stories that support my point. There is an extensive list of comments

that were solicited by an African-American woman on campus that details the criticisms of many racially subordinated students about the education that they are receiving at HGSE. I have also chosen this narrative style in place of a more research/historical look at the university and its legacy of oppressive practices. There are a number of publications that cover this history; see, for example, J. Trumpbour (1989). *How Harvard Rules: Reason in the Service of Empire.* Boston: South End Press.

2. In fact, everyone who worked in the offices (not the faculty) such as the registrars, financial aid people, admissions people, the *Harvard Educational Review* staff, and the Committee on Degrees, as well as the folks in the cafeteria, were enormously generous and open. I am extremely grateful to all these people.

3. I refer to myself as a teaching assistant. However, Harvard prefers the more sexist language of teaching fellow.

4. It is important to note that Macedo, at the recommendation of Bartolomé, was brought in as a visiting lecturer to temporarily teach while she was on leave.

5. I do not mean to imply that the internal biological predispositions, such as gender, sexuality, language faculties, or other cognitive capacities, are not connected to the social. In fact, the relationship is inextricable. It would be more productive for critical educators to move beyond the false binarisms of **structuralism** versus **poststructuralism,** modernism versus postmodernism, formalism versus postformalism, and so on, and instead begin to understand the complex matrix of relationships among these concepts so as to be able to critically appropriate and reinvent the theoretical tenets therein, and use them to inform our transformative practices. For example, in my mind there are important and complimentary insights in both structuralism and poststructuralism. Human beings are biologically predisposed with certain cognitive structures, such as the Language Acquisition Device, which endows humans with the ability to grow systems of communication (Chomsky, 1965). However, this device by no means shapes sociocultural identities, the ideological nature of surface languages, or the politics of exclusion in such onslaughts as the English Only Movement. Nor does the LAD determine whether kids in the ghetto are going to learn dominant languages.

6. It is important to note that a course in clinical research was required for doctoral students; however, there was no formal encouragement to take a course in antiracist multicultural education.

7. For an extensive discussion of the issues raised in *The Bell Curve,* see *Measured Lies: The Bell Curve Examined* (1996), edited by Joe Kincheloe, Shirley Steinberg, and Aaron Gresson, Saint Martin's Press, New York.

8. Although I by no means embrace imposed or de facto segregation, this short-term solution for dealing with the oppressive conditions of dominant institutions can be effective. The backlash from such efforts at group solidarity is often centered around the accusation that it represents a form of separatism, or balkinization. Blaming the victim, instead of addressing the unjust conditions within which a great many people live, conservatives of the likes of Arthur Schlesinger, E. D. Hirsch, William Bennett, and Diane Ravitch, among others, claim that these people will be responsible for the "disuniting of America"—as if it has ever been united.

9. Capitalism is a major force in shaping racism and other oppressive cultural manifestations. Although racism cannot solely be reduced to capitalist social relations, understanding the links is imperative (Du Bois, 1935).

10. *Liberal* carries very little meaning in that its semantic reality has shifted dramatically over time. Its present reification is also experiencing change. I use the term in an ambiguous way to refer to an ideological middle ground where one speaks of democracy but hides behind existing relations of power. For an interesting discussion of the transformations of the term *liberal,* see David Green's (1987) *The Language of Politics in America: Shaping Political Consciousness from McKinley to Reagan.* London: Cornell University Press.

11. However, cultural reproduction via the socialization process is by no means deterministic: culture is ever shifting and forming, and there is always room for teacher and student resistance and agency.

12. The additional information about the young black girls, the white woman who participated in the math exercise, and the black man was taken from conversations that I had with them after class.

13. It is important to note that the profits generated by such student projects are not shared with the editors. Although we do not receive a cent, I am glad that the money will fund new projects, as it did ours. The most important result is that educators around the country are reading the book and making themselves more aware of the issues that shape their lives. These benefits, both financial and pedagogical, are of extreme importance, especially when one board member rejected the proposal simply because he felt the central reason that I was interested in publishing the book was for self-promotion. I sarcastically asked him if self-demotion would make the book any more valuable.

14. If being cost-efficient were the excuse for such behavior, then it is important to note, if not obvious, that it would be more expensive to call the author, or to mail him the request, than it would be to simply copy the text. I am convinced that the issue was policy. It also could have been a diversionary tactic, that is, a way to block the critical nature of the manuscript from being published.

15. By no means am I implying that meritocracy exists in the United States. However, the *Harvard Educational Review*'s student-run editorial board, even with its exclusionary tendencies, is far more democratic in structure and practice than what the faculty desire to impose. The bottom line with the majority of manuscripts submitted by School of Education faculty was not that their work was not political enough; it simply was not good enough.

16. This statement should not be understood as a criticism of affirmative action, nor should it be interpreted to mean that racial representation is not important. It simply implies that Clarence Thomas, for example, does not represent the interests and struggles of the majority of African-Americans in this country.

6 Reading Between the Lines of E. D. Hirsch Jr.'s Core Knowledge Sequence

As I have been arguing throughout this book, critical literacy—that is, the ability to recognize and engage the values, beliefs, and interests embedded in the information to which we are exposed—is crucial to meaningful and transformative education. However, often educators are confused as to what this kind of analysis entails. In this chapter I intend to **deconstruct** the work of E. D. Hirsch Jr. in order to illustrate how critical analysis and theorizing function in action.

First of all, it is important to recognize that critical pedagogy is not simply (as it is often accused of being) some macro, **theoretical,** abstract undertaking in which realistic applications are beyond reach. On the contrary, there is an inextricable relationship between critical social theory and practice, a symbiosis that should inspire the reconceptualization of different ways of knowing that rupture entrenched epistemologies and can foster participatory spaces for the sharing and production of knowledge, as well as the mobilization of agency to effect changes in the world.

In light of the fact that E. D. Hirsch Jr.'s work, known as common cultural literacy (also referred to as core knowledge or core literacy), has been implemented in dozens of public school systems in more than forty states, it is imperative for educators to understand his plans for reforming public education. During an interview on National Public Radio's *Merrow Report,* on December 5, 1996, at the Harvard Graduate

School of Education, he stated: "I got into it [the Core Knowledge Sequence] for social justice. This is the most democratically conceived curriculum ever; it's not ideological." In this chapter I investigate and challenge, through a literature review, Hirsch's perspectives on democracy in public education in the United States, and consequently provide a clear picture of what his approach is attempting to accomplish and why. I describe his position on the following issues:

1. Culture
2. Multicultural education and common cultural literacy
3. Language

Each of these discussions is accompanied by an analysis of the central points raised, as well as a critique of the limitations and contradictions. In essence, I look at Hirsch's work in terms of what is there, what is not there, and what could and should be there.

Professional Biography

E. D. Hirsch Jr. is a professor at the University of Virginia, Charlottesville. He is a senior fellow of the National Endowment for the Humanities, a member of the federally sponsored Foundations of Literacy Project, and the founder and president of the Core Knowledge Foundation. His work has resulted in the development of an educational model referred to as a centrist approach, or the Core Knowledge Sequence, which includes a series of resource books for implementing specific content knowledge in schools.

Considered by many to be the pioneering figure of common cultural literacy, Hirsch has witnessed the implementation of his ideas nationwide. Such success has come with the support of William Bennett (the former chairman of the National Endowment for the Humanities and secretary of education in Ronald Reagan's second administration) and Diane Ravitch (who served from 1991 to 1993 as the assistant secretary for Educational Research and Improvement, and counselor to the secretary at the U.S. Department of Education, and who also co-authored the book *What Do Our 17-Year-Olds Know?* with Chester Finn Jr.—the assistant secretary and counselor to the secretary of the U.S. Department of Education from 1985 to 1988. In addition, Ravitch was the principal writer of the California K–12 history–social science curriculum).

What Are Hirsch's Views on Culture, Multicultural Education, Common Cultural Literacy, and Language?

Culture

In order to begin an analysis of an educator's theoretical and practical insights on diversity and multicultural education, an understanding of his or her conception of culture is essential. However, E. D. Hirsch Jr., throughout his work, chooses not to provide the reader with an in-depth explanation. Although he recognizes that all people "inhabit numerous local cultures and adopt hundreds of small-scale cultural roles within the large-scale culture" (1988a, p. 97), he fails to explore what constitutes and shapes these social phenomena, providing the following disclaimer:

> But this book *[Cultural Literacy]* is not, and no single book could be, an inquiry into the multifarious local and ethnic traditions that are found in the United States. It is for the Amish to decide what Amish traditions are, but it is for all of us to decide collectively what our American traditions are, to decide what "American" means on the other side of the hyphen in Italo-American or Asian-American. (1988a, p. 98)[1]

Consequently, Hirsch focuses his discussions on the formation and contents of national culture and its role in maintaining democracy and unity within the country.

The Formation and Contents of a Common National Culture. Hirsch believes that all national cultures (what he also refers to as "mainstream culture") undergo a similar formative process in which "nation builders" begin by assembling a collection of folk materials such as songs, dances, and legends. He states that these cultural artifacts are then reinterpreted by intellectuals to create a cultural foundation—"our common heritage"—upon which the country as a whole can thrive (1988a, p. 83).

Along with democracy, "standard" English, and federal legal codes, Hirsch contends that national culture is also made up of a "civil religion" that underlies our "civil ethos." This religion constitutes the broadly shared values of society:

> Our civil ethos treasures patriotism and loyalty as high, though perhaps not ultimate, ideals and fosters the belief that the conduct of the nation is guided by a vaguely defined God. Our tradition places importance on carrying the rites and ceremonies of our civil ethos and religion through the national flag, the national holidays, and the national anthem (which means

"national hymn"), and supports the morality of tolerance and benevolence, of the Golden rule, and communal cooperation. We believe in altruism and self-help, in equality, freedom, truth telling and respect for the national law. Besides these vague principles, American culture fosters such myths about itself as its practicality, ingenuity, inventiveness, and independent-mindedness, its connection with the frontier, and its beneficence in the world (even when its leaders do not always follow beneficent policies). It acknowledges that Americans have the right to disagree with the traditional values but nonetheless acquiesce in the dominant civil ethos to the point of accepting imprisonment as the ultimate means of expressing dissent. (1988a, p. 99)

Central to Hirsch's notion of national culture is the country's dependence on a body of common cultural knowledge. He insists that this foundation of knowledge ("our national vocabulary"), which includes a list of over five thousand names, phrases, dates, and concepts, should function as our shared public discourse with which we can communicate. "The anthropological view stresses the universal fact that a human group must have effective communications to function effectively, that effective communications require shared culture, and that shared culture requires transmission of specific information to children" (1988a, pp. xvi–xvii).

Although recognizing culture as "deliberately artificial" (1996, p. 235), and the role of "nation builders," Hirsch nonetheless insists that this shared culture of "essential names and concepts has arisen by historical accident" (1988a, p. 28). He states that, "History has decided what those elements are. They are the medium of public discourse, the instruments through which we are able to communicate our views to one another and make decisions in a democratic way" (1988a, p. 107). According to this leading proponent of common culture, without this body of knowledge, democracy and national unity cannot be sustained.

The Role of National Culture in Maintaining National Unity. Hirsch argues that historically "modern democratic nations arose at the same time as the great national literate languages, and ever since, democracy and literate culture have been essentially connected" (1988a, p. 106). In order to keep the country together politically, socially, and economically, he believes that a national culture should transcend regional and social class differences. However, he insists that, "The specific content of our common heritage is not and must not be detailed, unchanging, or coercive, because that would impinge on our equally fundamental principles of diversity, localism, and toleration" (1988a, p. 96). In fact, Hirsch argues that this country, out of legal and moral principle, has traditionally encouraged the development of local cultures, and that the national code, which has been designed to protect minorities against majorities, should continue to act as a safeguard for local and individual interests against the larger nation (1988a, p. 97).

For Hirsch, maintaining national culture has been pivotal in preserving unity throughout the States. He contends that because pluralism in this country has been a moderate tradition, we do not see the cultural animosities such as warring Serbs and Croates. From his point of view, the nation, in all of its diversity, has come to a general consensus about what it means to be American:

> After more than two hundred years of national life, the main elements of our vocabulary have transcended the sphere of contention and dispute. We do not argue whether Abraham Lincoln in his log cabin belongs in the vocabulary of literate Americans, any more than we argue about spelling. (1988a, p. 26)

> No matter how value-laden or partisan some of these common elements were in their origins long ago, they now exist as common materials of communication. (p. 107)

Hirsch's main point of concern is that this body of knowledge is no longer being adequately taught to up-and-coming generations.

The Role of Schools in Promoting National Culture. Hirsch insists that the information that we have traditionally anticipated our children to learn in school, in order that they be well versed in the national culture, is no longer prioritized, or even coherently promoted. Students are thus thought ill-prepared to fully participate in a democracy. Conversely, schools within his plans (which will be discussed later in more detail) play a crucial role in the intergenerational transmission of what he defines as "our literate" tradition. Within the microculture of educational institutions, he believes that common contents not only promote higher school morale and better teaching and learning but also a strong sense of community and common purpose (1993, p. 30).

Reading Between the Lines: What to Make of and Take from Hirsch's Perspectives on Culture. By ignoring the issues that many social theorists raise about the role of power and ideology in shaping culture and social relations, Hirsch fails to take into consideration how schools and other institutions nationwide function to legitimate particular experiences and worldviews at the expense of others, thus reproducing forms of inequality and oppression. He seems to believe that culture, history, and social reality are driven by mother nature, stating that, "Essential names and concepts have arisen by historical accident" (1988a, p. 28). "History has decided what those elements are" (p. 107).

In his interview on the *Merrow Report,* Hirsch stated that, "Culture is a natural phenomenon." Such an apolitical perspective contradicts his discussions of "a culture that is deliberately artificial" (1996, p. 235), and nation builders, in which a select group of humans actively construct the national culture. It also disregards his acknowledgment of historical struggle over national identity, found in the following statements:

> After more than two hundred years of national life, the main elements of our vocabulary have transcended the sphere of contention and dispute. We do not argue whether Abraham Lincoln in his log cabin belongs in the national vocabulary of literate Americans, any more than we argue about spelling. (1988a, p. 26)

> No matter how value-laden or partisan some of these common elements were in their origins long ago, they now exist as common materials of communication. (1988a, p. 107)

By depoliticizing culture, history, and difference, Hirsch ends up with a view of social reality that is not only abstracted from issues of power and ideology but also from the significant role that antagonistic social relations play in shaping experience, perception, national culture, and overall participation in public life. When reading his work, it is as if the political battles over identity, culture, **representation,** and social reality are all something of the past. He tells us that,

> So long as Blacks and Asians and Latinos remained invisible in our present they also remained invisible in our past. But the present has changed, and henceforth so must the past. . . . Events of recent years have redistributed power in the United States, and it is this change that lies behind the new multicultural redefinition of American history and literature. (1992, p. 5)

There is an enormous body of literature and research, which Hirsch neglects to engage, that discusses the current realities of what Pat Buchanan and many others across the ideological spectrum refer to as culture wars. Buchanan is very clear about his position: "Our Judeo-

Christian values are going to be preserved, and our Western heritage is going to be handed down to future generations, not dumped into some landfill called multiculturalism" (as cited in Macedo, 1994, p. 91). As the struggles over identity, across race, class, gender, sexual orientation, ability, and so on, are so prevalent in this country, it is either naive or malicious to imply, as Hirsch does, that "the Amish" (African-Americans, Latinos, women, gays and lesbians, Asians, and Native Americans, for that matter) "decide what Amish traditions are," and that "it is for all of us to decide collectively what our American traditions are, to decide what 'American' means" (1988a, p. 48).

Hirsch manages to cleanse culture and history of their multiple voices and dangerous memories in a way that makes the country appear as if there were actually a common culture (Macedo, 1994). His efforts to portray our national unity represent a refusal to identify the ubiquitous realities of social turmoil (except in a retrospective manner) that have and continue to be prevalent in the United States: for example, the Los Angeles uprisings, de facto racial segregation, crime, infant mortality, violence against women and gays, the extreme poverty that inflicts at least one in four children, and a long list of other forms of social strife and struggle.[2] Instead, he contends that because pluralism has been a moderate tradition in this country, "we do not see the cultural animosities."

> The deliberately artificial wall of separation [between church and state] helped to create and nurture a public domain of toleration and civility, while leaving everyone as free as possible in their private lives. It was a brilliant Enlightenment political innovation for encouraging internal peace and solidarity in a large nation, and it led to the development of a uniquely American public culture. (1996, p. 234)

From Hirsch's depoliticized perspective, culture is equated with the idea of cultured—that one is well educated in the sense that he or she has learned a particular body of knowledge. As Henry Giroux states,

> Culture in Hirsch's view is seen as a time capsule of past events, prevalent social idioms, and sanctioned codes of behavior of a given nation and merely presents itself for all to participate in its language and conventions. Culture is thereby reduced to a type of monumentalism, and the pedagogy through which it is expressed is organized around the process of transmission and the practice of moral and political regulation. (1992, p. 233)

A collection of dates, names, events, and beliefs does not solely capture the complexities of what shapes and reproduces culture.

Hirsch's desire for national unity is noble, though misguided. Democracy, as opposed to core knowledge, is what should bring us all together. Although he believes that both culture and democracy begin with a preestablished canon of knowledge—a literate tradition and language—he fails to recognize that the concepts of canon and participatory democracy are in fact a contradiction in terms. It is unity in diversity, and not conformity and commonality, which is supposed to bring this country together.

Hirsch's Views of Multiculturalism

Cognizant of the historically pluralistic nature of the United States, Hirsch believes that tolerance for diversity has been a fundamental part of our self-portrait—bringing us "a special strength and vitality" (1988a, p. 95). He acknowledges the movement developing in this country that is calling for school-based knowledge, especially in the areas of history and literature, to be more multicultural than it has been in the past: "Events of recent years have redistributed power in the United States, and it is this change that lies behind the new multicultural redefinition of American history and literature" (1992, p. 5). To accommodate positive social change, Hirsch invites people to work toward reforms that allow for a greater representation of women and those members of non-Western cultures. Schools are thought to be important agents in these reforms in that they help students learn to respect each other via a curriculum that includes the study of diverse peoples and cultures.

When it comes to multiculturalism, Hirsch believes that there are two predominant models that have developed over the years. He describes one as "progressive" because it welcomes all members of society and refers to this as "cosmopolitanism." The other model, which he characterizes as being "retrogressive," he outright rejects because he perceives it as "particularistic," "ethnocentric," and "separatist" in nature (1992, p. 3). Hirsch believes that as a nation we need to embrace the possibilities of "dual citizenship" in which we are all simultaneously part of our particular ethos and the larger cosmopolis (p. 3).

> Like Richard Rodriguez in *Hunger of Memory,* which is a modern American version of this theme, Virgil saw very clearly that the benefits conferred by Roman civilization entailed the pain of some cultural loss. But even as Virgil dramatized the poignancy of loss, he also foreshadowed a cosmopolitan future in which all of these diverse groups would come to live in peace and prosperity instead of living as before in conflict, poverty, and danger. (1992, p. 3)

Hirsch insists that the "ethnic loyalist's" perspective, which he feels embraces cultural separatism, disrupts the harmony of the larger cosmopolis, and that such exclusive loyalty also acts as an obstacle to educational excellence and fairness. A multicultural redefinition of this country, he argues, should avoid these pitfalls:

> It will do black American children little good, for example, to learn a lot about their African and African-American past if they still cannot read and write effectively, do not understand natural science, and cannot solve basic mathematical problems. The only kind of multiculturalism that can overcome these deficiencies is the kind that invites children to become active, effective members of the larger cosmopolis. (1992, Introduction)

A Critique of Traditional Pedagogy and Curricula.   Hirsch contends that the most significant diversity faced by our schools is not cultural but rather consists of a schizophrenia of academic preparation. He believes that students across the nation, even some that have attended the same schools, are exposed to very different kinds of curricular content. "The inevitable consequence of the shopping mall high school is a lack of shared knowledge across and within schools. It would be hard to invent a more effective recipe for cultural fragmentation" (1988a, p. 21).

The highly varied subject matter, which he often refers to as "cafeteria-style education," is thought to have led to what he describes as a steady decline of commonly shared information among members of society. Hirsch attributes this lack of curricular cohesion, which he correlates with low academic achievement, to what he considers a favorable view of content-neutral curricula. He believes that all students can succeed if they are freed of the limiting theories and practices that education professors and school administrators have followed over the past fifty years; theories and practices that have emanated from the work of such educators as Rousseau, Kilpatrick, and Dewey. As Hirsch stated during the *Merrow Report* interview, "Kilpatrick is the bad guy, the DNA spread from Columbia." He argues that a content-neutral conception of educational development has dominated American schools of education, and consequently, the curricula of public primary and secondary schools nationwide. He adamantly criticizes anyone who believes that a child's intellectual and social skills would develop naturally without regard to the specific content of education: "Only by piling up specific, communally shared information can children learn to participate in complex cooperative activities with other members of their community" (1988a, p. xv).

Hirsch insists that a great deal of today's youth lack the intergenerational information that writers of American books and newspapers have traditionally taken for granted among readers. He goes as far as to say that middle-level executives are unable to communicate effectively in business because they no longer share literate background knowledge.

Hirsch also insists that critical thinking and basic skills—what he considers to be the two areas of current focus in education—do not "enable children to create out of their own imaginations the essential names and concepts that have arisen by historical accident" (1988a, p. 28). He believes that a coherent approach to core knowledge provides the best of both worlds in that it not only presents an abundance of important information to memorize but does so (or should do so) in a manner that he sees as the most effective approach for increasing students' ability to think and question (1993, p. 24).

The Call for Common Cultural Literacy. A remedy to what he sees as the present crisis of cultural fragmentation in this country, Hirsch proposes that imparting traditional literate information will not only bring the nation closer together but will effectively contribute to higher literacy rates and social justice. Explaining the origins of this foundation, he tells us that a body of traditions has become fixed in the national memory and is thus central to our nation's identity. This information, which includes legends, names, and events, is thought to have entered the oral and written traditions of the country. He insists that people need to learn not only the grammar of standard English but also this national vocabulary. Hirsch argues that because the reader's mind is constantly inferring meanings that are not directly stated by the words of a text, but are nonetheless part of its essential content (1988a, p. 34), he or she needs to be well equipped with the necessary background information to make and understand the implied associations. Otherwise, this leading advocate of common cultural literacy believes that people will have a difficult time communicating with each other, even though technically they speak the same language (1988a, p. 4).

Cognitively, Hirsch subscribes to the idea that learning builds upon learning in a cumulative way. As such, the lack of learning in the early grades usually has a negatively cumulative effect (1993, p. 27). Believing that basic acculturation—that is, assimilation of a common national vocabulary—should largely be completed by age thirteen (1988a, p. 30), he tells us that cultural literacy, once lost in the early grades, is usually lost for good: "By the fourth grade, it is usually unbridgeable" (1996, p. 44).

Within this model of linguistic and cultural transmission, public education plays a central role by maintaining communicative standards as presented in national dictionaries, spelling books, pronunciation guides, grammar texts, and other core knowledge curricular materials. Hirsch insists that new theories of multicultural education should not interfere with this process:

> It should not be allowed to supplant or interfere with our schools' responsibility to ensure our children's mastery of American literate culture. . . . The acculturative responsibility of the schools is primary and fundamental. To teach the ways of one's own community has always been and still remains the essence of the education of our children who enter neither a narrow tribal culture nor a transcendent world culture but a national literate culture. For profound historical reasons, this is the way of the modern world. It will not change soon, and it will certainly not be changed by educational policy alone. (1988a, p. 18)

The Core Knowledge Sequence consists of a planned progression of specific knowledge in history, geography, mathematics, science, language arts, and fine arts. Hirsch emphasizes that this curricular model does not claim to teach the entirety of what schoolchildren should know but rather represents a "working agreement" regarding the minimum knowledge that children need to acquire. The Core Sequence was designed to take up 50 percent of a school's curriculum, which Hirsch believes leaves ample room for site-based governance, local requirements and emphases, and creative implementation.

The Multicultural Nature of the Core Knowledge Sequence. In order to be accepted nationwide, Hirsch tells us that the Core Knowledge Sequence has to be ratified by many ethnic groups. He claims that as a result of the diversity of groups that participated in its formation, the core curriculum is inherently multicultural. He invites the reader to consider the following guide for first-grade history:

> Introduce ancient civilizations and the variety of religions in the world, using maps of the ancient world. Specifics: *Egypt:* King Tutankhamen; Nile; Pyramids; Mummies; Animal gods; Hieroglyphics. *Babylonia:* Tigris and Euphrates; Hammurabi. *Judaism:* Moses; Passover; Chanukah. *Christianity:* Jesus. *Arabia:* Mohammed; Allah; Islam. *India:* Indus River; Brahma; Hinduism; Buddha. *China:* Yellow River; Confucius; Chinese New Year. (1991, p. 3)

Hirsch insists that any centrist curriculum must contain the following characteristics:

1. It encourages knowledge of and sympathy toward the diverse cultures of the world.
2. It fosters respect for every child's home culture as well as for the cosmopolitan school-based culture.
3. It gives all children competence in the current system of language and allusion that is dominant in the nation's economic and intellectual discourse. (1992, p. 6)

The Role of Core Literacy in Educating the "Disadvantaged." Hirsch argues that the United States has one of the most unjust educational systems in the developed world, which he feels greatly contributes to the condition of "disadvantaged" children (1991, p. 2). He believes that the best way to help such children (who have not had access to the background information and skills needed for schooling) overcome educational injustice is to provide them with the universally shared body of knowledge. Without such a foundation, he insists that many "minority students" will continue to fall behind their peers in academic achievement (1991, p. 1). Hirsch claims that bridging this gap would enhance the motivation, self-esteem, and performance of such children (1988a, p. 28). "Knowing that only a few hundred pages of information stand between the literate and the illiterate, between dependence and autonomy, should energize people to learn" (1988a, p. 143). Drawing a connection between background information and the ability to hold positions of responsibility and power, he hopes that blacks and other minorities will be able to assimilate core knowledge and thus improve their social and economic status (1988a, p. 10).

Reading Between the Lines: What to Make of and Take from Hirsch's Perspectives on Multicultural Education and Common Cultural Literacy. In light of the plethora of research and literature on multicultural education—as articulated in Chapter 1 of this book—Hirsch's reduction of this enormous diversity of perspectives into two camps is extremely problematic. Within his limited description of both models, this advocate of core knowledge not only fails to address cultural differences specifically in terms of race, gender, sexual orientation, and so forth, but he also chooses not to sufficiently outline how these ideological constructs actually function to shape cultural tensions and practices.

The multicultural paradigm that Hirsch embraces is thought to have played a significant role in promoting national literacy and solidarity, and "in creating and sustaining modern civilization" (1988a, p. 93). He selects the Ancient Greek term *cosmopolis* to describe his utopian vision.[3] It is interesting to note that the Greeks felt that foreigners were uncivilized, primitive barbarians who lacked the ability to think rationally. In fact, slaves and radical stratification along the lines of gender, class, religion, and language existed within their cosmopolis. As Jim Gee asserts, "Plato's perfect state was an authoritarian one based on the view that people are, by and large, born suited for a particular place in a naturally given hierarchy, with the 'philosopher-kings' (that is, Plato or people like him) at the top" (1996, p. 30).

With the oppressive practices and institutions that the United States has maintained, it sounds as if we have already achieved a cosmopolis. Any romanticized notion of modern civilization, in which "all of these diverse groups would come to live in peace and prosperity instead of living as before in conflict, poverty, and danger" (Hirsch, 1992, p. 3), which disregards the realities of today's social crises as well as the blood upon which this society has been built, needs to be seriously challenged.

Superficially dismissing the multicultural model that he describes as retrogressive, Hirsch gives no explanation as to why ethnic loyalties have arisen, thus obfuscating the realities of oppression and unfair social practices that are prevalent in the United States—that give rise to solidarity and struggle. In fact, Hirsch's tone throughout his work (for example, see the previous quote about Richard Rodriguez and the cosmpolis) sounds as if one of the central reasons that conflict, poverty, and discrimination exist is because certain groups simply refuse to assimilate.

> The principle of multiculturalism should be guided into this ecumenical, cosmopolitan direction for the good of the nation rather than fostering its all-too-prevalent tendency toward angry separatism and mutual hostility. (1996, p. 235)

> The interethnic hostilities that have intensified among us recently, the development of an us-versus-them mentality in political life, the astonishing indifference to the condition of our children—all bespeak a decline in the communitarian spirit, which used to be a hallmark of what Patterson calls our "ecumenical national culture." (1996, p. 238)

Critiquing Hirsch's description of certain groups as particularistic, Giroux rightly rebuts:

> Nor in a democratic society should subordinate groups attempting to fashion a pedagogy and politics of inclusion and cultural democracy be derisively labeled as particularistic because they have raised serious questions

regarding how the canon and public school curriculum work to secure specific forms of cultural authority or how the dynamics of cultural power works to silence and marginalize specific groups of students. (1994a, p. 334)

Opposed to practicing the kinds of dissent that Giroux feels are fundamental to a participatory democracy, like the Greek/Roman model that he embraces, Hirsch creates a false sense of public sharing:

> In our own day, the chief danger to this ecumenical, cosmopolitan public culture is not a religious but an ethnic sectarianism. The two kinds of sect, religious and ethnic, are highly similar in their divisiveness and their danger to the shared public sphere. Had the idea of ethnic strife been as present in the minds of the Founding Fathers as the idea of religious strife, our founding laws might have included a clause forbidding the establishment of a narrow ethnic culture. (1996, p. 234)

If we are to truly practice democracy, we are compelled to embrace, rather than eliminate, multiple dissenting publics with diverse concerns. As Nancy Fraser argues, we must "eradicate the underlying assumption that the institutional confinement of public life to a single, overarching public sphere is a positive and desirable state of affairs, whereas the proliferation of a multiplicity of publics represents a departure from, rather than an advance toward, democracy" (1994, p. 83).

Denying the validity of the criticism that common cultural literacy is exclusionary—that is, class-bound, not to mention racist, sexist, and excessively Western—Hirsch states that, "Characteristically, some of the most persistent elements of our national lore owe their longevity to human universality rather than conscious political design" (1988a, p. 89). He further argues that common cultural literacy "is primarily an instrument of communication among diverse cultures rather than a cultural or class instrument in its own right. In fact, one of the main uses of a national vocabulary is to enable effective and harmonious exchange despite personal, cultural, and class differences" (p. 104).[4] He acknowledges that such information has been more readily accessible to those who are wealthy enough to be educated than by poor people, but he argues that schools, with the help of Core Sequence Programs, could easily bridge this gap.

Hirsch believes that educational institutions have an important "controllable influence" on culture in terms of what children do and do not learn (1988a, p. 20). However, rather than questioning this power and its potentially abusive qualities, he acts as an apologist for the reproductive nature of schools. His argument is that educational policy always in-volves choices between degrees of worthiness, and those who have power in the present always determine what shall be selected and inter-preted from the infinite past. Rejecting what he seems to believe are the excesses of democracy, when it comes down to power and decision making, Hirsch sees the dispersion of educational authority as an insur-mountable obstacle to altering the fragmentation of the school curricu-lum (1988a, p. 19). It is troubling that Hirsch simultaneously supports and rejects monopolies:

> Philanthropists and capitalists have spent large sums to design "break-the-mold" schools. (1996, p. 60)

> These ideas [charter schools and choice] are based on the sound theory that parent empowerment would moderate the evils of institutional mo-nopoly through the power of competition. (1996, p. 61)

> Public schooling is under monopolistic control in almost every modern na-tion, and quality does not necessarily suffer as a result. (1996, p. 65)

Although Hirsch argues that no single national vocabulary is inherently superior or privileged above all others (1988a, p. 107), it is obvious that if his monolithic system of ideas were adopted nationwide it in fact would have a more significant impact and more recognition. During the *Merrow Report*, he revealed his ulterior motive, stating, "Fifty percent [of core knowledge in the school day] is as much as I can get away with."[5] Hirsch is obviously in support of a monopoly when his agenda is at the forefront. Although he claims that his fixed curricula "is not a *prescriptive* list of books, but rather, a *descriptive* list of the information actually possessed by literate Americans" (1988a, p. xiv), the title of the book—*What Every American Needs to Know*—contradicts his argument. Even his notion of "centrists," which he uses to describe those who support the idea of core knowledge in schools, gives the image of a dominant model.

Literacy within Hirsch's multicultural model is reduced to the ability to negotiate and converse through a monolithic body of knowledge—disregarding both the basics of reading and writing, and the need for critical thinking in order to make any real sense of what is being learned and communicated. Critical educators, on the other hand, recognizing and moving beyond functional literacy, demand that students also de-velop the kinds of awareness, or presence of mind, that help to identify and interact with the sociopolitical realities that shape their lives. Arguing that current dominant theories of education crush independence of mind (1996, p. 2), Hirsch also claims to embrace critical thinking in his Core Knowledge Sequence:

> Although teaching children national mainstream culture doesn't force them to accept its values uncritically, it does enable them to understand those values in order to predict the typical attitudes of other Americans. (1988a, p. 24)

> We are justifiably proud of the degree to which our children are encouraged to think for themselves, to be independent-minded, and critical of received ideas. (1996, p. 98)

However, when discussing the role of cultural literacy/core knowledge, consider the pedagogy of containment embedded in the language that he uses:

transmission (1988a, p. 84)
controllable, (1988a, p. 20)
basic acculturation should largely be completed by age thirteen
    (1988a, p. 30)
functional (1988a, p. xi)
universal literacy (1988a, p. 1)
background information stored in their minds (1988a, p. 2)
conservatism (1988a, p. 23)
techniques of conveying traditions (1988a, p. 25)
master the materials that authenticate membership (1988a, p. 30)
memorization to carry on their traditions (1988a, p. 30)
holding to its standards (1988a, p. 71)
to eliminate all other dialects, spellings, and pronunciation in order
    to create a single standard language (1988a, p. 77)
important legends, names, and events become fixed by constant
    usage (1988a, p. 90)
effective monoliteracy (1988a, p. 92)
national language is permanently fixed (1988a, p. 93)
American literacy must be to institute a policy of imparting com-
    mon information (1988a, p. 94)
our civic religion defines our broadly shared values as a society
    (1988a, p. 103)
no matter how value-laden or partisan some of these common ele-
    ments were in their origins long ago, they now exist as common
    materials of communication (1988a, p. 107)

children will become adults who cooperate (1992, p. 1); hard work
and the transmission of knowledge (1996, p. 6)
intellectual capital is *itself* the great all-purpose tool of adaptation
in the modern world (1996, p. 22)[6]

In this language of **cultural reproduction** we do not engage cultural
and linguistic traditions for their strengths and weaknesses but rather
uncritically pass them down. As such, students are relegated to the status of passive reproducers, rather than active producers of knowledge.
In fact, Hirsch openly contradicts his own call for critical thinking, stating, "Although 'critical thinking' has replaced the vocationalism of earlier decades as an aim that is superior to mere book learning, the same
anti-intellectual, anti-subject-matter, and supposedly anti-elitist bias
lies at its root" (1996, p. 114).[7]

Perhaps Hirsch's most contradictory statement about his position on
critical thinking is evident in the following quote: "We make social and
educational progress *only* by teaching myths and facts that are predominantly traditional" (1988a, p. xii). Acknowledging the fact that history
and truth are ideologically engineered—for example, he states that the
fabricated "story of the cherry tree is a useful illustration of the way our
national culture was formed" (1988a, p. 88)—Hirsch embraces historical
distortions and folklore as being essential to maintaining our national
identity. He disregards the fact that such myths only serve to prevent actual readings of social reality. Thus, truth telling, which is embraced as a
basic tenet of Hirsch's notion of civil ethos, also consists of a consciously
motivated form of distortion and public manipulation.

With such an apolitical approach to learning and literacy, it comes as
no surprise that at the Washington Core Knowledge School in Colorado,
there

> is near-scorn for consciousness-raising programs that mark the calendars
> of many public schools. DARE Day, for example, a drug education cam-
> paign sponsored by the federal Drug Abuse Resistance Education program,
> was practically ignored; the faculty didn't want to give up teaching time to
> make posters and ribbons. AIDS education, self-esteem raising, social ad-
> justment—at Washington these are perceived as mere digressions . . . even
> African-American history month gets scant attention. (Ruenzel, 1996, p. 28)

In fact, Hirsch refers to such goals as health and citizenship as nonacad-
emic (1996, p. 109). It is as if any movement away from the content of his
lists, especially in the name of ethics, civic responsibility, and moral development, is not educational. Thus, the real links between education

and democracy—the development of those qualities necessary to participate effectively in democratic structures—are ignored or discarded.

In Hirsch's case, the connection between critical thinking and creating socially responsible citizens is never really made. Although he states that, "The right to vote is meaningless if a citizen is disenfranchised by illiteracy or semiliteracy" (1988a, p. 12), he never explains exactly how assimilation of a body of knowledge can assist people in making critical and responsible decisions, or in effectively working against oppressive practices.

Within his discussions of helping the so-called disadvantaged, Hirsch manages to reduce the realities of poverty and oppression to issues of cultural literacy and educational theory:

> Illiterate and semiliterate Americans are condemned not only to poverty, but to the powerlessness of incomprehension. (1988a, p. 12)

> The social injustice that has resulted from our dominant educational theories . . . (1996, p. 4)

> Inferior education is today the primary cause of social and economic injustice. (1996, p. 43)

> Improving the effectiveness and fairness of education through enhancing both its content and its commonality has a more than educational significance. The improvement would, as everyone knows, diminish the economic inequalities within the nation. (1996, p. 238)

Rather than viewing educational institutions as reflections of the larger society, they are considered either relentless generators of, or all-encompassing panaceas to, social problems. Issues of socially sanctioned racism, sexism, classism, heterosexism, and ableism are left out of the picture, or dismissed.[8] Hirsch argues:

> 16 percent lower wages for Blacks of the same grade level completed is owing to the fact that Blacks have been on average less well educated by the schools. Most of the existing wage disparity, that is, some of the 12 out of the 16 percent, can be explained by a disparity in actual educational attainment . . . economic class more than race currently determines educational and economic attainment in the United States—a hopeful sign. (1996, p. 5)

From this myopic form of class analysis, poverty and all other kinds of discrimination are reduced not to capitalist social relations and institutionalized oppression but rather to school curriculum.[9]

Throughout his work, Hirsch insists that the reason we do not have the necessary core programs in our schools to eradicate illiteracy and poverty is because of the misguided theories of Rousseau, Kilpatrick, and Dewey. However, it is absolutely ridiculous to assume that theories of education, in and of themselves, cause racism, poverty, and all the other forms of social injustice. It is equally irresponsible to assume that illiteracy alone causes poverty, rather than the opposite way around. This alternative perspective calls for a more in-depth macroexamination of the unequal distribution of wealth and power in the United States, far beyond Hirsch's severely limited microexplanations based on whether students acquire a decontextualized, abstract body of knowledge.

For Hirsch, education via cultural literacy becomes the all-encompassing panacea for this country's social deterioration:[10]

> As the universal second culture, literate culture has become the common currency for social and economic exchange in our democracy, and the only available ticket to full citizenship. Getting one's membership card is not tied to class or race. Membership is automatic if one learns the background information and the linguistic conventions that are needed to read, write, and speak effectively. (1988a, p. 22).

> But an equally important contribution of the truly common school would be the strengthening of universal communicability and a sense of community within the public sphere. In the long run, that could be the common school's most important contribution to preserving the fragile fabric of our democracy. (1996, p. 238)

The idea that, "Knowing that only a few hundred pages of information stand between the literate and the illiterate, between dependence and autonomy, should energize people" (1988a, p. 143), is a deceitful misconception of the realities of discrimination in this country. African-American intellectuals, for example, walk up the street with a great breadth of knowledge and are still targeted and abused as "niggers."

Beyond placing the blame for social inequalities on schools, the deceit that Hirsch perpetuates also implicates **subordinated** parents and caregivers in their own, as well as society's, predicament—thus blaming the victims:

> We know that many children are too heavily influenced by the anti-academic values (usually defensive reactions) of their parents and peers. Every conscientious teacher, principal, and supervisor tries to counteract the

> anti-school ethic that is especially powerful and self-defeating among just those disadvantaged children who are most in need of a pro-school ethic. . . . Although few of us in education have the time or opportunity to abolish the anti-school ethic in all its defensive manifestations . . . (1987, p. 211)

> No nation has entirely overcome a correlation between social class and educational achievement, and none is likely to, since the home is an important educational institution in its own right. (1996, p. 226)

From his perspective, it is a fundamental injustice that what American children learn in school should be determined by whether their homes have given them the background knowledge they need for academic work (1991, p. 5).

Rather than engaging illiteracy and what causes cultural opposition to oppressive practices, Hirsch's position not only blames the victim but also aspires to abolish resistance to social injustice. At its very core, Hirsch's political posture represents an advanced form of social Darwinism—he is providing a survival kit and the rest is simply up to you. As such, the larger factors that lead to and perpetuate discrimination go unaddressed.[11] Critical pedagogues, on the other hand, take these issues head on. Instead of simply desiring in a patronizing way to "help the disadvantaged," they endeavor to create the pedagogical conditions within which educators, students, and their communities at large understand what constitutes disadvantaged in the first place. But Hirsch is not interested in alternative explanations for this country's problems.

On the *Merrow Report,* Hirsch argued against what he described as a progressive monopoly on schools, insisting that, "Schools of education should embrace heterodoxies rather than orthodoxies." However, when discussing multicultural education, he completely ignores, or hastily dismisses, the enormous body of research, as cited throughout this book, that deals with the sociohistorical, political, and cultural issues (what I refer to as the politics of motivation) that lead to a lack of academic achievement and school dropouts. A quick scan over his reference sections reveals this radical omission. For example, important insights about resistance theory and education (Fine, 1991; Fordham, 1988; Giroux, 1983; McLaren, 1986; Ogbu, 1987; Rampton, 1995; Solomon, 1992; Willis, 1977) are virtually nonexistent within his work. Once again contradicting himself, arguing earlier that parents create an antischool ethic, Hirsch actually argues that, "The claim that minority children resist 'assimilation' to school-based culture is not borne out by our experience" (1996, p. 287).

Hirsch simply rejects any and all opposition to his plans as

extremist (1992, p. 6)
anti-knowledge extremism (1996, p. 126)
over-facile dismissals that ought to be cut off at the pass (1996, p. 145)
mindless claims (1996, p. 155)
pandemic of mistaken ideas (1996, p. 230)
disabling indoctrination (1996, p. 230)
facile doctrines (1996, p. 241)
ideologues (1996, p. 112)
ideological phrase dropping (1988a, p. 106)[12]

He even suggests that all those opposed to his particular agenda are responsible for perpetuating the social problems facing this country:

> Those who evade the inherent conservatism of literacy in the name of anti-elitism are, in effect, elitists of an extreme sort. Traditionally educated and economically secure, these self-appointed protectors of minority cultures have advised schools to pursue a course that sentences minorities to illiteracy and poverty. (1988b, p. 25)

Hirsch compares opposition to his proposed changes as being

> not different in principle from the resistance to change exhibited by Soviet and Chinese bureaucrats. Stubborn traditions may succeed in perpetuating themselves through powerful bureaucracies, but a persistence in old ways in the face of new circumstances cannot succeed in creating a better life for the people of a nation. (1991, p. 9)[13]

It is interesting how he strategically uses 1950s McCarthy tactics to instill fear in people. His choice of the words *Soviet* and *Chinese* (implying communism) act as shock words that deter attention away from any kind of **counterdiscourse.** "American schools need to be transformed, and to accomplish that, many ideas (including even the pseudo-idea of 'radical transformation') need to be repudiated" (1996, p. 15). He accuses others of skirting "underlying complexities" by engaging in an us-versus-them, black-and-white debate (1996, p. 11); however, in essence, he is complicit in the very kinds of anti-intellectualism that he claims to abhor (1996, p. 106). Although Hirsch insists that "they [alternative perspectives] wither under close scrutiny" (1996, p. 15)—a kind of examination that he fails to illustrate—he himself, under analysis, is having a hard time holding water.

An important question that readily pops up when reading Hirsch concerns the "who" of the collective that supposedly participated in the production of the Core Knowledge Sequence. Throughout Hirsch's work the reader is often informed that parents, teachers, scientists, professional curriculum organizations, and experts on America's multicultural traditions were included in the process. In the acknowledgments of his newest book (1996) he states, "I ventured to ask the best scholars and scientists I could think of for criticisms." However, one never really knows exactly who these people/consultants were, or more importantly, what the criteria were for choosing them. He insists that, "Such people are a lot easier to find than publicized disputes suggest, and fortunately there are more centrists than there are extremists" (1992, p. 6). It seems obvious from this statement that so-called extremists were probably not invited to participate in this project, nor were there concerns addressed from afar. Had they been involved at any level, the fate of the final list certainly would have been different.[14]

Hirsch tells the reader that providing our children with traditional information ("national culture") in public schools by no means imposes a particular point of view: "Conservatives who wish to preserve traditional values will find that these are not necessarily inculcated by traditional education, which can in fact be subversive of the status quo" (1988a, p. 24). Unfortunately, instead of clearly articulating the necessary critical pedagogical conditions for engaging ideological diversity, he completely omits any explanation as to how such subversion comes to fruition. Hirsch's idea of multicultural participation is nothing more than an uncritical call for color coordination. For example, he praises the work of Richard Rodriguez, who is a staunch conservative and advocate for monolingual/monocultural education. Rodriguez by no means represents the general sentiments of the Latino/a community. By refusing to engage ideological diversity, Hirsch simply pays lip service to difference and democracy. Thus, the constant use of "we," "our," "us," and "a working agreement" throughout his work, especially when he rejects "a dispersion of educational authority" (1988a, p. 19), is disconcerting. The title of his new book (1996), *The Schools We Want and Why We Don't Have Them*, exacerbates this tension. Critical educators, on the other hand, offer a much more democratic theoretical framework for creating a pedagogy of inclusion, for engaging the politics of difference, and for working toward social change.

The idea of change in schools and society represents a major contradiction that is characteristic of Hirsch's work. While he calls for serious philosophical changes in approaches to schooling, changes that he claims will solve this country's plethora of social ills (needless to say, a major societal undertaking), he demands that our common body of knowledge and dominant culture remain virtually in tact:

> Common sense and experience both dictate caution in trying to revolutionize American culture through the school curriculum by neglecting or even rejecting the currently dominant culture. That would simply harm children who are in most need of help. In order to get a good job a young person must be able to communicate in speech and writing in the standard language and allusion-system of the marketplace. Since this system of intellectual currency is in broad use by millions of adults, it is a highly stable system that is slow to change. (1992, p. 7)

He further argues that, "The inherent conservatism of literacy leads to a subtle but unavoidable paradox: the goals of political liberalism require educational conservatism. We make social and economic progress *only* by teaching myths and facts that are predominantly traditional" (1988a, p. xii).

In his newest book he reiterates, "I would label myself a political liberal and an educational conservative. . . . The only practical way to achieve liberalism's aim of greater social justice is to pursue conservative educational policies" (1996, p. 6). Although he argues that, "Traditional education can be subversive of the status quo" (1988a, p. 24), thus admitting that the status quo is in fact conservative, he nevertheless demands that we as a nation accept the necessary conservatism that exists at the core of the national vocabulary, and that any significant change "occur with glacial slowness if it is to accommodate all the people and serve as our universal medium of communication" (p. 107). On a societal level, he asserts: "Some believe, erroneously, that our culture can be remade on a large scale by an act of common will. This is a false and damaging myth. Rapid, large-scale change is no more possible in the sphere of national culture than in the sphere of national language" (1988a, p. 91). Rejecting the forces of common will, Hirsch's rhetoric is bereft of a call for students to critically appropriate aspects of the dominant culture in order that they may simultaneously work to change it for the better.

This major contradiction around social transformation and conservatism remains unresolved throughout Hirsch's work. It seems that the idea of change is presented in a positive light only when it supports his position. When under heavy criticism that his curriculum is exclusionary and reproduces injustice, he suddenly embraces the reality that mainstream culture is constantly in flux and uses the way in which it appropriates new elements and rids itself of old ones to argue that literate culture is the most democratic in the country (1988a, p. 21). But Hirsch later warns us that cosmopolitan centrist curriculum must initiate evolutionary rather than revolutionary change in American culture (1992, p. 6). This notion of change creates the misperception that sociocultural transformations should follow a natural course from which a more just society simply evolves. This type of attitude—a form of antipolitics—induces political paralysis by crippling social agency and leaving democracy and justice to the winds of change. Within Hirsch's plan, the unequal power relations that drive social institutions, including schools, remain completely intact. All that he proposes to change are the educational theories that guide the development of curricula and that he feels deny access to educational success for what he refers to as disadvantaged students.

There is an uneasy feeling that I get when reading Hirsch's descriptions of subordinated groups in schools. He leaves me with a sense of indifference, even disdain, for local and ethnic cultures. They represent what he describes as "the narrow spheres of family, neighborhood, and region" (1988a, p. 21) and "narrow tribal cultures" (1988a, p. 18). He declares that, "While ethnicity may be an important defining part of an individual's identity, it is a presumption to insist that ethnicity defines one more essentially than do dozens of other social and temperamental determinants" (1992, p. 3). The reader never finds out what exactly the other significant factors are that define one's identity, whether in fact they are the very cultural impositions and practices against which subordinated groups are fighting.

Unlike critical educators who use more accurate terms such as oppressed to describe the realities of many subordinated groups in this country, Hirsch chooses more derogatory descriptors such as:

disadvantaged (1987, p. 212)
those unfortunates (1987, p. 213)
illiterate (1988a, p. xii)
semiliterate (1988a, p. 12)
cultural deprivation (1988a, p. 24, p. 114)
[not having] culturally adequate backgrounds (1988a, p. 27)
disadvantaged offspring (1991, p. 4)
permanently handicapped (1992, p. 5)

less fortunate children (1992, p. 5)

[as having] educational defects (1992, p. 7)

lagging members (1993, p. 27)

learning/knowledge/permanent deficits (1993, pp. 27–28)

academic handicaps (1996, p. 33)

students from less-good home schools (1996, p. 43)

slower children (1996, p. 90)

children whose first language is not English and whose families
    may be nonfunctional (1996, p. 92)

ways of monitoring students' progress in order to remedy their de-
    ficiencies (1996, p. 177)[15]

This language of deficiency generates the impression that there is something fundamentally wrong with these groups and that they are in need of fixing. The invaluable cultural knowledge that they posses, whether it is a product of a wealth of traditions or resistance to oppression, is at best glossed over and at worst completely ignored. For example, Hirsch contends that even with the inclusion of more multicultural materials, "We still face the task of giving all children a good education" (1992, p. 6). He also argues that, "It is impossible for a teacher to reach all children when some of them lack the necessary building blocks of learning" (1996, p. 33). These statements imply that the cultural/educational foundations of groups that fall outside of the "acceptable norm" are not "good," and that the "real" building blocks of learning and knowing can only exist within the confines of his list. The following quote speaks to his belief in the superiority of core knowledge in cognitive development: "Keith Stanovitch and his colleagues have shown that, after controlling for IQ, those who score well on cultural literacy tests have more fully developed cognitive abilities than the control group" (1996, p. 12).

Hirsch contends that the severe lack of core knowledge in schools permanently retards cognitive development (1996, p. 90). Arguing that basic acculturation—that is, assimilation of the national vocabulary—should largely be completed by age thirteen (1988a, p. 30), he believes that cultural literacy, once lost in the early grades, is usually lost for good (1988a, p. 31; 1991, p. 4). This sounds as if there is a prepubescent critical period, after which all those who have not learned the list—adults, immigrants, and so on—are doomed. Is this in fact an implicit assault on immigration; that is, if we cannot assimilate them and make them "productive" members of society, do we not let them in? Not only is the idea of a critical period completely unfounded but more importantly people—whether in international business, in a college classroom, on the train, or wherever—readily communicate without a shared culture. The idea that we cannot communicate beyond our own understandings and experiences is simply ridiculous.

In addition, the chronological dispersion of knowledge by age and grade presents a real dilemma. One of Hirsch's major complaints about mainstream practices is that there is no set curriculum, and that consequently there is a great deal of repetition of subjects. He argues that, "Gaps and repetition mean ignorance and narrowness; they mean huge opportunities lost" (1996, p. 158). The mystery is, without redundancy in his sequence, how will learners ever acquire a deep understanding of what they covered in the early grades? For example, "according to what every second grader needs to know," students at this level will study the controversy over slavery and other aspects of the Civil War. How can second graders achieve any real depth in that area, which will not be repeated in the later grades? When asked during the *Merrow Report* interview how he proposes to resolve this dilemma, Hirsch responded, "I don't know."

I am not implying that we cannot talk with young people about discrimination. We can, and we should. My basic point is that we need to foster a deep and evolving understanding, and not simply a "covered that" kind of attitude. Part of such an understanding would require connecting history with the immediacy of students' realities. It would entail moving beyond Hirsch's ideas about multicultural content that are based on a vague and apolitical relationship between nation and culture.

If educational justice really means equality of educational opportunity, as Hirsch suggests (1991, p. 2), then why would the realities and worldviews of all students not be central to the process of learning? Hirsch insists that changes brought on by "other groups are generously reflected in our list" (1988a, p. xii). However, his use of "generous," "tolerant" (1988a, p. 18), "accommodate" (1988a, p. 95), and "sympathy" (1992, p. 3) sounds as if those involved with providing core knowledge are being charitable in their handouts, and people on the receiving end should not look a gift horse in the mouth.

Illustrating his "generosity," while parading his list around as being multicultural, Hirsch offers the reader the example of "griot" (explaining that in West African oral cultures, the griot is the tale-teller and rememberer of traditions). Although this morsel of information is intriguing, it is not clear why such an object of knowledge should be prioritized over the existential realities of life in the ghetto in the United States. For example, this is not simply an issue, as Hirsch seems to argue, of including other national cultures (1988a, p. 107) (or reducing the concept of culture to nation) but rather should be about affirming and engaging the histories and immediacy of cultures within a nation. It is the very immediacy of oppression that "every American needs to know." Instead, Hirsch insists that we "not burden students with endless history that is irrelevant to current realities" (1992, p. 7). He never articulates what aspects of their social reality will be included in the educational process. As such, the traditions that have sustained the abject poverty and discrimination that many people experience on a daily basis are not critically interrogated and risk being simply passed on. This level of transmission is especially probable in public schools that promote uncritical pedagogical styles.

A major omission in Hirsch's work, a key to critical multicultural education, concerns the role of teacher political awareness and pedagogy. He never questions the cultural assumptions that teachers consciously and unconsciously wield in the classroom, and does not concern himself with the sources that generate such assumptions and biases. The importance of having reflective practitioners who take ownership of both theory and practice, who are critical of the knowledge that they are teaching, and who are sensitive to students' needs and realities, is reduced to the call for teachers to simply transmit, in whatever way they choose, his list of knowledge. There is virtually no concern for how things are taught, only for what is taught and when. In Hirsch's mind, fairness is equated with equal content, not with democratic social interaction in the classroom. In fact, during his public interview on the *Merrow Report,* in front of a full house at Harvard, he announced without a care, "I don't know much about pedagogy or self-esteem. I don't claim to know it firsthand." He was then asked if his curriculum was "a recipe." He responded, "Yes, the pedagogy is not important; the ingredients are." With this public confession, Hirsch falls into what he himself criticizes:

> Colleagues who are logicians by profession are not by reason of their specialty immune from sloppy and hasty judgments when they pronounce upon public policy and other complex subjects they know little about. Usually, it isn't the logical structure of people's inferences that chiefly causes uncritical thinking but, rather, the uninformed or misinformed faultiness of their premises. (1996, p. 136)

Pedagogy, that is, how we learn what we learn, is essential to the process of learning and knowing. Without a concern for how things are taught, we risk collapsing into Plato's dilemma: "The people are given the text for themselves, but then something must ensure they see it 'right'—not in reality through their own eyes, but rather from the perspective of an authoritarian institution that delimits correct interpretations" (Gee, 1996, p. 32). For example, Hirsch includes the terms *feminism* and *Marxism* in his list of "what every American needs to know," but he never makes the effort to ensure that students are exposed to multiple interpretations of these concepts—my explanation would be very different from former President George Bush's, for example.

Although claiming throughout his work that he has no political agenda, Hirsch is caught up in his own manipulative interpretations. For example, he abstracts the work of Antonio Gramsci, Paulo Freire, and Pierre Bourdieu from any sense of what these critical social theorists have been all about. He asserts,

> History has proved Gramsci to be a better theorist and prophet than Freire. Modern nations that have adopted Gramscian principles have bettered the condition and heightened the political, social, and economic power of oppressed classes of people. By contrast, nations (including our own) that have stuck to the principles of Freire have failed to change the social and economic status quo. (1996, p. 7)

This statement teaches readers who are generally unfamiliar with such critical work that Freire's anticolonial theory and literacy practices have been central to the educational process in the United States, when in fact they are rarely even studied, let alone implemented. On the other hand, Gramsci, a neo-Marxist, is made to look as if he believed in cultural reproduction of the dominant classes—an idea that could not possibly be any further from the truth. Hirsch describes him as saying, "The oppressed class should be taught to master the tools of power and authority—the ability to read, write, and communicate—and to gain enough traditional knowledge to understand the worlds of nature and culture surrounding them" (1996, p. 7).

What is missing here is Gramsci's call to be able to navigate the mainstream such that we can work to transform its oppressive qualities. From Hirsch's description, it is as if Gramsci were against critical **praxis.** It is interesting to note that neither Gramsci nor his most important concept of **hegemony** are in Hirsch's dictionary of "what every American needs to know." This is not surprising considering the critical nature of this Italian's work (which got him thrown in prison) and the definition of the term: *Hegemony* is used to express how certain groups manage to dominate others via the imposition of particular ideologies and forms of authority that result in the reproduction of social and institutional practices through which dominant groups maintain not only their positions of privilege and control but also the consensual support of other members (even those subordinated) of society. If anything, this definition provides an accurate window into the world/agenda of E. D. Hirsch Jr.

Hirsch plays the same game with the work of Pierre Bourdieu, another critical social theorist, by implying that he and his notion of **cultural capital** (that different forms of cultural knowledge, such as language, modes of social interaction, beliefs, and meaning, are valued hierarchically in society) support the call for common cultural literacy. Hirsch even replaces the concept of cultural capital with intellectual capital, implying that there is some universal human **foundation** of knowledge (1996, p. 20). Bourdieu, along with most critical pedagogues, would argue that only those characteristics and practices (i.e., cultural wealth) of the dominant paradigm will potentially facilitate academic achievement within mainstream schools that reflect the dominant exclusionary ideology. However, by no means do they present this insight with the intention of inspiring uncritical assimilation of such knowledge, simply ignoring the unequal power relations that exist in society across a politics of difference.

The idea that Hirsch has more in common with Gramsci and Bourdieu than does Freire is simply ridiculous and manipulative. Although Hirsch castigates self-interested ideology in education, he is implicated in this very practice. It is no wonder that he avoids the word *ideology* altogether. He states,

> The human disposition to preselect research results is sometimes called an "ideology," a word implying that beliefs are chosen primarily to promote self-interest or class interests. It is true that American educational ideas are not completely free from self-interested ideology, particularly in their self-aggrandizing stress on process. But I shall avoid the word "ideology." (1996, p. 71)

Ideological distortion on Hirsch's part is also embedded in the following statement: "Our current textbooks teach the past shortcomings of the United States" (1996, p. 94). We need simply read the debates over so-called revisionist history to realize the controversial and exclusionary treatment of history in schools (Carroll & Noble, 1988; Chomsky, 1993; Loewen, 1995; Marciano, 1997; Roediger, 1994; Said, 1993; Sochen, 1974; Spring, 1994; Zinn, 1980, 1990). Ironically, Hirsch poses the following question to readers: "How can we protect ourselves and our students from oversimplifications, lies, and scapegoating conspiracy theories?" (1996, p. 155). Unfortunately, he exonerates himself from any association with the conditions that he describes. In fact, the answer to this question is critical literacy, and not blind adherence to Hirsch's mythically neutral body of knowledge.[16]

Perhaps the most hypocritical aspect of Hirsch's work concerns the fact that while he is engaged in a debate over cultural politics, he considers himself neutral—"non-ideological." As a staunch **modernist,** he believes an objectively verifiable reality can be achieved, and that the Core Knowledge Sequence is the sole key to that apolitical world. The summary and conclusion of his newest book begins with the subtitle "Practical Effectiveness, Not Ideology" (1996, p. 215). Along these same lines, consider the following quotes:

> In a conflict between ideology and reality, reality always trumps. (1996, p. 104)

> In good medical research, too, practical aims decide what questions get asked and what money gets allocated, but the answers and the results of this applied research are dictated by the realities, not the preferences . . . it [reality] determines what actually happens in the world. (1996, p. 128)

> My main task will be to show that the larger, oft-repeated criticisms of objective tests are *not* valid. (1996, p. 177)[17]

> One barrier to developing such expertise has been the politicization of educational issues that are at the bottom technical rather than political. (1996, p. 66)

> But it would be a grave oversimplification of my theme if the reader inferred that this book merely invites a revival of our Enlightenment educational traditions in order to counterbalance our too-dominant Romantic ones. That is certainly part of my message, but to overstress it would misleadingly suggest that the main issue is philosophical or ideological. On the contrary, the main issue is practical. (1996, p. 216)

> This is the most democratically conceived curriculum ever, it's not ideological. (*Merrow Report,* 1996)

In Hirsch's world, as practice is removed from theory, which is then removed from ideology, education becomes a technical, rather than political and ethical, issue.

In the twisted spirit of **positivism,** Hirsch would have us believe that, "Science is a neutral servant of our educational purposes" (1987, p. 216). However, it is only the research that supports his basic premise that is deemed legitimate and objective:

> No one can be confident that preselection is not driving his or her own interpretation of scientific research. Yet when there is a clear conflict between widely accepted mainstream science and the science cited by educational experts, it seems reasonable to conclude that mainstream science, being more diversified and disinterested, is more likely to be correct. (1996, p. 71)

In other words, the research that he cites from so-called refereed scientific books (1996, p. 182) is mainstream and thus acceptable, while he describes the rest as follows:

impractical, misleading, and simply untrustworthy (1996, p. 83)
nonrefereed (1996, p. 93)
clothed in the authority of science (1996, p. 131)
quasi-scientific (1996, p. 246)
preponderous rhetoric (1996, p. 246).

I am not arguing that informative research is an impossibility. My point is that we need to vigilantly recognize its inherently ideological nature. Hirsch lacks both this recognition (except for when he refers to research that contests his own position) and a sufficient amount of empirical studies to support his arguments. In the end, he creates the very dogma that he vociferously rejects.

Hirsch also wants us to believe that knowledge is objective and neutral, "at least in those areas like math and science and the basic facts of history and geography, which, unlike sex education, are not and should not be subjects of controversy" (1996, p. 37). Rejecting any claim to a universal foundation for truth and culture, as well as any claim to objectivity, critical pedagogy reveals that educational practices and knowledge are always produced within particular social and historical conditions, and therefore any understanding of their production and dissemination must be accompanied by an investigation of their relation to ideology and power. The question is: Whose interpretations of the world, whose "basic facts of history," for example, will be used? Responding to the criticism that his core knowledge list is exclusionary, Hirsch tells us that many national cultures (e.g., Spain, Germany, France, etc.) are neglected in our national vocabulary, but we are compelled to keep English culture as the dominant part of our national vocabulary for purely functional reasons (1988a, p. 107).

By insisting that science, knowledge, and education can be neutral, Hirsch works to hide the ideological nature of his own work. For example, he changed the name of his agenda from common cultural literacy to core knowledge. His public reasoning is that, "'Cultural' raised too many extraneous questions, whereas the term 'Core Knowledge' better described the chief aim of the reform" (1996, p. 13). However, the strategic use of *core* in place of *cultural* functions to obfuscate the ideological nature of Hirsch's curricula, as if *core* implies universality. The use of *cultural*, on the other hand, begs potentially transformative questions about everyday politics, especially the inherently political nature of schooling.

Hirsch's View of Language: In Defense of a Standard Language

E. D. Hirsch believes that in order to promote effective nationwide communications and meet the demands of modern technology and bureaucratic and economic structures, the United States is compelled to use a linguistic standard (1988a, pp. 2, 75, 92). He celebrates the idea that this country has "fortunately" been handed down a written language (grammar, spelling, and pronunciation), one that articulates such important documents as the Declaration of Independence and the Constitution (1988a, p. 91). He states that, "Although standard written English has no intrinsic superiority to other languages and dialects, its stable written forms have now standardized the oral forms of the language spoken by educated Americans" (1988a, p. 3).

Hirsch asserts that the best and most efficient way to "standardize and stabilize" a language is to emulate the European experience, that is, "fix upon a single dialectal norm, freeze its grammar at a particular time, fix standard spellings, and fix pronunciations that are reasonably well represented by the spellings" (1988a, p. 77). The language, except for the addition of new vocabulary, becomes "an immovable, almost unchanging substance" (1988a, p. 93). Advocating for unity, Hirsch believes that a national language is capable of "overcoming" the plethora of regional and ethnic variations of communication (1988a, pp. 82, 93).

The Rejection of Bilingual Education. Embracing the Jeffersonian notion of pluralism, which cherishes a diversity of traditions, values, and points of view, Hirsch nonetheless rejects the idea of bi/multilingualism in the United States, especially in the schools. Citing what he refers to as "our most ardent supporters of cultural pluralism"—among them, William James and Horace Kallen—he contends that they in fact did not support multilingualism but rather imagined that diversity in the United States would flourish within the parameters of a common language— "literate English" (1988a, p. 96).

Hirsch believes that foreign languages are only appropriate if they are not learned and utilized at the expense of the national standard. He insists that linguistic pluralism on a national level would bring about "cultural fragmentation, civil antagonism, illiteracy, and economic-technological ineffectualness" (1988a, p. 92):[18]

> Toleration of diversity is at the root of our society, but encouragement of multilingualism is contrary to our traditions and extremely unrealistic. Defenders of multilingualism should not assume that our Union has been preserved once and for all by the Civil War, and that we can afford to disdain the cultural and educational vigilance exercised by other modern nations. To think so complacently is to show a fundamental misunderstanding of the role of national literacy in creating and sustaining modern civilization. (1988a, p. 93)

Using China to illustrate his point, Hirsch concludes that because of its diversity and multilingualism ("a polyglot nation of mutually unintelligible dialects") it is unable to function successfully as a modern industrial and economic unit (1988a, p. 76).

The Relationship Between Language and Culture. Equating language with national culture—"A nation's language can be regarded as a part of its culture, or conversely, its culture can be regarded as the totality of its language" (1988a, p. 84)—Hirsch insists that people in this country need to learn not only the grammar of standard English but also the "national vocabulary." As such, notable names and events can be conceived of as both part of our culture and as part of our shared language. For Hirsch, formal education should play an important role in this process of linguistic and cultural transmission by maintaining communicative standards as presented in national dictionaries, spelling books, pronunciation guides, grammar texts, and his Core Knowledge Sequence.

Reading Between the Lines: What to Make of/Take from Hirsch's Perspectives on Language. When addressing language, Hirsch completely ignores the plethora of research that articulates the importance of multilingual education. Perhaps the most salient contradiction to his idea of core knowledge is his disregard for the realities of knowledge transfer (let alone linguistic, cognitive, and literacy transfer) from one's first language to the second, as supported in the research literature on bilingual education (Carrell, Devine, & Eskey, 1990; Cummins, 1979, 1981, 1988, 1994; Gass & Schachter, 1989; Gee, 1996; Hakuta, 1986; McLaughlin, 1987; O'Malley & Chamot, 1993; Reynolds, 1991).[19] In other words, why should a fourth grader who speaks Spanish not continue to learn content at his or her age level, rather than waiting until his or her English abilities are high enough—a matter of years. Through the lens of his own twisted logic about a critical period deadline to acquiring cultural literacy, Hirsch seems to want the student to miss the boat. Otherwise, he would be an avid supporter of bilingual education.

Although Hirsch claims to embrace Jeffersonian pluralism, which has encouraged a diversity of traditions, values, and opinions, he neglects to explore the inextricable relationship between these cultural phenomena and language—language being codified culture. Recognizing the fact that all of us inhabit numerous local cultures and adopt hundreds of small-scale cultural roles within the large-scale culture, and claiming that the American tradition encourages the development of all these local cultures and associations as a matter of fundamental legal and ethical principle—"Our code is designed to protect local and individual interests against the wider nation, just as it is designed to protect minorities against majorities" (1988a, p. 97)—he nonetheless fails to understand how language mediates such cultural differences. He also ignores how languages are all socially and ideologically developed, context specific, and always in need of interpersonal negotiation for clarity of intent. For example, when I say "good education," and William Bennett uses the exact same words, we are in fact talking about two very different things. Hirsch's final chapter, "Critical Guide to Educational Terms and Phrases," in his newest book (1996), provides a case and point: Few of the definitions, in which he inserts his own take on these terms, fit my own interpretations and uses. Nonetheless, Hirsch refutes this link between ideology and language: "But whether a word is learned by targeted practice or by the contextual method of enriched language use, its actual meaning is, for the most part, just a brute fact" (1996, p. 111).[20]

It is curious to note that in reference to other English-speaking countries that protest the foreign, all-too-English character of traditional elements of words such as *Achilles, Scrooge, Falstaff,* and *Cinderella,* Hirsch describes such dissent as "grumblings" and argues that "they [such words] are probably here to stay, because they form a useful basis for international exchanges in English" (1988a, p. 75). It appears that no matter what the country may be, for him the cultural associations embedded in core knowledge, for all those who have been exposed to it, are universal. Although he argues that there is a need to understand more than simply the words, but the context as well (1988a, p. 3), he fails to recognize the realities of multiple cultural interpretations within a single language (realities defined by social class, gender, race, etc.), let alone across national borders.

Hirsch admits that education helps to keep the national language stable by holding it to standards that are set forth in national dictionaries, spelling books, pronunciation guides, and grammars; however, he once again fails to adequately theorize how dominant languages are implicated in the suppression of others. He simply exonerates himself from the accusation of perpetuating injustice by claiming that the national standard and literacy belong to everyone. Hirsch's reluctance to name this process of silencing is evident in the assertion that linguistic uniformity inside nations is a "self-conscious political and educational arrangement" (1988a, p. 71). His use of the term *political* is ambiguous: If it refers to the democratic process, then it is extremely problematic—as stated in the U.S. Constitution, there is no official national language. As such, Spanish, especially considering the conquest of Mexican territory and Puerto Rico, is by no means a "foreign" language, as Hirsch would have us believe.

The use of "self-conscious arrangement" in the above statement is also an inaccurate description. A quick look at the histories of exclusion of such groups as Puerto Ricans, Native Hawaiians, African-, Asian- Mexican-, and Native-Americans in the United States, and it becomes obvious that the use of "self-conscious arrangement" is merely a distorted and euphemistic portrayal of ideological and physical domination.

Hirsch also neglects to recognize the fact that even in the cases where English is one's primary language, success is not so easily guaranteed. For example, African-Americans have been speaking English for centuries and still remain socially, economically, and politically subordinated (Macedo, 1994). So, what are the motives behind this leading proponent of common culture's attitudes toward language? Perhaps the answer to this question is evident in his use of the terms *overcoming* (1988a, p. 93), *eliminating* (1988a, p. 77), and *transcending* (1988a, p. 82) when discussing the fate of regional and ethnic variations of language. He seems to have no real need for such systems of cultural expression.

Hirsch's claim to a language of universal communication reflects a major flaw in current mainstream efforts in multicultural education: Many educators, as well intentioned as they may be, believe that diversity can be negotiated solely through standard English. If multicultural education is to really come to fruition, then, instead of imposing a mythical standard, it is important that students learn to cross linguistic borders of difference in order to understand others and to make themselves understood. Although he claims to support multiculturalism, Hirsch works against it. Although he admits that, "The acquisition of literacy is a non-natural, culture-specific process that is not universal" (1996, p. 147), he nonetheless argues that, "The complexities of classroom instruction are so great, and the cultural and personal variables so numerous, that it is the better part of wisdom not to advocate highly specific classroom practices" (p. 230).[21]

Such a position renders null and void the pedagogical importance of the social construction of literacies, learning and language styles, and cognitive skills (Au & Jordan, 1981; Bakhtin, 1981; Gee, 1996; Giglioli, 1972; Heath, 1983; Holland & Quinn, 1995; Lankshear, 1997; Lee, 1992; Michaels, 1981; Moll, 1990; Schieffelin & Ochs, 1992; Voloshinov, 1986; Vygotsky, 1978; Wertsch, 1991). Hirsch thus disregards how we improve teaching by accommodating and building from such roots.[22] These differences are overshadowed by an unrelenting adherence to **dominant discourse,** a position that is fundamentally antidemocratic and antimulticultural.[23]

Conclusion

As responsible practitioners it is important that we explore the multiplicity of theoretical and practical insights from across the spectrum of developing and established multicultural educational camps. These models have an enormous implicit and explicit impact on the national struggles over education in the United States. However, as this particular literature review (an exercise in critical pedagogy) illustrates, it is crucial that we not simply adopt at face value such theoretical and practical ideas. Because of the ways in which people, such as E. D. Hirsch Jr., present their agendas in a deceivingly positive light, we need to engage, critically appropriate, and reinvent these works. This entails developing the necessary presence of mind and consequential critical understanding of the sociocultural context within which such theories and practical applications were generated (Bartolomé, 1994). It also demands that we constantly question the plethora of theories, including our own, to ensure that they do not simply become a new totalizing narrative, a new colonial model.

It is crucial that teachers be reflective practitioners such that they develop a theoretical understanding of culture, multicultural education, and language. We should avoid Hirsch's notion that something can be "too theory-ridden to be reliable beacons for public policy" (1996, p. 7). It is my belief that a multicultural pedagogy should embrace theory—understanding the why of what we do—creativity, and resistance to domination as positive cultural acts. It should also engender social transformation through hope, human agency, and an undying belief (regardless of the complexities and contradictions inherent in a politics of difference) in achieving social and educational justice through real democratic struggle and praxis.

Notes

1. This failure to provide a more detailed definition of culture is consistent throughout Hirsch's entire body of work.

2. When Hirsch does acknowledge opposition to dominant cultural practices and institutions, he summarily dismisses or simply romanticizes them. Consider the following example, which contradicts his valorization of the separation of church and state: "Secularists who deplore any public references to God and regard benevolent social ideas as ultimate civil principles, are, in the end, just another species of hyphenated Americans—secularist-Americans—who form a large class but acquiesce in the second side of the American hyphen like most of us who sing the national hymn, pledge allegiance ('under God') to the flag, know that all are 'endowed by their Creator' with inalienable rights" (1988a, p. 99). In this case, all those who work for change are thought to nonetheless abide by the contrived patriotism/loyalty that, according to Hirsch, underlies "our civil ethos."

3. The example that I have provided in this chapter speaks of Roman cosmopolitanism. In fact, Hirsch makes references to both. My critiques of Greek civilization also apply to the Romans.

4. Hirsch differentiates between culture and social class in this statement, as if class, which shapes our physical beings, values, attitudes, social relations, and language (hooks, 1994), does not significantly define the everyday/cultural realities of people.

5. It comes as no surprise that Hirsch looks to the rich and the press for support. The twist is that he speaks of these forces as if they are outside of, rather than the constructors of mainstream society: "The special advantage of private philanthropy is its ability to *oppose* received opinion and resist the dominant tide" (1996, p. 64); "The press is the best agency for challenging the intellectual status quo and for bringing issues out into the daylight" (1996, p. 68).

6. Hirsch actually argues that strategic teaching—that is, getting students to take control of their own learning—is detrimental. He (1996) states, "In fact, there are good grounds for suspecting that a strong emphasis on metacognitive instruction can sometimes hinder student progress, particularly among slow or disadvantaged children" (p. 139). "Any extra burden of self-conscious monitoring is much heavier for slower students than it is for students who have already automated many processes" (p. 141). In other words, give them the robot track. Hirsch actually argues that, "We must not accept the claim that knowing how to learn (which is an abstract skill that does not even exist) is more important than having a broad foundation of factual knowledge that really does enable further learning" (1996, p. 216).

7. He erroneously suggests that critical pedagogy assumes an antiknowledge posture. As argued in Chapter 1 of this book, critical education simply approaches objects of knowledge in a very different way than that of a pedagogy of transmission. The basic reasoning is that facts are fine, but we need to understand where they come from. In many cases, Hirsch simply equates critical (as in ideological analysis) with the depoliticized notion of higher-order thinking skills.

8. When discussing race, Hirsch (1996) states, "Researchers were able to factor out the influences of poverty, race, single-parent households, and a lack of parental education in order to isolate the effects of school changing alone. Even with these adverse influences factored out" (p. 35), Hirsch, perhaps subconsciously, believes that race, rather than racism, is what has the adverse effect.

9. The only time that he mentions any real concern for discrimination is in reference to standardized testing: "Humanists who would be horrified at the stereotyping of people take delight in stereotyping objective tests" (1996, p. 191).

10. It is important to note that all the countries that Hirsch praises for having what he refers to as "whole-class instruction" combined with a "knowledge-based curriculum," have enormous troubles with racism, xenophobia, sexism, homophobia, poverty, and other forms of social injustice.

11. For example, Hirsch equates boredom and humiliation in the classroom with a lack of shared understanding, with no analysis of oppressive social interactions and identities in the educational process (1996, p. 25).

12. He (1996) claims that Jonathan Kozol's book, *Savage Inequalities*, "dramatized" the injustices inflicted on the poor (p. 5). The word "dramatized," in place of "clearly articulates," acts as a way to suggest that Kozol exaggerates the realities of the oppressed, thus showing Hirsch's own ideological proclivities.

13. He also equates the need for educational change in the United States to faulty economic theories that have, in his mind, led to the fall of communism (1996, p. 2).

14. For an alternative list, see Macedo's (1994) chapter, "Our Common Culture," in *Literacies of Power: What Americans Are Not Allowed to Know*. Boulder: Westview.

15. During his interview on the *Merrow Report*, he argued that some students were "behind for innate reasons, or cultural, I mean disadvantaged . . . some kids are lazier than others." In his most recent book, he also states that, "The schools have recently been quite reluctant to teach oral grammar or orthoepy,

on the mistaken assumption that standard oral speech is 'white' speech rather than simply standard educated speech" (1996, p. 274). This statement implies that all other languages are not educated speech.

16. He also distorts the public's impression of research in stating that, "But the research literature offers not one example of successful implementation of progressivist methods in a carefully controlled longitudinal study" (1996, p. 216).

17. Hirsch (1996) states, "I will use the term 'standardized test' to mean any objective test, or combination of objective and performance tests, that yields the same score for the same performance, no matter who is doing the scoring" (1996, p. 179). "I view the war on standardized tests as mainly a disheartened, scapegoating attempt to shoot the messenger that is bringing the bad news. Educators would hardly be so preoccupied with attacking standardized tests, and blaming them for the ineffectiveness and inequity of American schooling, if those machine-scored messengers were bringing less depressing bulletins, or if educators had workable ideas about how to make the results better" (p. 180).

18. Hirsch insists that with two dominant languages inside a nation, "neither can yield to the other except by strife or vigorous intervention in the educational system" (1988a, p. 93). He rejects the argument that countries such as Switzerland are prime examples of the possibilities of multilingualism, contending that Switzerland's apparent success at "multi*literacy* (as distinct from multilingualism)" is the result of "a small, intensive, centralized educational system that, coupled with universal military service, enables the Swiss to communicate with one another despite their linguistic handicaps" (1988a, p. 92).

19. The list of research, books, and edited collections that support the idea of transfer is far too extensive to include here. The point is that Hirsch sees no need in engaging this work in any depth or mentioning it at all.

20. Again, when the research supports his point of view, Hirsch happily, or perhaps unconsciously, contradicts himself. Although he argues that meaning is fixed, he has an about-face when the idea of constructivism supports his position: "The only way a student can understand what a teacher or anyone else is saying is through a complex, sometimes strenuous activity of constructing meaning from words. Hearing a lecture—in the event that one is understanding it—requires an active construction of meaning. Listening, like reading, is far from being a passive, purely receptive activity" (1996, p. 134). Hirsch never explains what this process, the production of meaning, entails.

21. Knowing virtually nothing about language acquisition, Hirsch makes a stab at the universal nature of developing speech. He states, "In sum, language development, psychomotor development, and (to a more variable degree) basic conceptual development do appear to follow a temporal sequence that can reasonably be called 'natural' because it is a sequence that has been shown to be transcultural and universal" (1996, p. 88). "The child's acquisition of oral-aural speech is an evolutionary based, natural process, universal in all human groups" (1996, p. 147). However, because of his ignorance in the field of linguistics, he is unable to reconcile the structural/poststructural (nature versus nurture) binarism. What he argues should be a scientific battle over reality collapses into dogma.

22. Virtually denying the cultural aspects of learning, Hirsch argues that play is the same across cultures, "is universal in children" (1996, p. 87). He needs to

read the research (e.g., Roopnarine, Johnson, and Hooper, 1994) that explores the diverse ways in which different cultures play and interpret play.

23. The list of researchers who have investigated this connection is far too extensive to include here. The point is that the socially constructed literacies are virtually ignored. In fact, at one point he contradicts his acknowledgment that literacy is a "non-natural culture-specific process that is not universal" (p. 147), stating that, "Variations in ability are caused by individual differences that are innate, hence natural, and beyond remedy" (1996, p. 87).

Afterword

A Pedagogy of Entrapment

Donaldo Macedo

Against a landscape of unrelenting assault on public schools and public school teachers, Pepi Leistyna's book *Presence of Mind: Education and the Politics of Deception* is not only timely, but it also brilliantly addresses the fundamental question that reactionary educators and politicians have conspicuously failed to raise. In Massachusetts, "fifty-nine percent of 1,800 education students taking first-ever certification exams in April have failed."[1] While there has been a barrage of teacher bashing in the media and political circles, very few people are asking the simple yet crucial question: Who has trained these teachers? In fact, even when the chairman of the State Board of Education, James F. Carlin, demanded "almost immediate feedback from college professors on how schools of education can better prepare graduate students [with the threat that] he will not tolerate defensiveness or oblique educational rhetoric,"[2] the chairman of the board got precisely what he would not tolerate: defensiveness and oblique educational rhetoric.

Unfortunately, the chairman of the board is betrayed by his own rhetoric to the extent that he is part and parcel of a social order that supports a form of education designed to deskill and domesticate teachers only later to blame them for the skills that they do not have and the general failure of public schools. This "politics of deception," as Leistyna calls it, is very much like a pedagogy of entrapment where the system requires of students, including teachers, what it does not give them. That is, schools of education, by and large, are informed by an ideology characteristic of the Trilateral Commission whose members, among them the former President Jimmy Carter, referred to schools as "institutions responsible for the indoctrination of the young."[3] As Noam Chomsky describes, the Trilateral Commission argued that schools should be institutions for indoctrination, "for imposing obedience, for blocking the possibility of independent thought, and they play an institutional role in a system of control and coercion."⁴ This pedagogy of containment invariably has given rise to an instrumentalist and domesticating education that sets the stage for the anesthetization of the mind, as poet John Ashbery (1977) eloquently captured in "What Is Poetry?":

> *In school*
> *All the thoughts got combed out:*
> *What was left was like a field.*⁵

The educational "comb" for those teachers who have blindly accepted the dominant ideology on education is reflected in an instrumentalist literacy characterized by mindless, meaningless drills and exercises given "in preparation for multiple choice exams and writing gobbledygook in imitation of the psycho-babble that surrounds them."⁶

In *Presence of Mind: Education and the Politics of Deception*, Pepi Leistyna not only critiques the domesticating nature of instrumentalist approaches to education that are designed, along the lines of the Trilateral Commission, to produce readers who meet the basic requirements of our contemporary society, but he also points to another culprit found in the highest level of literacy: specialism and hyperspecialization. The instrumentalist approach to literacy, even at the highest level of specialism, functions to domesticate the consciousness via a constant disarticulation between the narrow reductionistic reading of one's field of specialization and the reading of the universe within which one's specialism is situated. This inability to link the reading of the word and the world is part of a literacy for stupidification that, at best, produces semiliterates. Thus, we should not at all be surprised that 59 percent of teachers who took the first state-mandated certification exam failed. In fact, this so-called teacher failure serves as a prime example of the highest level of literacy for stupidification. In other words, at the lowest level of instrumental literacy, a semiliterate needs the word but is unable to read the world. At the highest level of instrumental literacy achieved via specialization, the semiliterate is able to read the text of his or her specialization, but is ignorant of all other bodies of knowledge that constitute the world of knowing. This semiliterate specialist was characterized by Ortega y Gasset (1932) as a "learned ignoramus." That is to say, "He is not learned, for he is formally ignorant of all that does not enter into his specialty; but neither is he ignorant, because he is a 'scientist' and 'knows' very well his own tiny portion of the universe."[7]

Instead of bashing teachers we should put the blame squarely on institutions such as schools of education that have trained them in an approach that abstracts methodological issues from their ideological contexts, and consequently ignores the interrelationship between sociopolitical structures of a society and the act of learning and knowing. In part, the exclusion of social, cultural, and political dimensions from learning and teaching practices gives rise to an ideology of cultural reproduction that produces individuals who are deskilled and acritical—without much independent thought.

In *Presence of Mind: Education and the Politics of Deception*, Pepi Leistyna convincingly demonstrates the aversion in the culture of schools of education, in general, and at the Harvard Graduate School of Education (HGSE) in particular, toward critical social theory and the development of independent critical thought. This is abundantly clear in an HGSE professor's written comments on Pepi Leistyna's research paper:

> The assumption that ideological sophistication is a sign of cultural progress ignores the fact that many people just don't give a damn about this kind of complex verbalization. They may be temperamentally bent toward building, or singing, or hoeing corn. So the problem for me is to prevent the *over-interpretive egghead* from claiming a special corner on sacred (significant) knowledge—but still get his or her due. It always makes me a little wary about the extent to which the critical theorists (Freire, Giroux, etc.) appreciate the great range of talents of people who are not so much deluded by all this professional garbage as they are bent toward other enterprises that have little to do with complex elaboration of language. So they often cannot protect themselves, either from specialized professors of literacy or specialized professors of critical literacy.

This comes from a department, a culture in general, that pontificates about intellectual rigor and yet allows a graduate course on the politics of literacy to be taught without any reference to Freire. The syllabus for this course further revealed its hidden politics: The professor even allotted one week to cover the politics of literacy in Latin America without any reference to the renowned Brazilian educator. In the reading assignments for critical literacy, the most well-known critical literacy authors in the United States, such as Henry Giroux, bell hooks, Linda Brodkey, and Peter McLaren, were also missing. Not requiring students to read Freire in a graduate course on the politics of literacy, which covers both literacy in

Latin America and critical literacy, is tantamount to offering an introduction to linguistics without mentioning Noam Chomsky, or an introduction to British literature without mentioning William Shakespeare. Not only is this evidence of the fear that many professors feel toward Freire's critical theories, but it also points to an extreme level of academic dishonesty and the ahistorical nature of the course. One may disagree with Freire's theories, but one cannot arrogantly ignore the best-known literacy educator in the world. Failure to expose students of literacy to such work is not only a form of anti-intellectualism but also a de facto censorship. Here is where the HGSE faculty mantra of objectivity and scientific rigor is subverted by a more insidious force: ideology. But what can one expect from a culture in which another professor responded to Freire's death in the following manner: "Freire's coming to Harvard would have made twenty students very happy, while making the rest of the students extremely unhappy. Now he is dead and we are all unhappy."

This comment regarding Freire's death not only epitomizes the level of dehumanization and insensitivity that exists at the highest level of education, but it also points to the arrogance (which borders on stupidification—what Leistyna refers to as "the arrogance of ignorance") ascribed to many professors by the sheer power, resources, and authority of institutions such as Harvard. Many of these professors' identities are tied solely to Harvard's prestige, which gives many of them the illusion that they can dismiss any body of knowledge, views, or perspectives that does not conform to their preestablished ways of seeing the world. In fact, if one applies rigorous standards of the academy, one soon realizes (1) that, with a handful of exceptions, most of the professors at HGSE are not among the most-cited educators in the United States, much less in the world; (2) that their work has done little to advance the present theoretical debate in the field; and (3) that they have contributed few earth-shaking ideas that might help to raise schools—particularly urban schools, with their outrageously high dropout rate and high numbers of students who graduate as semiliterates—out of their moribund condition. On the contrary, most of these schools are very much informed by the positivistic and management models that characterize the very ideologies and cultural practices to which Freire was in opposition all his life.

A permanent feature of the HGSE faculty discourse is the call for objectivity and scientific rigor; this can be seen, for example, in the comments on Leistyna's term paper on the political nature of bilingual education: "These are unsupported politically motivated claims! [The professor called for] a more linguistic analysis." As Leistyna recounts, this same professor told him: "I hope you have been reading some hard science." When I told Linda Brodkey, an English professor at the University of California in San Diego, she laughingly asked: "Why doesn't this professor use her scientific methods to determine what the scientists in the Harvard yard think about the scientific research conducted at the Harvard Graduate School of Education?" She later added that, "At best she will be told that they don't know of any and, at worse, she will be an object of laughter." By and large, the laughter is justified, because academic work in schools of education is often restricted to derivative analysis in which students, and sometimes professors, are reduced to working with secondary and tertiary texts. Take the doctoral program in Language and Literacy at HGSE, for instance. A student can earn a doctorate in language studies without any exposure to contemporary linguistic theories. In fact, to my knowledge, there is not a single course in linguistic theory through which students could, on the one hand, be exposed to contemporary theories in the field of linguistics and, on the other hand, develop tools to understand how theory informs the complex universe of language acquisition, development, and use.

When the suggestion was made that the program should begin to offer at least a module in linguistics, the idea was dismissed with the claim that students did not really need linguistics. Instead, the graduate students in the Language and Literacy Program organize workshops for those students who come into the program without any knowledge of linguistics. This position not only makes a mockery of the complex field of study that informs all language realizations, but it also points to the atheoretical posture of those professors who hide their anti-intellectualism in the false call for scientific rigor.

Given the anti-intellectual posture of many School of Education professors, a posture that is manifested either through censorship of certain bodies of knowledge or through the disarticulation between the theories of discipline and the empirically driven and self-contained studies, it becomes obvious why these pseudoscientists

do not challenge the territorialization of university intellectual activity or in any way risk undermining the status and core beliefs of their fields. The difference [for scientists] is that this blindness or reluctance often contradicts the intellectual imperatives of the very theories they espouse. Indeed, only a theorized discipline can be an effective site for general social critique— that is, a discipline actively engaged in self-criticism, a discipline that is a locus for struggle, a discipline that renews and revises its awareness of its history, a discipline that inquires into its differential relations with other

academic fields, and a discipline that examines its place in the social formation and is willing to adapt its writing practices to suit different social
functions.[8]

As the theoretical requirements make abundantly clear, the decision
of the Language and Literacy Program faculty not to expose students to
the theoretical linguistics that inform their field of study, and the arrogant dismissal of Freire's social critical theories of literacy, unveil the ideology behind the prescription that Leistyna should have been "reading
some hard science." They expose the almost illusory and schizophrenic
educational practice in which "the object of interpretation and the content of the interpretive discourse are considered appropriate subjects
for discussion and scrutiny, but the interests of the interpreter and the
discipline and society he or she lives are not."[9]

The disarticulation between the interpretive discourse and the interests of the interpreter is often hidden in the false call for objectivity that
denies the dialectical relationship between subjectivity and objectivity.
The false call for objectivity is deeply ingrained in a positivistic method
of inquiry. In effect, this has resulted in an epistemological stance in
which scientism and methodological refinement are celebrated while
"theory and knowledge are subordinated to the imperatives of efficiency
and technical mastery, and history is reduced to a minor footnote in the
priorities of 'empirical' scientific inquiry."[10] Perhaps it is this devaluation
of history that enabled a professor at HGSE to tell the international student who was a doctoral candidate "not to cite too many historical
sources. In the United States, any research that is more than five years
old is considered dated." The blind celebration of empiricism has created a culture in which pseudoscientists, particularly in schools of education, who engage in a form of "naive empiricism," believe "that facts
are not human statements about the world but aspects of the world itself."[11] According to Michael Schudson (1978):

> This view was insensitive to the ways in which the "world" is something
> people construct by the active play of their minds and by their acceptance
> of conventional—not necessarily "true" ways of seeing and talking. Philoso-
> phy, the history of science, psychoanalysis, and social science have taken
> great pains to demonstrate that human beings are cultural animals who
> know and see and hear the world through socially constructed filters.[12]

It is the same celebration of research methodologies over theory and
knowledge that led some senior professors at HGSE to worry that the
Harvard Educational Review was becoming biased toward publishing

critical work that was, according to them, filled with "political rhetoric" rather than research-based scientific articles informed by empirical evidence. Two students on the board of the *Harvard Educational Review* told me that they were reprimanded by some senior professors because they were publishing too many works by Freire, Giroux, Macedo, and Aronowitz, among other critical writers. This not only represents a form of censorship through intimidation, but it is also a distortion of reality since the *Harvard Educational Review* historically has not been in the forefront of publishing critical works. What is really happening is that, through peer review, the works of some senior professors are being rejected while articles by Freire and other critical writers are being published. In other words, these professors seemed to feel that the referee process through peer review can only be considered objective if it reproduces the dominant ideology and maintains the status quo. This is where the call for objectivity and scientific rigor is subverted by the weight of its own ideology.

These professors do not realize that there is a large body of critical literature that interrogates the very nature of what they consider research. Critical writers such as Donna Haraway,[13] Linda Brodkey, Roger Fowler, Greg Myers, among others, have painstakingly demonstrated the erroneous claim of "scientific" objectivity that permeates all forms of empirical work in social sciences. According to Linda Brodkey (1996), "Scientific objectivity has too often and for too long been used as an excuse to ignore a social and hence, political practice in which women and people of color, among others, are dismissed as legitimate subjects of research."[14]

The blind belief in objectivity not only provides pseudoscientists with a safe haven from which they can attempt to prevent the emergence of counterdiscourses that interrogate "the hegemony of positivism and empiricism,"[15] but it is also a practice that generates a form of folk theory concerning objectivity believed only by nonscientists. In other words, as Brodkey would so eloquently put it, "that any and all knowledge, including that arrived at empirically, is necessarily partial, that is, both an incomplete and an interested account of whatever is envisioned."[16] In fact, what these pseudoscientists consider research, that is, work based on quantitative evaluation results, can never escape the social construction that generated these models of analysis from which the theoretical concepts are always shaped by the pragmatics of the society that devised these evaluation models in the first place.[17] If the results are presented as facts that were originally determined by a particular ideology, these facts cannot in themselves illuminate issues that lie outside of their ideological construction.[18]

I would warn educators that these evaluation models can provide answers that are correct and nevertheless without truth. A study that concludes that African-American students perform way below white mainstream students in reading is correct, but such a conclusion tells us very little about the material conditions with which African-American students work in the struggle against racism, educational tracking, and the systematic negation and devaluation of their histories. I would propose that the correct conclusion rests in a full understanding, which Leistyna provides, of the ideological elements that generate and sustain the cruel reality of racism and economic oppression. Thus, an empirical study will produce conclusions without truth if it is disarticulated from the sociocultural reality within which the subjects of the study are situated. For example, an empirical study designed to assess reading achievement of children who live in squalid conditions must factor in the reality faced by these children as accurately described by Jonathan Kozol (1996):

> Crack-cocaine addiction and the intravenous use of heroin, which children I have met here call "the needle drug," are woven into the texture of existence in Mott Haven. Nearly 4,000 heroin injectors, many of whom are HIV-infected, live here. Virtually every child at St. Ann's knows someone, a relative or neighbor, who has died of AIDS, and most children here know many others who are dying now of the disease. One quarter of the women of Mott Haven who are tested in obstetric wards are positive for HIV. Rates of pediatric AIDS, therefore, are high.
>
> Depression is common among children in Mott Haven. Many cry a great deal but cannot explain exactly why. Fear and anxiety are common. Many cannot sleep. Asthma is the most common illness among children here. Many have to struggle to take in a good deep breath. Some mothers keep oxygen tanks, which children describe as "breathing machines," next to their children's beds. The houses in which these children live, two-thirds of which are owned by the City of New York, are often as squalid as the houses of the poorest children I have visited in rural Mississippi, but there is none of the greenness and the healing sweetness of the Mississippi countryside outside their windows, which are often barred as protection against thieves.[19]

An empirical study that neglects to incorporate in its design the cruel reality just described (and this is often the case in our supposedly classless society) will never be able to fully explain the reasons behind the poor performance of these children. Although pseudoscientists will go through great lengths to prevent their research methodologies from being contaminated by the social ugliness described by Kozol—so that they can safeguard their "objectivity" in, say, their study of under-achievement of children who live in ghettos—the residents of these ghettos have little difficulty understanding the root causes of their misery, described by a community resident named Maria:

> If you weave enough bad things into the fibers of a person's life—sickness and filth, old mattresses and other junk thrown in the streets, ugly ruined things and ruined people, a prison here, sewage there, drug dealers here, the homeless people over there, then give us the very worst schools anyone could think of, hospitals that keep you waiting for ten hours, police that don't show up when someone's dying . . . you can guess that life will not be very nice and children will not have much sense of being glad of who they are. Sometimes it feels like we have been buried six feet under their perceptions. This is what I feel they have accomplished.[20]

What Maria would probably say to researchers is that we do not need another doctoral dissertation to state what is so obvious to the people sentenced to live in this form of human misery. In other words, by locking children in material conditions that are oppressive and dehumanizing, we are invariably guaranteeing that they will be academic under-achievers. Once the underachievement is guaranteed by these oppressive conditions, it is then very easy for research studies (as described in *The Bell Curve*),[21] which, in the name of objectivity, are disarticulated from the political and social reality that have shaped and maintained these oppressive conditions, to conclude that blacks are genetically wired to be intellectually inferior to whites. Along the same lines, an empirical study that concludes that children who engage in dinner conversation with their parents and siblings achieve higher rates of success in reading is not only academically dishonest, but also misleading to the degree that it ignores the class and economic assumptions that all children are guaranteed daily dinners in the company of their parents and other siblings.

What generalizations can such a study make about the twelve million children who go hungry every day in the United States? What can a study of this type say to the thousands upon thousands of children who are homeless, who do not have a table, and who sometimes do not have food to put on the table that they do not have? A study that makes such sweeping and distorted generalizations about the role of dinner conversations in reading achievement says little about children whose houses are without heat in the winter, houses that reach dangerously cold conditions, leading a father of four children to remark: "You just cover up . . . and hope you wake up the next morning."[22] If the father really believes the study results, he will suggest to his children, after they have all made it through another freezing night alive, that they should have a conversation during dinner the next night since it will be helpful in their reading development should they be lucky enough to make it through another night alive. What dinner conversation would the Haitian immigrant, Abner Louima, have with his children after being brutally sodomized with a toilet plunger by two white policemen in a New York police precinct? Would his children's reading teacher include as part of his or her literacy development the savage acts committed by the white New York police against their father?

These questions make it clear how distorted empirical study results can be when they are disconnected from the sociocultural reality that informs the study to begin with. In addition, such distortion feeds into the development of stereotypes that, on the one hand, blame the victims for their own social misery and, on the other hand, rationalize the genetic inferiority hypotheses that are advanced by such pseudoscholars as Charles Murray and the former Harvard professor Richard Hernstein. Empirical studies often neglect to point out how easily statistics can be manipulated to take away the human face of the subjects of study through a process that not only dehumanizes, but also distorts and falsifies the reality.

The inability to link research with larger critical and social issues often prevents educators not only from engaging in a general critique of the social mission of their own educational enterprise, but also from acknowledging their roles as gatekeepers in order to reproduce the dominant social (dis)order. In *Presence of Mind: Education and the Politics of Deception,* Pepi Leistyna painstakingly demonstrates how schools of education obediently implement the Trilateral Commission's proposal that schools become "institutions for the indoctrination of the young."

Leistyna courageously denounces educators' complicity with the oppressive conditions of students, who by virtue of their race, ethnicity (what he refers to as "racenicity"), class, gender, and language are not treated with the dignity and respect they deserve. After reading *Presence of Mind,* one soon realizes that most of the so-called objective educators will become at best paternalistic missionaries or, at worst, literacy and poverty pimps who make a living from the human misery with which they are in ideological complicity. In short, *Presence of Mind* energetically reminds us about the social (dis)order that, according to Jean Paul Sartre, "sanctions misery, chronic hunger, ignorance, or, in general, subhumanity."[23]

The book pointedly unmasks educators who refuse to transform the ugliness of human misery, social injustices, and inequalities in the name of science and objectivity. These reactionary educators for domestication are the foot soldiers and cultural commissars of the present education malaise. The present so-called failure of public school teachers represents what Paulo Freire viewed as the ultimate victory of the system in that the cultural commissars who are responsible for educational policy are colonizers who, as Sartre so poignantly stated, "will change nothing and will serve no one, but will succeed only in finding moral comfort in malaise."[24]

Donaldo Macedo
Distinguished Professor of
Liberal Arts and Education

Notes

1. Ebbert, S. (1998). "Carlin Demands Teacher Strategy from Colleges." *The Boston Globe*, July, 3, p. B1.

2. Ebbert, op. cit., p. B1.

3. Chomsky, N. (1988). *Language and Politics*, C. P. Otero (ed.). New York: Black Rose Books. p. 681.

4. Chomsky, op. cit., p. 681.

5. Ashbery, J. (1977). "What Is Poetry." In: *Houseboat Days: Poems by John Ashbery.* New York: Penguin Books, p. 4.

6. Courts, P. L. (1991). *Literacy and Empowerment: The Meaning Makers.* South Hadley, MA: Bergin and Garvey. p. 4.

7. Gasset, O. (1932). *The Revolt of the Masses.* New York: Norton, p. 111.

8. Nelson, C. (1997). *Manifesto of a Tenured Radical.* New York: New York University Press. p. 19.

9. Nelson, op. cit., p. 19.

10. Giroux, H. (1983). *Theory and Resistance in Education: A Pedagogy for the Opposition.* South Hadley, MA: J. F. Bergin Publisher, p. 87.

11. Schudson, M. (1978). *Discovering the News: A Social History of American Newspapers.* New York: Basic Books. p. 6.

12. Schudson, op. cit., p. 6.

13. For a comprehensive and critical discussion of scientific objectivity, see Haraway, D. (1988). "Situated Knowledges: The Science Question in Feminism and the Privilege of Partial Pespective." *Feminist Studies*, Vol. 14, pp. 575–599.

14. Brodkey, L. (1996). *Writing Permitted in Designated Areas Only.* Minnesota: Minnesota University Press, p. 10.

15. Brodkey, op. cit., p. 8.

16. Brodkey, op. cit., p. 8.

17. Fowler, R. (1979). *Language and Control*. London: Routledge & Kegan Paul, p. 192.

18. Myers, G. (1986). "Reality, Consensus, and Reform in the Rhetoric of Composition Teaching." *College English*, Vol. 48, No. 2 (February).

19. Kozol, J. (1996). *Amazing Grace: The Lines and the Conscience of a Nation*. New York: Harper Perennial. p. 4.

20. Kozol, op. cit., p. 39.

21. Hernstein, R., & Murray, C. (1994). *The Bell Curve: Intelligence and Class Structure in American Life*. New York: The Free Press.

22. Kozol, J. (1996). *Amazing Grace: The Lines and the Conscience of a Nation*. New York: Harper Perennial, p. 39.

23. Sartre, J. P. (1965). "Introduction." In: *The Colonizer and the Colonized*. Boston: Beacon Press, pp. xxiv–xxv.

24. Sartre, op. cit., p. xxvi.

Glossary

My objective in providing these heuristics should not be misinterpreted as an endorsement of fixed definitions and the mechanical process of rote memorization. I am simply attempting to provide readers unfamiliar with this work with the necessary signposts to enter discussions based on my sense of semantic reality. Reflective reading should always be a challenge to push us beyond our immediate ability and understanding. As these ideas vary from author to author, instead of being uncritically consumed, they should be understood, linked to one's own experience, and subsequently re-created to fit one's particular needs in defining the world around them.

Americanization: Americanization is the socializing process through which individuals lose their cultural identity as the language, values, and beliefs of the dominant white majority are imposed. Within such a process schools are seen as an integral agent of assimilation.

Anticolonialism: Anticolonial theoretical frameworks and practices confront the ideologies, authority, discourses, and social relations that have driven the oppressive legacy of colonialism and imperialism that structure Western institutions, practices, knowledge, representations, and texts. I prefer the use of *anti* as opposed to *post* because *post* implies that colonization is finished, which it is not.

Banking model of education: The banking model of education occurs when teachers perceive students as empty containers that need to be filled with preestablished bodies of knowledge. The narrowly defined facts and pieces of information that are transmitted are often disconnected from both teachers' and students' sociocultural realities. Students are thus treated as objects that are acted upon, rather than as knowledgeable participants in the construction of deep and meaningful learning experiences.

Commodification: Commodification is the process by which culture is increasingly being held captive by the materialistic logic of capitalism in which everything/everybody is reduced to objects/commodities and thus to its/their market value. The consequence of this process is that people become uncritical tools of production and consumption—commodified. In this sense, schools function merely as adjuncts to corporations and the marketplace.

Counterdiscourse (countervailing ideologies, counterhegemonic practices): Counterdiscourses are languages of critique, demystification, and agency capable of contesting dominant oppressive ideologies and practices.

Critical thinking (critical consciousness/critical inquiry): Not to be confused with what is traditionally thought of as the higher-order thinking skills (problem-solving skills), critical in this sense implies being able to understand, analyze, pose questions, and affect and effect the sociopolitical and economic realities that shape our lives.

Cultural capital: Cultural capital refers to Pierre Bourdieu's concept that different forms of cultural knowledge, such as language, modes of social interaction, beliefs, and meaning, are valued hierarchically in society. Critical pedagogues argue that only those characteristics and practices (i.e., cultural wealth) of the dominant paradigm will facilitate academic achievement within mainstream schools that reflect the dominant exclusionary ideology.

Cultural relativism: Cultural relativism argues that no culture is better or worse than another, that they are simply different. The problem with cultural relativism is that the presupposition is that all cultures exist on a level playing field, rather than within unequal relations of power that value certain identities at the exclusion of others. An additional problem with this framework is that it denies the possibility for taking an ethical stance; for example, Adolf Hitler's cultural reality is not simply different in a way that should be romanticized.

Cultural reproduction: Critical social theorists argue that dominant ideologies and knowledge are built into social institutions that both privilege and exclude particular perspectives, voices, authorities, and representations. Within theories of cultural reproduction, schools, teachers, and curricula are viewed as mechanisms of ideological control that work to reproduce and maintain dominant beliefs, values, norms, and oppressive practices. This reproductive process is mediated, in part, through the hidden curriculum—the hidden agenda of maintaining the status quo through specific schooling practices. However, contemporary interpretations of reproduction theory do perceive culture as ever shifting and forming, and, as such, there is always room for teacher and student agency.

Cultural worker: A cultural worker (transformative intellectual or public intellectual), in the best light, is an educator who critically engages learning (wherever it may take place) with the goal of working pedagogically and politically to ensure the development of a socially responsible citizenry and a critical, multicultural democracy. However, in the negative sense, public figures, such as talk hosts, are also cultural workers in that their interpretations can shape the ways in which different cultural groups interact by distorting the ways in which identities are depicted or represented in the mainstream.

Culture (cultural politics): Refuting the modernist notion of positivism, which, through claims to objectivity, truth, and certainty, defends a scientific basis for the study of culture, critical pedagogy focuses on the idea that cultures are always produced within particular social and historical conditions, and that any understanding of their production, reproduction, and representation is inherently subjective—that is, determined by one's own experiences, beliefs, values, and interests. Critical pedagogy views culture as a terrain of lived experiences and institutional forms organized around diverse elements of pleasure, struggle, and domination. In other words, culture embodies the lived experiences and behaviors that are the result of the unequal distribution of power along such lines as race, gender, class, age, and sexual orientation. As people interact with existing institutions and social practices in which the values, beliefs, bodies of knowledge, styles of communication, and biases of the dominant culture are imposed, they are often stripped of their power to articulate and realize their own goals. For example, the efforts in the United States to enforce a common culture (an unnegotiated foundation of values, ethics, meaning, histories, and representations—our cultural heritage) or a common sense (a selective view of social reality in which difference is viewed as deviant or a deficit) are, in fact, the imposition of a homogenizing social paradigm (known as ideological domination or hegemony) that grossly limits the possibility for a critical multicultural democracy. As class and race are inextricably related to culture in the United States, middle-class realities are certainly different from those of the working/lower class, as black and Latino/a are to white; the critical question is: Whose realities and interests are defining what it means to be American? Focusing on the imposition of particular values in society, as well as the antagonistic relations and the resistance (opposition) that surfaces as a response to such domination, critical pedagogues view the contemporary cultural landscape as a terrain of conflict of differences.

Deconstruction: Generally associated with the work of French theorist Jacques Derrida, deconstruction is an analytic process through which the deep, unconscious meaning of texts is examined. Within a critical pedagogical framework, deconstruction often refers to the analytic process of taking apart (i.e., dissecting, critically inquiring, problematizing) a phenomenon in order to understand its construction.

Deficit model: The deficit model is used to explain the low academic achievement of students from oppressed groups as being due to individual or group pathology, cultural deprivation, or genetic limitations (e.g., cognitive and linguistic deficiencies, poor motivation). Students perceived in this fashion are in need of fixing (if we could only identify the right schematic), or, at worst, culturally or genetically deficient and beyond repair.

Dialectics: While there are a number of definitions and interpretations of dialectics, for the general purpose of critical pedagogy this concept refers to the interconnecting and contradicting relationships that constitute a particular phenomenon, for example, among the economic, political, social, and cultural dimensions of society. A dialectical analysis is also often used to show how every idea, or force, has its opposite/contradiction. For example, the dialectic of *oppressor* is the reality of the *oppressed*. Such an analysis holds both opposing concepts together at once to see how they interconnect and play off each other.

Dialogue: Rejecting the style of education in which students are passive recipients of preestablished knowledge, critical pedagogy, which calls for the use of dialogue, facilitates critical interaction between teachers and learners. Such dialogues need to be infused with ideological analysis (theory that helps to make sense of the world) and political action capable of eradicating oppressive practices and institutions both in education and society. As such, a dialogue is never simply a conversation, a description, or a therapy session.

Discourse: A discourse represents the ways in which reality is perceived through and shaped by historically and socially constructed ways of making sense, that is, language, complex signs, and practices that order and sustain particular forms of social existence. These systems of communication, which are constructions informed by particular ideologies, play a significant role in shaping human subjectivities, social realities, and actions, and can work to either confirm or deny the life histories and experiences of the people who use them. If the rules that govern what is acceptable in a particular society are exclusive, discourse can be a major site of contention in which different groups struggle over meaning and ideology.

Domesticate: Domesticate refers to the process by which people learn to internalize the dominant values, behaviors, and thus discourses that render individuals and groups unable, or unwilling, to recognize oppressive practices. Similar concepts are manufacturing consent, anesthetizing, and colonizing the mind.

Dominant culture: As Antonia Darder (1991) argues, "Dominant culture refers to ideologies, social practices, and structures that affirm the central values, interests, and concerns of those who are in control of the material and symbolic wealth in society" (p. 30).

Dominant ideologies: Dominant ideologies are bodies of ideas held by cultural groups that are politically, socially, and economically in positions of power and are therefore able to impose on the greater society, through various social institutions and practices, particular traditions, bodies of knowledge, language uses, values, norms, and beliefs (discourse styles), usually at the expense of others.

Essentialism: Essentialism ascribes a fundamental nature or a biological determinism to humans (e.g., men are naturally aggressive, women are naturally nurturing, all blacks are the same, etc.) through attitudes about identity, experience, knowledge, and cognitive development. Within this monolithic and homogenizing view, categories such as race and gender become gross generalizations and single-cause explanations about individual character.

False consciousness: Linked to the notion that social institutions such as schools are agents of ideological control that work to reproduce dominant beliefs, values, norms, and forms of oppression, false consciousness is the point at which members of society buy into their own exploitation and subordination, and become uncritical tools of production and consumption. The concept is no longer readily used because the dialectic/opposite of *false* implies that there is a *true* consciousness. In that emancipation is always uncertain, contextual, and incomplete, this idea of universal truth is rejected by critical pedagogy. More contemporary concepts referring to a similar phenomenon are domesticated, mystification of social reality, dysconsciousness, anesthetized, the social construction of not seeing, manufactured consent, and colonization of the mind.

Foundationalism: Foundationalism refers to the central core of knowledge, morals, and social standards (what is perceived as a set of absolute truths) upon which a modernist society is built. Critical social theories contest foundationalism and the myth of universality because they obfuscate the power relations that impose particular forms of authority, social relations, bodies of knowledge, and worldviews.

Frankfurt School: The Frankfurt School, a German institute of social research frequented by the likes of Marcuse, Fromm, Horkheimer, Adorno, Habermas, Arendt, Brecht, Lukacs, and many others, had an enormous impact on the sociological, political, and cultural environment throughout this century. It was from this institute that the term *critical theory* and its ideas evolved.

Grand, totalizing, and **master narratives:** These narratives represent any macrotheories that attempt to explain social reality in its entirety. However, such explanations, by subsuming every aspect into one narrowly defined lens, are overly simplistic in that they suppress differences into homogenizing schemes. For example, the modernist claim to universality, or the Marxist notion that class struggle is the unifying principle of human history, is a totalizing narrative. In the case where there is a monopoly on the power structure in a particular social order, some of these theories (master narratives) have a large impact on the structure of society.

Hegemony: Hegemony, as derived from the work of Italian theorist Antonio Gramsci, is used to express how certain groups manage to dominate others. An analysis of hegemony is especially concerned with how the imposition of particular ideologies and forms of authority results in the reproduction of social and institutional practices through which dominant groups maintain not only their positions of privilege and control but also the consensual support of other members (even those subordinated) of society.

Hidden curriculum: This term refers to the unspoken agenda in schools that socializes students into the dominant ideology and discourse in which they become uncritical tools of the work force. The hidden curriculum functions to erase or distort the experiences and perceptions of individuals and groups from specific backgrounds, such as class, race, gender, and sexual orientation.

Historical amnesia: This term implies that people develop a limited and limiting sense of history through the socializing process in which selective historical memories are imposed. Historical amnesia is used to explain how negative memories and/or memories that threaten or question the status quo are excluded from public consciousness and classroom inquiry. How, for example, do the histories of women, blacks, Native Americans, working-class groups, and others whose past experiences contradict the moral foundation of the existing dominant structures of society get eliminated or simply rewritten? Critical pedagogy calls for the resurrection of such memories and buried knowledge for the purpose of creating more critically democratic societies.

Identity politics: Identity politics encompasses an analysis of the lived experiences of an individual group, for example, women, gays, blacks, or the working class. *See also* **politics of difference.**

Ideology: Ideology is used throughout this book to describe a body of beliefs and values that inform one's/a group's/an institution's actions. As humans are cultural beings, we all work from an ideological position, regardless of where we are situated on the political spectrum.

Internalized oppression: Internalized oppression occurs when members of an oppressed group, after a period of abuse and criticism, come to believe in the dominant group's description of them as inferior. As a result of such oppression, people often attempt to assimilate into the dominant culture. Although calling for an understanding of this psychological phenomenon, critical pedagogy nevertheless insists that it not simply be reduced to the level of the individual. Psychology in the critical sense is shaped by one's sociocultural reality, and thus any understanding of the individual would require an examination of the root cause of that psychological state, which pertains to the realm of ideology.

Learned helplessness: Learned helplessness occurs when a person has been systematically told that he or she does not possess the necessary intelligence to complete particular tasks, and thus comes to believe in his or her own inabilities. In the end, students subjected to such oppressive conditions no longer try.

Location: *See* **Positionality.**

Logocentrism/Cartesian logic: Associated with the work of Descartes, who proposed a form of linear causality and a foundation for knowledge, modernist epistemologies center on the idea that there are universal truths, absolute logic, and thus common sense in the world. These absolutes (logocentrics or Cartesian logic) are thought to be the building blocks of society.

Manufacture consent: Manufacturing consent refers to the process through which an individual or group internalizes certain values (or is indoctrinated), and thus conforms with particular practices, which are usually oppressive in nature. Other similar terms are domesticate, anesthetize, colonize the mind, dysconsciousness, and the social construction of not seeing.

Marginalize: To marginalize is to force an individual or group out of mainstream society, limiting their access to political and economic power, or to push ideas and concepts that conflict with dominant ideologies to the fringes of academic debate, labeling them as important only to special-interest groups. While critical pedagogy is certainly concerned with understanding the lives of those on the margins (and creating self-empowering conditions to escape and transform oppressive practices), one of its central purposes is to deconstruct the ideologies and practices of the existing dominant center that in fact creates such segregation.

Meritocracy: Under the assumption that institutions in this society are equally responsive to all groups, regardless of race, class, gender, sexuality, and so on, meritocracy refers to a system of education where the so-called talented are advanced by virtue of their achievements.

Modernity: *See* **Postmodernism/modernity.**

Object/subject of history: Critical pedagogy calls for a person to be an active participant and not simply an entity to be acted upon, manipulated, and controlled as an object of history. It is believed that only as active, critical subjects are we able to make substantive change. In the literature the term *objectification* is used to refer to people being seen/acted upon as objects. This is the process through which one becomes the object of learning strategies (for example, "This is designed for African-Americans, you're black, therefore . . . "), rather than a knowledgeable participant in the construction of deep and meaningful learning experiences.

Political awareness/clarity/presence of mind: Not to be confused with political correctness, political awareness/clarity (which Paulo Freire throughout his work refers to as conscientization) is the awareness of the historical, sociopolitical, economic, cultural, and subjective reality that shapes our lives, and our ability to transform that reality.

Politics of difference: Politics of difference refers to the multiple and interconnecting relationships across such ideological categories as race, class, gender, sexual orientation, disability, age, religion, and so forth. Unlike identity politics, which focus on the interests of a particular group (e.g., women, gays, working class, African-Americans, etc.), a politics of difference also looks at intragroup diversity.

Positionality (location, subject position, situated): Coming out of feminist scholarship, position or location refers to the place that a person occupies within a set of social relationships. This position is often determined by such categories as gender, class, race, language, sexual orientation, age, and physical ability.

Positivism: Associated with the Enlightenment and modernism, positivism refers to a defense of a scientific basis for the study of culture. As such, knowledge and reason are seen as neutral and universal, rather than as social constructions that reflect particular interests and ideologies. Refuting this prevailing notion, critical pedagogy focuses on the idea that any examination of culture is inherently subjective, that is, influenced by one's own experiences, beliefs, values, and interests. *See also* **technocratic.**

Postmodernism/modernity: There is no generic definition of either modernity or postmodernity. In fact, positions within these frameworks are often contradicting. This particular explanation will simply compare and contrast some specific points of modernism and postmodernism that are central to critical pedagogy (the individual, knowledge, schools). **The individual:** The individual in the modernist (or liberal humanist) sense is considered to be an independent and rational being who is predisposed to be motivated toward social agency and emancipation—what Descartes believed to be the existence of a unified self. Postmodernists, on the other hand, do not believe that the mind has an innate universal structure or essence. They contend that consciousness and the self are socially and historically constructed, and are constantly changing within shifting contexts. Emancipation is also seen as uncertain and incomplete. **Knowledge:** Modernist epistemologies center around the idea that universal truths, absolute logic, or common sense (referred to as *logocentrism* or *Cartesian logic*—associated with the work of Descartes, who proposed a form of linear causality) are a foundation for knowledge, morals, and social standards (referred to as *foundationalism*), and that society can and should be built upon these values and truths. Positivism is the philosophy associated with modernity, which makes claims to objectivity, truth, and certainty, in defense of a scientific basis for the study of culture. Universal reason and objectivity are seen as the source for knowledge and emancipation. Postmodernists are radically opposed to any homogenizing and constricting social paradigm, and reject a scientific basis for the study of culture and of the possibilities of truth, certainty, and objectivity. They reject positivism, instrumental reason, and any theory that subsumes every aspect of social reality into one totalizing theory that goes unquestioned (these all-encompassing theories are referred to as grand, master, or totalizing narratives). Postmodernists do not believe that the mind has an innate, universal structure; rather, they see consciousness, identities, and meaning as socially and historically produced. Universals are thus rejected in the name of difference and diversity, and the uncertainty of knowing the world in a fixed and assured way. As postmodernists confront the relationships among power, ideology, and knowledge, critical pedagogy concerns itself with having students examine the values, assumptions, ideologies, and interests reflected in bodies of knowledge so that they are able to recognize whose interests have been advanced at the expense of others. Students within this process become knowledge producers rather than uncritical reproducers. **Schools:** Modernists believe that schools can contribute to the development of a democratic and egalitarian social order. Postmodernists argue that the modernist foundations of positivism, instrumental reason, universal knowledge, and bureaucratic control have historically been injected into public schools—that in fact they are at the center of curriculum, educational theory, and practice—and frequently operate in oppressive ways to shape the manner in which people interact and relate to each other with an agenda of constructing forms of gender, sexual, linguistic, racial, and socioeconomic domination. Critical pedagogues thus contend that schools do not provide the opportunity for self-empowerment and democratic struggle, in that multiple voices cannot be heard because of the modernist belief in objective truth, which means that only one voice is given legitimacy, and only one truth, one reality, will be heard.

Poststructuralism: While poststructuralism holds certain assumptions about language, discourse, and identity, it is important to note that it does not constitute a unified field. A major influence in the development of postmodern thought, poststructuralists reject the notion of universal truth, and that the mind has an innate, universal structure. They also reject the possibility of conducting an objective study of culture. Consciousness, identities, meaning, and cognitive development are seen as socially and historically produced within the politics of everyday life. Poststructuralism works from the premise that language/discourse constitutes rather than merely reflects reality. Discourse in this sense refers to the way reality is perceived through and shaped by historically and socially constructed ways of making sense—that is, languages, complex signs, and practices that order and sustain particular forms of social existence. As such, systems of communication, which are all social and historical constructions informed by particular ideologies, play a significant role in shaping human subjectivities and reality, and can work to either confirm or deny the life histories and experiences of the people who use them.

Praxis: Praxis is the relationship between theoretical understanding and critique of society (that is, its historical, ideological, sociopolitical, and economic influences and structures) and action that seeks to transform individuals and their environment. Arguing that people cannot transform a given situation through awareness or the best of intentions, or through unguided action, Paulo Freire defines praxis throughout his work as a dialectical movement that goes from action to reflection and from reflection upon action to a new action.

Problematize: Associated with critical thinking/inquiry (that is, being able to understand, analyze, and affect the sociohistorical, economic, cultural, and political realities that shape our lives), problematizing is the process of posing questions in order to deconstruct a particular phenomenon so as to understand its construct. The term *deconstruct* is often used to describe this same process.

Public intellectual: *See* **Cultural worker.**

Public sphere: Public spheres in the critical sense are public arenas for citizens in political participation, outside of direct government and economic influence and intervention, that are enacted through dialogue and debate. Schools are envisioned by critical pedagogues as public spheres, wherein classrooms are active sites of public intervention and social struggle, rather than mere adjuncts of corporate and partisan interests. Because mainstream society is constituted by particular oppressive ideologies, these critical spheres are also referred to as counterpublics.

Racialization: Racialization is the process in which the color of one's skin takes on sociocultural characteristics/significance, which in turn shape perceptions of identity by virtue of race.

Reductionistic: To be reductionistic is to simplify a particular phenomenon so as to mask its complexity. For example, arguing that social reality is shaped solely by socioeconomic status and class conflict obscures the multiple and interconnecting relationships of other significant human experiences (such as race, gender, and sexual orientation) and their effects on perception and struggle.

Representational politics: Public media, such as film, television, and magazines, work to actively control the ways in which identities are depicted in the mainstream. These images/representations can stereotype, silence, marginalize, or distort. Curricula also function in this way by depicting and/or shaping the identities of students. This struggle over identity and representation—that is, over who has the power to fashion images and identities, and with what agenda in mind—is referred to as representational politics.

Resistance/oppositional identity: Resistance (oppositional identity) has traditionally been attributed to deviant behavior, individual pathology, learned helplessness, cultural deprivation, and genetic flaws. Critical pedagogy, on the other hand, sees resistance as a legitimate (though not always conscious) response to domination, used to help individuals or groups deal with oppressive social conditions and injustice. From this perspective, resistance in any form should be part of a larger political project that is working toward change.

Sociohistorical: A sociohistorical lens works from the assumption that we are never independent of the social and historical forces that surround us. That is, we all inherit beliefs and values—ideologies—that need to be critically understood and transformed where necessary. Arguing that history is not predetermined, critical pedagogy contends that we should be active subjects of history (shapers of history), rather than objects that are acted upon, manipulated, and controlled.

Stupidification: Coined by Donaldo Macedo, this term refers to a process of deskilling and dumbing-down people, via indoctrination, so that they are unable to critically read the world around them.

Subjectivity: Subjectivity in the liberal humanist sense is described as being constructed by the independent choices and intentions of the individual. Rejecting the notion of an autonomous being, subjectivity in the critical sense is more of a product of historical, cultural, social, linguistic, and institutional structures and constraints. As such, subjectivity is always forged within particular relations of power. Only through critical consciousness, or what I call presence of mind, can subjectivities be shaped in a liberatory way.

Subject position: *See* **Positionality.**

Subordinated cultures: Subordinated refers to cultural groups that have been historically, politically, socially, and economically disempowered in the greater society. The use of *minority* is problematic in that it speaks of numerical minority rather than the oppressive conditions within which people live. In addition, as a marker of low status, the term *minority* has historically been used to categorize racially subordinated groups.

Technocratic (technicians/technicists): Emanating from the positivist tradition, technocratic models, which conceptualize teaching as a discrete and scientific undertaking, embrace depersonalized solutions for education that often translate into the regulation and standardization of teacher practices and curricula, and rote memorization of selected facts that can easily be measured through standardized testing. As such, the role of the teacher is reduced to that of an uncritical, objective, and efficient distributor of information.

Text: A text implies any aspect of reality that transfers meaning. This may include, but is not limited to, aural, visual, and printed materials. Examples of text include written passages, oral communication, music, body language, and visual representations such as movies, advertisements, photographs, and paintings.

Theory: Theory is the ability to interpret, critique, and draw generalizations. That is, it is the ability to make sense of the world around you—it is the "why" of "what" happened. As culture changes with the shifting sociopolitical landscape, theory must always be subjected to critical engagement and change.

Voice: Voice simply refers to people's authentic self-expression, with an understanding that people are situated in personal histories of engagement with their surroundings/communities through which voice is shaped by class, race, gender, sexuality, and so forth. Finding one's/using one's voice refers to a quality of authenticity, that one is speaking with integrity and from a position of self-empowerment, or even liberation.

References

Aguirre, A., & Baker, D. (1995). *Sources: Notable Selections in Race and Ethnicity.* Guilford: Dushkin Publishing Group.

Alba, R. D. (1990). *Ethnic Identity: The Transformation of White America.* New Haven: Yale University Press.

Allen, T. (1994). *The Invention of the White Race.* London: Verso.

Anyon, J. (1988). "Social Class and the Hidden Curriculum of Work." In: *Curriculum: An Introduction to the Field,* J. R. Gress (ed.). New York: McCutchan.

Anzaldúa, G. (1988). "Tlilli, Tlapalli: The Path of the Red and Black Ink," In: *Multicultural Literacy: Opening the American Mind,* R. Simonson & S. Walker (eds.). Saint Paul: Gray Wolf Press.

Anzaldúa, G. (1990). "How to Tame a Wild Tongue." In: *Out There: Marginalization and Contemporary Cultures,* R. Ferguson, M. Gever, T. Minh-ha, & C. West (eds.). Cambridge: MIT Press.

Apple, M. W. (1990). *Ideology and Curriculum.* New York: Routledge.

Apple, M. (1993). *Official Knowledge: Democratic Education in a Conservative Age.* New York: Routledge.

Apple, M. (1996). *Cultural Politics & Education.* New York: Teachers College Press.

Aronowitz, S. (1992). *The Politics of Identity: Class, Culture, Social Movements.* New York: Routledge.

Aronowitz, S. (1993). *Roll Over Beethoven: The Return of Cultural Strife.* London: Wesleyan University Press.

Au, K. H., & Jordan, C. (1981). "Teaching Reading to Hawaiian Children: Finding a Culturally Appropriate Solution." In: *Culture and the Bilingual Classroom,* H. T. Trueba, G. P. Guthrie, & K. H. Au (eds.). Rowley, MA: Newbury House.

Baker, H. A., Jr. (1991). Foreward: *"There Aint't No Black in the Union Jack": The Cultural Politics of Race and Nation.* Chicago: University of Chicago Press.

Bakhtin, M. M. (1981). *The Dialogic Imagination.* Austin: University of Texas Press.

Baldwin, J. (1985). *The Price of the Ticket: Collected Nonfiction 1948–1985.* New York: St. Martin's.

Bartolomé, L. (1994). "Beyond the Methods Fetish, Toward a Humanizing Pedagogy." *Harvard Educational Review,* Vol. 64, No. 2, Summer, pp. 173–191.

Bellant, R. (1991). *Old Nazis, the New Right, and the Republican Party: Domestic Fascist Networks and Their Effects on U.S. Cold War Politics.* Boston: South End Press.

Bennett, W. (1992). *The De-Valuing of America.* New York: Summit.

Bennett, W. (1996). *The Book of Virtues for Young People: A Treasury of Great Moral Stories.* Parsippany, NJ: Silver Burdett Press.

Berube, M., & Nelson, C. (1995). *Higher Education Under Fire: Politics, Economics, and the Crisis of the Humanities.* New York: Routledge.

Best, S., & Kellner, D. (1991). *Postmodern Theory: Critical Interrogations.* New York: Guilford Press.

Bloch, M., & Tabachnick, B. (1994). "Improving Parent Involvement as School Reform: Rhetoric or Reality." In: *Changing American Education: Recapturing the Past or Inventing the Future,* K. Borman & N. Greenman (eds.). New York: SUNY Press.

Bloom, A. (1987). *The Closing of the American Mind.* New York: Simon & Schuster.

Borman, K., & Greenman, N. (1994). *Changing American Education: Recapturing the Past or Inventing the Future.* New York: SUNY.

Bourdieu, P., & Passeron, J. C. (1977). *Reproduction in Education, Society, and Culture.* London: Sage.

Bowker, A. (1993). *Sisters in the Blood: The Education of Women in Native America.* Newton, MA: WEEA Publishing.

Bowles, S., & Gintis, H. (1976). *Schooling in Capitalist America: Educational Reform and the Contradictions of Economic Life.* New York: Basic Books.

Bowser, B., & Hunt, R. (1996). *Impacts of Racism on White Americans,* 2nd ed. London: SAGE.

Brandt, R. (1989). "On Parents and Schools: A Conversation with Joyce Epstein." *Educational Leadership,* Vol. 47, No. 2, pp. 24–27.

Bryan, D. (1993). "Teaching for Global Responsibility Through Student Participation in the Community." In: *Promising Practices in Teaching Social Responsibility.* S. Berman & P. La Farge (eds.). New York: SUNY Press.

Buchanan, P. (1992). "Yes Mario, There Is a Culture War!" *Chicago Tribune,* September 14, p. 17.

Cabral, A. (1973). *Return to the Source: Selected Speeches by Amilcar Cabral.* New York: Monthly Review Press.

Carby, H. (1993). "Encoding White Resentment: *Grand Canyon*—A Narrative for Our Times." In: *Race, Identity, and Respresentation in Education,* C. McCarthy & W. Crinchlow (eds.). New York: Routledge.

Carlson, D. (1997). *Making Progress: Education and Culture in New Times.* New York: Teachers College Press.

Carrell, P.; Devine, J.; & Eskey, D. (1990). *Interactive Approaches to Second Language Reading.* New York: Cambridge University Press.

Carroll, P., & Noble, D. (1988). *The Free and the Unfree: A New History of the United States.* New York: Penguin.

Castenell, L., & Pinar, W. (1993). *Understanding Curriculum as Racial Text: Representation of Identity and Difference in Education.* New York: SUNY.

Cheney, L. (1988). *Humanities in America: A Report to the President, the Congress, and the American People.* Washington, DC: National Endowment for the Humanities.

Chomsky, N. (1965). *Aspects of the Theory of Syntax.* Cambridge, MA: MIT Press.

Chomsky, N. (1992). *What Uncle Sam Really Wants.* Berkeley, CA: Odonian Press.

Chomsky, N. (1993). *Year 501: The Conquest Continues.* Boston: South End Press.

Chosmky, N.; Leistyna, P.; & Sherblom, S. (1995). "A Dialogue with Noam Chomsky." *Harvard Educational Review,* Vol. 65, No. 2, Summer, pp. 127–144.

Cummins, J. (1979). "Linguistic Interdependence and the Educational Development of Bilingual Children." *Review of Education Research,* Vol. 49, pp. 222–251.

Cummins, J. (1981). "The Role of Primary Language Development in Promoting Educational Success for Language Minority Students." In: *Schooling and Language Minority Students: A Theoretical Framework.* Los Angeles: California State Department of Education, Evaluation, Dissemination, and Assessment Center.

Cummins, J. (1988). *Empowering Minority Students.* Sacramento, CA: California Association for Bilingual Education.

Cummins, J. (1994). "From Coercive to Collaborative Relations of Power in the Teaching of Literacy." In: *Literacy Across Languages and Cultures,* B. M. Ferdman, R. M. Weber, & A. Ramirez (eds.). Albany: State University of New York Press.

Daniels, J. (1997). *White Lies: Race, Class, Gender, and Sexuality in White Supremacist Discourse.* New York: Routledge.

Darder, A. (1991). *Culture and Power in the Classroom: A Critical Foundation for Bicultural Education.* New York: Bergin & Garvey.

Davies, D. (1988). "Benefits and Barriers to Parent Involvement." *Community Education Research Digest,* Vol. 2, No. 2, pp. 11–19.

Davies, J. (1996). *Educating Students in a Media Saturated Culture.* Lancaster, PA: Technomic.

Davis, F. J. (1991). *Who Is Black: One Nation's Definition.* University Park: Pennsylvania State University Press.

Delgado-Gaitan, C. (1990). *Literacy for Empowerment: The Role of Parents in Children's Education.* London: Falmer Press.

Delgado, R., & Stefancic, J. (1997). *Critical White Studies: Looking Behind the Mirror.* Philadelphia: Temple University Press.

Delpit, L. (1993). "The Silenced Dialogue: Power and Pedagogy in Educating Other People's Children." In: *Beyond Silenced Voices: Class, Race, and Gender,* L. Weis & M. Fine (eds.). New York: SUNY.

Dent, G. (1992). *Black Popular Culture.* Seattle: Bay Press.

DeVos, G. A. (1967). *Japan's Invisible Race: Caste in Culture and Personality.* Berkeley: University of California Press.

Dines, G., & Humez, J. (1995). *Gender, Race, and Class in Media: A Text-Reader.* London: Sage.

D'Souza, D. (1992). *Illiberal Education: The Politics of Race and Sex on Campus.* New York: Vintage Books.

D'Souza, D. (1995). *The End of Racism.* New York: Free Press.

Du Bois, W.E.B. (1935). *Black Reconstruction in America, 1860–1880.* New York: Atheneum.

During, S. (1993). *The Cultural Studies Reader.* New York: Routledge.

Dyer, R. (1988). "White." *Screen,* Vol. 29, No. 4, pp. 44–64.

Dyer, R. (1993). *The Matter of Images: Essays on Representations.* New York: Routledge.

Dyer, R. (1997). *White.* New York: Routledge.

Dyson, M. (1993). *Reflecting Black: African-American Cultural Criticism.* Minneapolis: University of Minnesota Press.

Dyson, M. (1994). "The Politics of Black Masculinity and the Ghetto in Black Film." In: *The Subversive Imagination: Artists, Society, and Social Responsibility,* C. Becker (ed.). New York: Routledge.

Everhart, R. (1983). *Reading, Writing, and Resistance.* Boston: Routledge.

Fanon, F. (1967). *Black Skin White Masks.* New York: Grove Press.

Feagin, J., & Vera, H. (1995). *White Racism.* New York: Routledge.

Ferguson, R. (1990). "Introduction: Invisible Center." In: *Out There: Marginalization and Contemporary Cultures,* R. Ferguson, M. Gever, T. Minh-ha, & C. West (eds.). Cambridge, MA: MIT Press.

Ferrell, J., & Sanders, C. (1995). *Cultural Criminology.* Boston: Northeastern University Press, 1995.

Fine, M. (1991). *Framing Dropouts: Notes on the Politics of an Urban Public High School.* New York: SUNY.

Fine, M.; Weis, L.; Powell, L.; & Wong, L. Mun (1997). *Off White: Readings on Race, Power, and Society.* New York: Routledge.

Fiske, J. (1994). *Media Matters.* Minneapolis: University of Minnesota Press.

FitzGerald, F. (1986). *Cities on a Hill: A Journey Through Contemporary American Cultures.* New York: Simon and Schuster.

Fordham, S. (1988). "Racelessness as a Factor in Black Students' School Success: Pragmatic Strategy or Pyrrhic Victory?" *Harvard Educational Review,* Vol. 58, No. 1, pp. 54–84.

Fordham, S., & Ogbu, J. (1986). "Black Students' School Success: Coping with the 'Burden of Acting White.'" *Urban Review,* Vol. 18, No. 3, pp. 176–206.

Foucault, M. (1972). *Power/Knowledge: Selected Interviews & Other Writings—1972–1977.* New York: Pantheon.

Frankenburg, R. (1993). *The Social Construction of Whiteness: White Women, Race Matters.* Minneapolis: University of Minnesota Press.

Frankenburg, R. (1994). "Whiteness and Americanness: Examining Constructions of Race, Culture, and Nation in White Women's Narratives." In: *Race,* S. Gregory & R. Sanjek (eds.). New Brunswick, NJ: Rutgers University Press.

Frankenburg, R. (1997). *Displacing Whiteness: Essays in Social and Cultural Criticism.* London: Duke University Press.

Franklin, J. H. (1995). "Ethnicity in American Life: The Historical Perspective." In: *Sources: Notable Selections in Race and Ethnicity,* A. Aguirre & D. Baker (eds.). Guilford, CT: Dushkin Publishing Group.

Fraser, N. (1989). *Unruly Practices: Power, Discourse, and Gender in Contemporary Social Theory.* Minneapolis: University of Minnesota Press.

Fraser, N. (1994). "Rethinking the Public Sphere: A Contribution to the Critique of Actually Existing Democracy." In: *Between Borders: Pedagogy and the Politics of Cultural Studies.* H. Giroux & P. McLaren (eds.). New York: Routledge.

Freire, P. (1970). *Pedagogy of the Oppressed.* New York: Seabury Press.

Freire, P. (1985). *The Politics of Education: Culture, Power, and Liberation.* New York: Bergin & Garvey.

Freire, P., & Macedo, D. (1987). *Literacy: Reading the Word and the World.* New York: Bergin & Garvey.

Freire, P., & Macedo, D. (1996). "A Dialogue: Culture, Language, and Race." In: *Breaking Free: The Transformative Power of Critical Pedagogy,* P. Leistyna, A.

Woodrum, & S. Sherblom (eds.). Cambridge, MA: Harvard Educational Review Press.

Fusco, C. (1988). "Fantasies of Oppositionality," *Afterimage Magazine,* Vol. 16, December, pp. 6–9.

Fusco, C. (1995). *English Is Broken Here: Notes on Cultural Fusion in the Americas.* New York: The New Press.

Gans, H. (1979). "Symbolic Ethnicity: The Future of Ethnic Groups and Cultures in America." *Ethnic and Racial Studies,* Vol. 2, pp. 1–20.

Gass, S., and Schachter, J. (1989). *Linguistic Perspectives on Second Language Acquisition.* New York: Cambridge University Press.

Gates, H. L., Jr. (1992). *Loose Canons: Notes on the Culture Wars.* New York: Oxford University Press.

Gee, J. P. (1990). "Discourses, Socio-culturally Situated Educational Theory, and the Failure Problem." Paper presented at the University of Delaware.

Gee, J. P. (1996). *Social Linguistics and Literacies: Ideology in Discourses.* London: Taylor & Francis.

Gibson, M. A. (1976). "Approaches to Multicultural Education in the United States: Some Concepts and Assumptions." *Anthropology and Education Quarterly,* Vol. 7, pp. 7–18.

Giglioli, P. (1972). *Language and Social Context.* London: Penguin.

Gilroy, P. (1987). *"There Aint't No Black in the Union Jack": The Cultural Politics of Race and Nation.* Chicago: University of Chicago Press.

Gilroy, P. (1993). *The Black Atlantic: Modernity and Double Consciousness.* Cambridge: Harvard University Press.

Giroux, H. (1983). *Theory and Resistance in Education: A Pedagogy for the Opposition.* South Hadley, MA: Bergin & Garvey.

Giroux, H. (1988). *Teachers as Intellectuals: Toward a Critical Pedagogy of Learning.* New York: Bergin & Garvey.

Giroux, H. (1992). *Border Crossings: Cultural Workers and the Politics of Education.* New York: Routledge.

Giroux, H. (1993). *Living Dangerously: Multiculturalism and the Politics of Difference.* New York: Peter Lang.

Giroux, H. (1994a). "Insurgent Multiculturalism and the Promise of Pedagogy." In: *Multiculturalism: A Critical Reader,* D. Goldberg (ed.). Cambridge, MA: Blackwell.

Giroux, H. (1994b). *Disturbing Pleasures: Learning Popular Culture.* New York: Routledge.

Giroux, H. (1994c). "Doing Cultural Studies: Youth and the Challenge of Pedagogy." *Harvard Educational Review,* Vol. 64, No. 3, Fall, pp. 278–308.

Giroux, H. (1996). *Fugitive Cultures: Race, Violence, and Youth.* New York: Routledge.

Giroux, H. (1997). *Channel Surfing: Race Talk and the Destruction of Today's Youth.* New York: St. Martin's Press.

Giroux, H., & Penna, A. (1979). "Social Education in the Classroom: The Dynamics of the Hidden Curriculum." *Theory and Research in Social Education,* Vol. 7, No. 1, Spring, pp. 21–42.

Giroux, H., & Purple, D. (1982). *The Hidden Curriculum and Moral Education: Illusion or Insight.* Berkeley: McCutchan.

Giroux, H.; Simon, R.; & Contributors (1989). *Popular Culture: Schooling & Everyday Life.* New York: Bergin & Garvey.

Gless, D., & Smith, B. (1992). *The Politics of Liberal Education.* London: Duke University Press.

Goldberg, D. T. (1993). *Racist Culture: Philosophy and the Politics of Meaning.* Cambridge, MA: Blackwell.

Goldberg, D. (1994). *Multiculturalism: A Critical Reader.* Cambridge, MA: Blackwell.

Goldfield, M. (1992). "The Color of Politics in the United States: White Supremacy as the Main Explanation for the Peculiarities of American Politics from Colonial Times to the Present." In: *The Bounds of Race,* D. LaCapra (ed.). Ithaca, NY: Cornell University Press.

Goldfield, M. (1997). *The Color of Politics: Race and the Mainsprings of American Politics.* New York: The New Press.

Goodlad, J. (1994). *Educational Renewal: Better Teachers, Better Schools.* San Francisco: Jossey-Bass.

Gordon, B. M. (1985). "Teaching Teachers: 'Nation at Risk' and the Issue of Knowledge in Teacher Education." *The Urban Review,* Vol. 17, pp. 33–46.

Gould, S. J. (1981). *The Mismeasure of Man.* New York: W. W. Norton.

Granat, D.; Hathaway, P.; Saleton, W.; & Sansing, J. (1986). "Blacks and Whites in Washington: How Separate? How Equal? A Special Report." *The Washingtonian,* Vol. 22, pp. 152–182.

Gray, A., & McGuigan, J. (1993). *Studying Culture: An Introductory Reader.* London: Edward Arnold.

Gray, H. (1995). *Watching Race.* Minneapolis: University of Minnesota Press.

Greene, M. (1996). "Plurality, Diversity, and the Public Space." In: *Can Democracy Be Taught: Perspectives on Education for Democracy in the United States, Central and Eastern Europe, Russia, South Africa, and Japan,* A. Oldenquist (ed.). Bloomington, IN: Phi Delta Kappa Educational Foundation.

Grossberg, L.; Nelson, C.; & Treichler, P. (1992). *Cultural Studies.* New York: Routledge.

Habermas, J. (1962). *The Structural Transformation of the Public Sphere: An Inquiry into a Category of Bourgeois Society.* Cambridge, MA: MIT Press.

Hakuta, K. (1986). *Mirror of Language.* New York: Basic Books.

Hall, S. (1995) "The Whites of Their Eyes: Racist Ideologies and the Media." In: *Gender, Race and Class: A Text-Reader,* G. Dines & J. Humez (eds.). Thousand Oaks, CA: Sage.

Hall, S.; Held, D.; Hubert, D.; & Thompson, K. (1996). *Modernity: An Introduction to Modern Societies.* Cambridge, MA: Blackwell.

Halliday, M.A.K. (1976). *Language as a Social Semiotic.* London: Edward Arnold.

Haney Lopez, I. F. (1996). *White by Law: The Legal Construction of Race.* New York: New York University Press.

Haymes, S. (1995). "White Culture and the Politics of Racial Difference: Implications for Multiculturalism." In: *Multicultural Education, Critical Pedagogy, and the Politics of Difference,* C. Sleeter & P. McLaren (eds.). New York: SUNY.

Heath, S. B. (1983). *Ways with Words: Language, Life, and Work in Communities and Classrooms.* Cambridge: Cambridge University Press.

Hechter, M. (1974). *Internal Colonialism: The Celtic Fringe in British National Development.* Berkeley: University of California Press.

Hechter, M. (1978). "Group Formation and the Cultural Division of Labor." In: *American Journal of Sociology,* Vol. 84, pp. 293–318.

Herman, E., & Chomsky, N. (1988). *Manufacturing Consent: The Political Economy of the Mass Media.* New York: Pantheon Books.

Hernstein, R., & Murray, C. (1994). *The Bell Curve: Intelligence and Class Structure in American Life.* New York: The Free Press.

Hill, M. (1997). *Whiteness: A Critical Reader.* New York: New York University Press.

Hirsch, E. D., Jr. (1987). "Restoring Cultural Literacy in the Early Grades." In: *Taking Sides: Clashing Views on Controversial Educational Issues,* J. Noll (ed.). Guilford, CT: Dushkin Publishing Group, 1993.

Hirsch, E. D., Jr. (1988a). *Cultural Literacy: What Every American Needs to Know.* New York: Vintage.

Hirsch, E. D., Jr. (1988b). "A Postscript by E. D. Hirsch, Jr." *Change,* July/August, p. 25.

Hirsch, E. D., Jr. (1991). "Fairness and Core Knowledge." Paper presentation. Sponsored by The Core Knowledge Foundation, Charlottesville, VA.

Hirsch, E. D., Jr. (1992). "Toward a Centrist Curriculum: Two Kinds of Multiculturalism in Elementary School." Paper presentation. Sponsored by The Core Knowledge Foundation, Charlottesville, VA.

Hirsch, E. D., Jr. (1993). "The Core Knowledge Curriculum: What's Behind Its Success?" *Educational Leadership,* May, pp. 23–30.

Hirsch, E. D., Jr. (1996). *The Schools We Need, Why We Don't Have Them.* New York: Doubleday.

Holland, D., & Quinn, N. (1995). *Cultural Models in Language and Thought.* New York: Cambridge University Press.

Hollins, E.; King, J. E.; & Hayman, W. (1994). *Teaching Diverse Populations: Formulating a Knowledge Base.* New York: SUNY Press.

hooks, b. (1981). *Ain't I a Woman: Black Women and Feminism.* Boston: South End Press.

hooks, b. (1989). *Talking Back: Thinking Feminist, Thinking Black.* Boston: South End Press.

hooks, b. (1990). *Yearning: Race, Gender, and Cultural Politics.* Boston: South End Press. See especially Chapter 15: "Choosing the Margin as a Space for Radical Openness."

hooks, b. (1992). *Black Looks: Race and Representation.* Boston: South End Press.

hooks, b. (1993). *Sisters of the Yam: Black Women and Self-Recovery.* Boston: South End Press.

hooks, b. (1994). *Teaching to Transgress: Education as the Practice of Freedom.* New York: Routledge.

Jenks, C. (1993). *Culture: Key Ideas.* New York: Routledge.

Jones, L. (1963). *Blues People: The Negro Experience in White America and the Music That Developed from It.* New York: Morrow Quill Paperbacks.

Kelly, E. (1995). *Education, Democracy, & Public Knowledge.* Boulder: Westview Press.

Kimbal, R. (1990). *Tenured Radicals: How Politics Has Corrupted Our Higher Education.* New York: Harper Perennial.

Kincheloe, J., & Steinberg, S. (1996). "A Tentative Description of Post-Formal Thinking: The Critical Confrontation with Cognitive Theory." In: *Breaking Free: The Transformative Power of Critical Pedagogy,* P. Leistyna, A. Woodrum, & S. Sherblom (eds.). Cambridge, MA: Harvard Educational Review Press.

King, J. E. (1994). "The Purpose of Schooling for African American Children: Including Cultural Knowledge." In: *Teaching Diverse Populations: Formulating a Knowledge Base,* E. Hollins, J. E. King, & W. Hayman (eds.). New York: SUNY Press.

Kluegel, J. R. (1990). "Trends in Whites' Explanation of the Black–White Gap in Socioeconomic Status, 1977–1989." *American Sociological Review,* Vol. 55, pp. 512–525.

Kluegel, J. R., & Smith, E. R. (1982). "Whites' Beliefs About Black Opportunity." *American Sociological Review,* Vol. 47, No. 4, pp. 518–532.

Kluegel, J. R., & Smith, E. R. (1983). "Affirmative Action Attitudes: Effects of Self-Interest, Racial Affect, and Stratification Beliefs on Whites' Views." *Social Forces,* Vol. 61, No. 3, pp. 797–824.

Knowledge Unlimited (1987). *The Golden Door: Our Nation of Immigrants.* Video.

Kushnick, L. (1996). "The Political Economy of White Racism." In: *Impacts of Racism on White Americans,* 2nd ed., B. Bowser & R. Hunt (eds.). London: Sage.

Ladson-Billings, G., & Henry, A. (1990). "Blurring the Borders: Voices of African Liberatory Pedagogy in the United States and Canada." *Journal of Education,* Vol. 172, No. 2, pp. 72–88.

Lambert, W., & Taylor, D. (1990). *Coping with Cultural and Racial Diversity in Urban America.* New York: Praeger.

Lankshear, C. (1997). *Changing Literacies.* Philadelphia: Open University Press.

Lankshear, C., & McLaren, P. (1993). *Critical Literacy: Politics, Praxis, and the Postmodern.* New York: SUNY.

Lee, D. (1992). *Competing Discourses: Perspectives and Ideology in Language.* New York: Longman.

Lefkowitz, M. (1996). *Not Out of Africa: How Afrocentrism Became an Excuse to Teach Myth as History.* New York: Basic Books.

Leistyna, P., & Woodrum, A. (1996). "Context and Culture: What Is Critical Pedagogy." In: *Breaking Free: The Transformative Power of Critical Pedagogy,* P. Leistyna, A. Woodrum, & S. Sherblom (eds.). Cambridge, MA: Harvard Educational Review Press.

Leistyna, P.; Woodrum, A.; & Sherblom, S. (1996). *Breaking Free: The Transformative Power of Critical Pedagogy.* Cambridge, MA: Harvard Educational Review Press.

Levin, M. A. (1987). "Parent–Teacher Collaboration." In: *Critical Pedagogy & Cultural Power,* D. Livingston & Contributors (eds.). New York: Bergin & Garvey.

Lieberson, S., & Waters, M. (1986). "Ethnic Groups in Flux: The Changing Ethnic Responses of American Whites." *Annals of the American Academy of Political and Social Science,* Vol. 487, September, p. 264.

Lipman, S. (1994). *Culture and Anarchy: Matthew Arnold.* New Haven: Yale University Press.

Loewen, J. (1995). *Lies My Teacher Told Me: Everything Your American History Textbook Got Wrong.* New York: The New Press.

Lott, T. (1994). "Black Vernacular Representation and Cultural Malpractice." In: *Multiculturalism: A Critical Reader,* D. Goldberg (ed.). Cambridge, MA: Blackwell.

MacCannell, D. (1989). *The Tourist: A Theory of the Leisure Class.* New York: Schocken Books.

MacCannell, D. (1992). *Empty Meeting Grounds: The Tourist Papers.* London: Routledge.

Macedo, D. (1994). *Literacies of Power: What Americans Are Not Allowed to Know.* Boulder: Westview.

MacLeod, J. (1987). *Ain't No Making It: Leveled Aspirations in a Low-income Neighborhood.* Boulder: Westview Press.

MacLeod, J. (1991). "Bridging School and Street." *Journal of Negro Education,* Vol. 60.

Marable, M. (1992). "Blueprint for Black Studies and Multiculturalism." *The Black Scholar,* Summer.

Marciano, J. (1997). *Civic Illiteracy and Education: The Battle for the Hearts and Minds of American Youth.* New York: Peter Lang.

Marcuse, H. (1955). *Eros and Civilization: A Philosophical Inquiry into Freud.* Boston: Beacon Press.

Marshal, G. (1994). *The Concise Oxford Dictionary of Sociology.* New York: Oxford University Press.

Massachusetts Department of Education (1997). "English Language Arts Curriculum Framework." Boston: The Commonwealth of Massachusetts Department of Education.

McBrien, J. L., & Brandt, R. (1997). *The Language of Learning: A Guide to Education Terms.* Alexandria, VA: Association for Supervision and Curriculum Development.

McCaleb, S. P. (1994). *Building Communities of Learners: A Collaboration Among Teachers, Students, Families, and Community.* New York: St. Martin's Press.

McCarthy, C. (1993). "After the Canon: Knowledge and Ideological Representation in the Multicultural Discourse on Curriculum Reform." In: *Race, Identity, and Representation in Education,* C. McCarthy & W. Crinchlow (eds.). New York: Routledge.

McCarthy, C., & Crinchlow, W. (1993). *Race, Identity, and Representation in Education.* New York: Routledge.

McCarthy, C.; Rodriguez, A.; Meecham, S.; David, S.; Wilson-Brown, C.; Godina, H.; Supryia, K. E.; & Buendia, E. (1997). "Race, Suburban Resentment, and the Representation of the Inner City in Contemporary Film and Television." In: *Off White: Reading on Race, Power, and Society,* M. Fine, L. Weis, L. Powell, & L. Mun Wong (eds.). New York: Routledge.

McIntosh, P. (1990). "White Privilege: Unpacking the Invisible Knapsack." *Independent School,* Winter, pp. 31–36.

McIntyre, A. (1997). *Making Meaning of Whiteness: Exploring Racial Identity with White Teachers.* New York: SUNY.

McLaren, P (1986). *Schooling as a Ritual Performance.* London: Routledge & Kegan Paul.

McLaren, P. (1994). "White Terror and Oppositional Agency." In: *Multiculturalism: A Critical Reader,* D. Goldberg (ed.). Cambridge: Blackwell.

McLaren, P. (1995). *Critical Pedagogy and Predatory Culture: Oppositional Politics in a Postmodern Era.* New York: Routledge.

McLaughlin, B. (1987). *Theories of Second-Language Learning.* London: Edward Arnold.

Memmi, A. (1965). *The Colonizer and the Colonized.* Boston: Beacon Press.

Menchaca, M., & Valencia, R. (1990). "Anglo-Saxon Ideologies in the 1920s–1930s: Their Impact on the Segregation of Mexican Students in California." *Anthropology & Education Quarterly,* Vol. 21, pp. 222–246.

Mercer, K. (1994). *Welcome to the Jungle: New Positions in Black Cultural Studies.* New York: Routledge.

Michaels, S. (1981). "Sharing Time: Children's Narrative Styles and Differential Access to Literacy." *Language in Society,* Vol. 10, pp. 423–442.

Mills, C. Wright (1959). *The Sociological Imagination.* London: Oxford University Press.

Mills, C. (1997). *The Racial Contract.* London: Cornell University Press.

Minh-ha, Trinh T. (1989). *Woman, Native, Other.* Bloomington: University of Indiana Press.

Miramontes, O.; Nadeau, A.; & Commins, N. (1997). *Restructuring Schools for Linguistic Diversity: Linking Decision Making to Effective Programs.* New York: Teachers College Press.

Mitchell, C., & Weiler, K. (1991). *Rewriting Literacy: Culture and the Discourse of the Other.* New York: Bergin & Garvey.

Mohanty, C. T. (1990). "On Race and Voice: Challenges for Liberal Education in the 1990s." *Cultural Critique,* Vol. 18, No. 14, Winter, pp. 179–208.

Mohanty, C. T.; Russo, A.; & Torres, L. (1991). *Third World Women and the Politics of Feminism.* Indianapolis: University of Indiana Press.

Moll, L. (1990). *Vygotsky and Education: Instructional Implications and Applications of Sociohistorical Psychology.* New York: Cambridge University Press.

Moll, L.; Diaz, S.; Estrada; & Lopes, L. M. (1991). "Making Contexts: The Social Construction of Lessons in Two Languages." In: *Cross-Cultural and Communicative Competencies,* S. Arivzu & M. Saravia-Shore (eds.). New York: Horizon Press.

Molnar, T. (1995). *Authority and Its Enemies.* London: Transaction Publishers.

Morrison, T. (1992). *Playing in the Dark: Whiteness and Literary Imagination.* New York: Vintage.

Mun Wah, L. (1994). *The Color of Fear.* Oakland, CA: Stir Fry Productions. Video.

Natambu, K. (1992). "Nostalgia for the Present: Cultural Resistance in Detroit 1977–1987." In: *Black Popular Culture,* G. Dent (ed.). Seattle: Bay Press.

Newfield, C., & Strickland, R. (1995). *After Political Correctness: The Humanities and Society in the 1990s.* Boulder: Westview Press.

Ngugi Wa Thiong'o (1986). *Decolonizing the Mind: The Politics of Language in African Literature.* London: James Currey.

Nieto, S. (1992). *Affirming Diversity: The Sociopolitical Context of Multicultural Education.* New York: Longman.

Novick, M. (1995). *White Lies, White Power.* Monroe, ME: Common Courage Press.

Oakes, J. (1985). *Keeping Track: How Schools Structure Inequality.* New Haven, CT: Yale University Press.

Ogbu, J. (1987). "Variability in Minority Responses to Schooling: Nonimmigrants vs. Immigrants." In: *Interpretive Ethnography of Education,* G. Spindler & L. Spindler (eds.). Hillsdale, NJ: Lawrence Erlbaum Associates.

O'Malley, J. M., & Chamot, A. U. (1993). *Learning Strategies in Second Language Acquisition.* New York: Cambridge University Press.

Omi, M., & Winant, H. (1994). *Racial Formation in the United States: From the 1960s to the 1990s.* New York: Routledge.

Outhwaite, W., & Bottomore, T. (1993). *The Blackwell Dictionary of Twentieth-Century Social Thought.* Cambridge, MA: Blackwell.

Pierce, B. N. (1995). "Social Identity, Investment, and Language Learning." *TESOL Quarterly,* Vol. 29, No. 1, Spring, pp. 9–29.

Pink, W., & Borman, K. (1994). "Community Involvement and Staff Development in School Improvement." In: *Changing American Education: Recapturing the Past or Inventing the Future?* K. Borman & N. Greenman (eds.). New York: SUNY.

Popkewitz, T. (1992). "Culture, Pedagogy, and Power: Issues in the Production of Values and Colonization." In: *What Schools Can Do: Critical Pedagogy and Practice,* K. Weiler & C. Mitchell (eds.). New York: SUNY Press.

Porter, R. P. (1990). *Forked Tongue: The Politics of Bilingual Education.* New York: Basic Books.

Pratte, R. (1983). "Multicultural Education: Four Normative Arguments." *Educational Theory,* Vol. 33, pp. 21–32.

Rampton, B. (1995). *Crossing Language and Ethnicity Among Adolescents.* New York: Longman.

Ravitch, D. (1983). *The Troubled Crusade: American Education 1945–1980.* New York: Basic Books.

Ravitch, D. (1995a). *Debating the Future of American Education: Do We Need National Standards and Assessments?* Washington, DC.: The Brookings Institute.

Ravitch, D. (1995b). *National Standards in American Education: A Citizen's Guide.* Washington, DC.: The Brookings Institute.

Ravitch, D., & Finn, C. (1987). *What Do Our 17-Year-Olds Know? A Report on the First National Assessment of History and Literature.* New York: Harper & Row.

Reeves, J., & Campbell, R. (1994). *Cracked Coverage: Television News, The Anti-Cocaine Crusade, and the Reagan Legacy.* Durham, NC: Duke University Press.

Reynolds, A. (1991). *Bilingualism, Multiculturalism, and Second Language Learning: The McGill Conference in Honour of Wallace E. Lambert.* London: Lawrence Erlbaum Associates.

Rhodes, J. (1995). "The Visibility of Race and Media History." In: *Gender, Race and Class: A Text-Reader,* G. Dines & J. Humez (eds.). Thousand Oaks, CA: Sage.

Riggs, M. (1987). *Ethnic Notions: Black People in White Minds.* San Francisco: California Newsreel.

Roberts, L. W., & Clifton, R. A. (1982). "Exploring the Ideology of Canadian Multiculturalism." *Canadian Public Policy,* Vol. 7, No. 1, pp. 88–94.

Rodriguez, R. (1982). *Hunger of Memory: The Education of Richard Rodriguez.* New York: Bantam Books.

Roediger, D. (1991). *The Wages of Whiteness: Race and the Making of the American Working Class.* London: Verso.

Roediger, D. (1994). *Towards the Abolition of Whiteness.* New York: Verso.

Roopnarine, J.; Johnson, J.; & Hooper, F. (1994). *Children's Play in Diverse Cultures.* New York: SUNY Press.

Rosaldo, R. (1993). *Culture and Truth: The Remaking of Social Analysis.* Boston: Beacon.

Rose, T. (1994). *Black Noise: Rap Music and Black Culture in Contemporary America.* London: Wesleyan University Press.

Royer, J., & Feldman, R. (1984). *Educational Psychology: Applications and Theory.* New York: Knopf.

Ruenzel, D, (1996). "By the Book." *Teacher Magazine,* August, p. 28.

Said, E. (1993). *Culture and Imperialism.* New York: Knopf.

Samuels, D. (1991). "Rap on Rap." *The New Republic,* Vol. 11, November, pp. 24–26.

Sarup, M. (1993). *An Introductory Guide to Post-Structuralism and Postmodernism.* Athens, GA: The University of Georgia Press.

Schieffelin, B., & Ochs, E. (1992). *Language Socialization Across Cultures.* New York: Cambridge University Press.

Schlesinger, A., Jr. (1991). "The Disuniting of America: What We All Stand to Lose If Multicultural Education Takes the Wrong Approach." *American Educator,* Winter, pp. 14–33.

Schlesinger, A., Jr. (1992). *The Disuniting of America: Reflections on Multicultural Society.* New York: Norton.

Scott, J. (1990). *Domination and the Arts of Resistance: Hidden Transcripts.* New Haven: Yale University Press.

Seiter, E. (1995). "Different Children, Different Dreams: Racial Representation in Advertising." In: *Gender, Race and Class: A Text-Reader,* G. Dines & J. Humez (eds.). Thousand Oaks, CA: Sage.

Sholle, D., & Denski, S. (1994). *Media Education and the (Re)Production of Culture.* Westport, CT: Bergin & Garvey.

Simon, R. (1992). *Teaching Against the Grain.* New York: Bergin & Garvey.

Simon, R., & Willensky, J. (1980). "Behind a School Literacy Policy: The Surfacing of a Hidden Curriculum." *Journal of Education,* Vol. 162, No. 1, Winter.

Sklar, H. (1993). "Young and Guilty by Stereotype." *Z Magazine,* Vol. 6, No. 7/8, July/August, p. 53.

Sleeter, C. (1993). "White Teachers Construct Race." In: *Race and Representation in Education,* C. McCarthy & W. Crichlow (eds.). New York: Routledge.

Sleeter, C., & Grant, C. (1988). *Making Choices for Multicultural Education: Five Approaches to Race, Class, and Gender.* New York: Merrill.

Sleeter, C., & McLaren, P. (1995). *Multicultural Education, Critical Pedagogy and the Politics of Difference.* New York: SUNY.

Smith, A. W. (1981). "Racial Tolerance as a Function of Group Position." *American Sociological Review,* Vol. 46, No. 5, pp. 558–573.

Snauwaert, D. (1993). *Democracy, Education, and Governance: A Developmental Conception.* New York: SUNY Press.

Sochen, J. (1974). *Herstory: A Woman's View of American History.* New York: Alfred Publishing.

Solomon, R. P. (1992). *Black Resistance in High School: Forging a Separatist Culture.* New York: SUNY.

Spener, D. (1996). "Transitional Bilingual Education and the Socialization of Immigrants." In: *Breaking Free: The Transformative Power of Critical Pedagogy,* P. Leistyna, A. Woodrum, & S. Sherblom (eds.). Cambridge: Harvard Educational Review Press.

Spring, J. (1994). *Deculturalization and the Struggle for Equality: A Brief History of the Education of Dominated Cultures in the United States.* New York: Mc-Graw-Hill.

Squire, C. (1997). "Who's White? Television Talk Shows and Representations of Whiteness." In: *Off White: Readings on Race, Power, and Society,* M. Fine, L. Weis, L. Powell, & L. Mun Wong (eds.). New York: Routledge.

Strinati, D. (1995). *An Introduction to Theories of Popular Culture.* New York: Routledge.

Suina, J. (1988). "Epilogue: And Then I Went to School." In: *Linguistic and Cultural Influences on Learning Mathematics,* R. Cocking & J. Mestre (eds.). Hillsdale, NJ: Lawrence Erlbaum Associates.

Sullivan, E. (1990). *Critical Psychology and Pedagogy: Interpretation of the Personal World.* New York: Bergin & Garvey.

Szkudlarek, T. (1993). *The Problem of Freedom in Postmodern Education.* London: Bergin & Garvey.

Terry, R. (1970). *For Whites Only.* Grand Rapids, MI: Erdmans.

Terry, R. (1981). "The Negative Impact on White Values." In: *Impacts of Racism on White Americans,* 1st ed., B. Bowser & R. Hunt (eds.). Newbury Park, CA: Sage.

Torres-Guzman, M. E. (1995). "Recasting Frames: Latino Parent Involvement." In: *Policy and Practice in Bilingual Education: Extending the Foundations,* O. Garcia & C. Baker (eds.). Philadelphia: Multilingual Matters LTD.

Torres-Guzman, M. E.; Mercado, C. I.; Quintero, A.; & Rivera Viera, D. (1994). "Teaching and Learning in Puerto Rican/Latino Collaboratives: Implications for Teacher Education." In: *Teaching Diverse Populations: Formulating a Knowledge Base,* E. Hollins, J. E. King, & W. Hayman (eds.). New York: SUNY Press.

Turner, B. (1996). *The Blackwell Companion to Social Theory.* Cambridge, MA: Blackwell.

Vallance, E. (1973). "Hiding the Hidden Curriculum." *Curriculum Theory Network,* Vol. 4, No. 1, p. 6.

Villegas, A.M. (1988). "School Failure and Cultural Mismatch: Another View." *The Urban Review,* Vol. 20, No. 4, pp. 253–263.

Voloshinov, V. N. (1986; orig. 1929). *Marxism and the Philosophy of Language.* Cambridge, MA: Harvard University Press.

Vygotsky, L. S. (1978). *Mind in Society: The Development of Higher Psychological Processes.* Cambridge, MA: Harvard University Press.

Walker-Moffat, W. (1995). *The Other Side of the Asian American Success Story.* San Francisco: Jossey-Bass.

Wallace, M. (1990). *Invisibility Blues: From Pop to Theory.* New York: Verso.

Webster's II New Riverside Dictionary (1984). New York: Houghton Mifflin Company.

Weis, L. (1985). *Between Two Worlds: Black Students in an Urban Community College.* New York: Routledge.

Wellman, D. T. (1977). *Portraits of White Racism.* New York: Cambridge University Press.

Wertsch, J. (1991). *Voices of the Mind: A Sociocultural Approach to Mediated Action.* Cambridge, MA: Harvard University Press.

West, C. (1993). "The New Cultural Politics of Difference." In: *Beyond a Dream Deferred: Multicultural Education and the Politics of Excellence,* B. Thompson & S. Tyagi (eds.). Minneapolis: University of Minnesota Press.

Williams, R. (1976). *Keywords: A Vocabulary of Culture and Society.* New York: Oxford University Press.

Willis, P. (1977). *Learning to Labor: How Working Class Kids Get Working Class Jobs.* New York: Columbia University Press.

Wilson, J. (1995). *The Myth of Political Correctness: The Conservative Attack on Higher Education.* London: Duke University Press.

Winant, H. (1995). "Dictatorship, Democracy, and Difference: The Historical Construction of Racial Identity." In: *The Bubbling Cauldron: Race, Ethnicity, and the Urban Crisis,* M. P. Smith & J. R. Feagin (eds.). London: University of Minnesota Press.

Yinger, J. M. (1994). *Ethnicity: Source of Strength? Source of Conflict?* New York: SUNY.

Zinn, H. (1980). *A People's History of the United States.* New York: Harper & Row.

Zinn, H. (1990). *Declarations of Independence: Cross-Examining American Ideology.* New York: Harper Perennial.

Index

Index